TEACHING READING COMPREHENSION PROCESSES

TEACHING READING COMPREHENSION PROCESSES

Judith Westphal Irwin
Loyola University of Chicago

Prentice-Hall, Inc., Englewood Cliffs, New Jersey 07632

Library of Congress Cataloging in Publication Data

Irwin, Judith Wesphal.
  Teaching reading comprehension processes.

  Includes bibliographies and index.
  1. Reading comprehension. I. Title.
LB1050.45.I79 1985   428.4′3   85-3630
ISBN 0-13-895269-8

428.43
Ir9I
139812
Sept. 1986

© 1986 by Prentice-Hall, Inc., Englewood Cliffs, New Jersey 07632

Printed in the United States of America

10 9 8 7 6 5 4 3 2 1

Editorial/production supervision and
  interior design: Virginia Cavanagh Neri
Cover design: Wanda Lubelska Design
Manufacturing buyer: Barbara Kelly Kittle

ISBN 0-13-895269-8 01

Prentice-Hall International (UK) Limited, *London*
Prentice-Hall of Australia Pty. Limited, *Sydney*
Editora Prentice-Hall do Brasil, Ltda., *Rio de Janeiro*
Prentice-Hall Canada Inc., *Toronto*
Prentice-Hall Hispanoamericana, S.A., *Mexico*
Prentice-Hall of India Private Limited, *New Delhi*
Prentice-Hall of Japan, Inc., *Tokyo*
Prentice-Hall of Southeast Asia Pte. Ltd., *Singapore*
Whitehall Books Limited, *Wellington, New Zealand*

CONTENTS

Preface   ix

**PART ONE   TEACHING BASIC
COMPREHENSION PROCESSES**

One   Comprehension Processes: An Overview   1

Traditional Subskills Models and
        Methods   2
Comprehension Processes   2
Comprehension Contexts   7
Defining Comprehension   9
An Example   10
A Final Note   11
Self-check Test   12
Suggested Activities   13
References   13

Two   Teaching Microprocesses   15

Basics for Teaching Comprehension   15
Chunking   18

Microselection   22
Summary   24
Self-check Test   24
Suggested Activities   25
References   25

Three   **Teaching Integrative Processes   27**

Understanding Anaphora   28
Understanding Connectives   33
Slot-Filling Inferences   37
A Final Look at Integrative Processes   39
Summary   39
Self-check Test   40
Suggested Activities   40
References   43

Four   **Teaching Macroprocesses   44**

Story Grammars   45
Organizational Patterns in Expository
          Materials   48
Macroselection   57
Macrorules and Summarizing   58
Summary   62
Self-check Test   64
Suggested Activities   64
References   66

Five   **Teaching Elaborative Processes   68**

Elaborative Processes   68
Predictions   69
Other Prior-Knowledge Elaborations   73
Mental Imagery   74
Affective Responses   76
Higher-Level Thinking Responses   78
Final Considerations for Teaching
          Elaboration   82
Summary   83
Self-check Test   84
Suggested Activities   84
References   85

Six   **Teaching Metacognitive Processes   86**

Reading for Meaning: Comprehension
          Monitoring   87
Reading for Remembering: Study
          Skills   89
Basic Processes, Comprehension Contexts
          and Metacognitive Decisions   96
Summary   97

Self-check Test   97
Suggested Activities   99
References   99

**PART TWO   FACTORS THAT AFFECT
COMPREHENSION PROCESSES**

Seven   Individual Reader Contexts: Who Is Reading?   101

Prior Knowledge   102
Motivation and Interest   110
Cultural Differences   111
Decoding Fluency   112
Summary   113
Self-check Test   113
Suggested Activities   114
References   114

Eight   Text Contexts: What Is Being Read?   117

Readability Formulas   118
Assessing "Processability"   118
The Readability Checklist   121
Matching Students with Materials   124
Academic Learning Time   125
Summary   126
Self-check Test   126
Suggested Activities   127
References   127

**Nine   Situational Contexts: Why, When, and Where Are They
              Reading?   129**

The Comprehension Task   129
The Social Context   134
Classroom Environment   137
Summary   138
Self-check Test   138
Suggested Activities   139
References   140

PART THREE   PUTTING IT ALL TOGETHER

Ten   Asking Questions   141

Questioning Taxonomies   142
Planning for Questioning   150
Involving Students in Questioning   153
A Final Note   154

Summary   155
Self-check Test   155
Suggested Activities   155
References   156

Eleven   **Informal Comprehension Assessment   158**

Traditional Measures of Comprehension
     Ability   158
Informal Assessment for the Classroom
     Teacher   159
The Comprehension Assessment
     Checklist   160
Observation in Remedial Situations   160
Analyzing Free Recall   167
Summary   169
Self-check Test   172
Suggested Activities   172
References   173

Twelve   **General Procedures for Teaching Comprehension
Processes   174**

Toward a Model of Direct Comprehension
     Instruction   174
Putting It Together: The Active Reading
     Comprehension Activity   181
Summary   189
A Final Note: The Outer Context   189
Self-check Test   190
Suggested Activities   190
References   190

Thirteen   **Developmental and Remedial Applications: Some
Examples   192**

A Brief Review   192
Teaching Comprehension in Reading
     Groups   195
Teaching Comprehension in Remedial
     Situations   197
Teaching Comprehension in the Content
     Areas   198
It's Your Turn!   201

Index   203

PREFACE

This is a book about teaching people how to understand what they read. The activities suggested are all based on the assumption that the students can already read the individual words: the purpose of these activities is to help people who can already read words to better understand sentences, paragraphs, articles, chapters, books, and so on.

Thus, this book is intended for all teachers. Elementary school teachers who overtly teach reading skills can use the material in this book to teach reading better. Secondary school and content-area teachers can use the suggestions in this book to help their students better understand the reading materials used in their courses.

This book is also intended for use as a college text for reading methods courses at both the undergraduate and graduate levels. For undergraduates preparing to be teachers, it will provide many useful ideas for their future teaching careers. For graduate students, reading researchers, and my colleagues who are training such, this book is intended to provide a review and synthesis of the current state of the art in comprehension research as well as a new application of theory to practice.

The title of this book, *Teaching Reading Comprehension Processes,* reflects the fact that the pedagogy suggested herein is based on recent discourse processing research in such fields as reading, cognitive psychology, information processing, and psycholinguistics. The premise is that now that we can describe some of the processes involved in comprehension, we can devise even more effective ways for helping students to use those processes. Thus, as the title suggests, this book is about teaching comprehension as a unified set of processes.

A second special feature of the pedagogy in this text is that it attempts to integrate discourse processing research with general principles of good teaching. Basic themes include the importance of providing each student with activities at his or her level of competence, using ongoing assessment for instructional choices, using direct instruction and modeling, teaching skills in a variety of meaningful contexts, integrating holistic and subskill approaches, and encouraging students to take an active role in their own learning.

Finally, the theory explained in this book represents an attempt to define comprehension in relation to all of the contexts that affect it. This is not an easy task! Comprehension involves a complex interplay of reader, text, and situational contexts that can be only partially specified.

Part One of this text presents a general model of the comprehension process that has emerged from recent research. This model is not the only one possible, nor is it final and complete; instead, I have tried to present a model that synthesizes current research in a way that is usable in the classroom. Thus, for each process described, specific teaching activities are suggested for both developmental and remedial situations. These suggestions are largely drawn from the plethora of recent articles presenting new and exciting ways to teach comprehension.

Part Two deals with the reader, text, and situational contexts each teacher must consider every time he or she teaches comprehension. A description of the importance of each context is followed by the implications for teaching. For instance, Chapter Seven presents ways for teachers to build background and increase motivation. Chapter Eight shows teachers how to examine reading materials critically, and Chapter Nine includes a demonstration of how to choose reading purposes and methods.

Part Three contains discussions of the general methodologies that can be used to teach reading comprehension. In Chapter Ten, a new taxonomy for questions is presented along with the distinction between product and process questions. Chapter Eleven describes an informal, multicontext approach to assessment, and Chapter Twelve presents an overall structure for organizing lessons.

In writing this book, I have attempted to describe, synthesize, and apply everything I know about reading comprehension. I have tried to make new research theories and terminology understandable and usable without losing the complexity of the analysis. Above all, I have tried to write a book that will liberate teachers from being managers of meaningless activities as well as liberate students from being passive recipients of meaningless drill. There is much in current research that can help with this, and I have attempted to communicate it here.

ACKNOWLEDGMENTS

The author wishes to thank her students for their numerous helpful suggestions, Sarah Shaftman and Susane Karlin for their editorial assistance, Patrick Bidelman for his sample text material, and Kenneth Smith for his story, "The Magic Prince." She also wishes to thank her reviewers at Prentice-Hall, Inc., those who have kindly granted reprint permission for previously published material, and all the friends and colleagues who have contributed indirectly but substantially with their patient advice and support.

Judith Westphal Irwin

ONE
COMPREHENSION
PROCESSES: *An Overview*

All good skill instruction is based on an understanding of the skill being taught. Thus, a book on teaching reading comprehension must include a description of the reading comprehension process itself. Indeed, one of the big problems in designing methods for teaching comprehension has been that comprehension is such a complex process that it has been difficult to understand fully.

In this chapter you will find an introduction to the new description of reading comprehension on which this book is based. First, the five types of processes that seem to occur during comprehension are briefly described. Following this is a discussion of the factors that influence what a reader understands when he or she reads. Finally, a definition of comprehension is presented.

Take some time to familiarize yourself with the new vocabulary introduced in this chapter, but don't be concerned if the new concepts are still a little unclear. This is just an introduction! All of these new terms will be discussed in more depth later in this book. In fact, you may wish to read this chapter again after you have finished reading all of Parts One and Two.

TRADITIONAL SUBSKILL MODELS AND METHODS

If we were to begin with an examination of how comprehension has traditionally been taught, we would see that it is usually taught in the form of isolable subskills. Students are given worksheets or are asked questions that require them to do things such as making comparisons, finding main ideas, recalling sequences, and so forth. Recently, however, this subskill model of comprehension has received considerable criticism. Though, certainly, some of the activities have been worthwhile, there are some problems with this approach worthy of note.

First, there is no available research to support any one list of skills or, indeed, to substantiate the theory that there are separable skills in the first place (see Rosenshine, 1980). As a result, lists of subskills vary considerably in terms of what skills they include. In a study of five commonly used lists, Rosenshine (1980) found that although there were several skills found on all the lists, there were many more that were unique to the separate lists. As a result, there has been very limited consistency in what has been taught as comprehension.

Another problem with the traditional subskills approach is the fact that the skill lists and the related activities tend to be based on the premise that comprehension is a passive, static process. Activities generally have a "one right answer" approach and are based on the assumption that the one right answer is to be found in the reading selection itself. There is little evidence of an awareness of the active nature of the reading process or of the facts that different people view things differently and that reading strategies are related to purposes and situations. Thus, many of these instructional programs produce passive readers who cannot comprehend in realistic situations that require active inference and strategy selection.

COMPREHENSION PROCESSES[1]

Perhaps, instead of lists of isolable subskills, we need a model of what is actually happening when a reader comprehends. Perhaps, if we can understand how comprehension occurs, then we can teach students to do it. The model presented in this book, though not necessarily a perfect replica of the process, represents an attempt to model comprehension in a way that is instructionally useful. It is largely based on the models presented by cognitive psychologists (Just & Carpenter, 1980; Kintsch & van Dijk, 1978; Rumelhart, 1976), although it also integrates much of the recent research conducted by reading educators.

[1]See Chapters Two through Six.

All of this research seems to indicate that there are at least five processes that proceed simultaneously during comprehension. Each of these processes involves a variety of subprocesses. The basic processes to be discussed in Part One of this book are diagrammed in Figure 1-1. Let's look at each one of the basic processes separately before discussing how they fit together in one unitary act. (Remember, don't worry if you find these hard to understand. Each will be discussed in more detail in future chapters.)

Microprocesses

The reader's first task is to derive meaning from the individual idea units in each sentence and to decide which of these ideas to remember. *The initial chunking and selective recall of individual idea units within individual sentences can be called* **microprocessing**.

Assuming that the meanings of individual words are understood (see Chapter Seven), at least two processing skills are required for the understanding of individual sentences. The first is the ability to group words into meaningful phrases. This is often called "chunking," and it involves a basic understanding of syntax and its use in written language. For instance, in sentence 1a, a reader would need to realize that "red" should be grouped with "balloon" because it tells what kind of balloon, that "slowly" similarly modifies "disappeared" rather than "balloon," and so forth.

1a.   The red balloon slowly disappeared into the blue sky.

A good reader would automatically "chunk" the sentence in this fashion while reading, and research indicates that good and poor comprehenders often differ in their responsiveness to these boundaries between meaningful phrases (Cohen & Freeman, 1978; Levin & Kaplan, 1970; and others). A second major skill required for microprocessing is the ability to select what idea units to remember. For example, when reading sentence 1a, a reader might choose to remember only that a balloon disappeared. If another idea, such as the fact that the balloon was red, was particularly important to the progress of the narrative that fact might also be remembered. As students mature, they are asked to read longer and longer passages. It is clearly impossible to remember every detail (without extensive application of study strategies), and good readers select what is important in each sentence, retaining only that information in memory (Kintsch & van Dijk, 1978).

Integrative Processes

Readers can recall what they read only if the individual ideas are connected into a coherent whole (Kintsch & van Dijk, 1978; Thorndyke, 1976; and others). This means that the relationships between clauses and/or be-

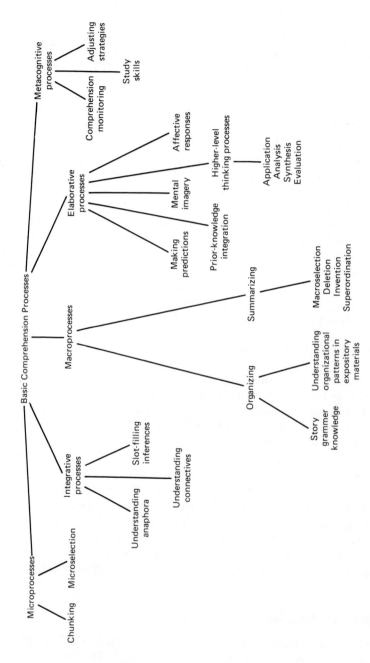

4

FIGURE 1-1

tween sentences must also be comprehended. *The process of understanding and inferring the relationships between individual clauses and/or sentences can be called* **integrative processing**.

Integrative processing requires the ability to do such things as identifying pronoun referents, inferring causation and sequence, and making other relevant inferences about the total situation being described. For instance, for sentences 1b and 1c, several inferences could be made to integrate these ideas.

1b. John went to the store.
1c. He was hungry.

First, one must infer that "he" refers to John. Second, one might infer that he went to the store *because* he was hungry. This would involve the added inferences that the store sold food and that he was going to buy some. (Note the amount of active inferring necessary to understand the relationships between two very simple sentences!)

Macroprocesses

Ideas are connected and retained in memory more effectively if they are organized around an overall organizational pattern. The main topics in an organized text make up a kind of summary. *The process of synthesizing and organizing individual idea units into a summary or organized series of related general ideas can be called* **macroprocessing**.

At least two skills are necessary for macroprocessing. The first is the ability to select the general ideas and to summarize the passage. This can also involve such things as deleting unimportant information and identifying or constructing general or main idea statements that summarize a large number of details.

The second major macroprocessing skill is the ability to use the author's general organizational pattern to organize one's own memory representation. Research has repeatedly shown that students who use the author's organizational pattern when they recall something they have read tend to recall more than those who do not (Meyer, Brandt, & Bluth, 1980) .

Elaborative Processes

As we read, we often make inferences not necessarily intended by the author and not required for a literal interpretation. For instance, we may make a prediction about what might happen, we may form a vivid mental picture, or we may think about how the information relates to something similar we have experienced. *The process of making inferences not necessarily intended by the author can be called* **elaborative processing**.

Research indicates that elaborations help us to recall the text. In general, readers who make elaborations recall more than those who do not (see Reder, 1980). It is important to note, however, that elaborations must have some relationship to the text. Inappropriate elaborating may actually interfere with comprehension of the author's intended message.

Metacognitive Processes

Metacognition may be loosely defined as conscious awareness and control of one's own cognitive processes. This involves knowing when one does or does not understand something and knowing how to go about achieving a cognitive goal, such as successful comprehension or long-term recall. *The process of adjusting one's strategies to control comprehension and long-term recall can be called* **metacognitive processing**.

Study skills are the most common of the metacognitive skills. Rehearsing, reviewing, underlining, and note-taking are all metacognitive processes that facilitate remembering. At a more basic level, checking an earlier part of the text to resolve an inconsistency, and even just being aware that something is unclear, are examples of ways that readers can have control over their own comprehension.

The Total Comprehension Process

We are now ready to begin to define comprehension itself. On the basis of the previous discussion, we can define comprehension as

> [the] process in which a reader understands and selectively recalls ideas in individual sentences (microprocesses), understands and/or infers relationships between clauses and/or sentences (integrative processes), organizes and synthesizes the recalled ideas into general ideas (macroprocesses), and make inferences not necessarily intended by the author (elaborative processes). The reader controls and adjusts these processes according to the immediate goal (metacognitive processes). All these processes occur virtually simultaneously, constantly interacting with each other (interactive hypothesis).

The *interactive hypothesis* was added to this definition to stress that these processes do not occur separately. We must assume that they occur almost simultaneously in no prespecified order, and that they interact with each other. This is reflected in the fact that each process can, in some situations, contribute to the success of another. For instance, understanding the organization (macroprocess) can help a reader to infer intersentential relationships (integrative process). Elaborating on one detail (elaborative process) can lead to recalling other details selectively (microprocess). This *interactive hypothesis* has important implications for teaching, which will be discussed throughout this book.

Now we have a definition that seems to describe comprehension in terms of what is actually happening when a reader comprehends. Can we

now teach students to comprehend everything, just by teaching these processes? Unfortunately, the answer is probably no. This definition still doesn't
really explain why students who *can comprehend* in one situation *cannot comprehend* in another or why students with *similar* abilities often seem to perform *differently* at the same task. To understand these phenomena, we must
understand how the comprehension process is influenced by the total context in which it occurs.

COMPREHENSION CONTEXTS

It is impossible to separate any act of comprehension from the contextual
factors that influence it (see Spiro, 1980). The individual reader's characteristics (reader context), the specific text being read[2] (text context), and the
total situation (situational context) all exert a strong influence on what is
comprehended.

Comprehension is an active process to which each reader brings his or
her individual attitudes, interests, expectations, skills, and prior knowledge
(reader context). Because the writer's message can never be entirely explicit, the reader must actively infer and interpret what is on the page in the
light of what he or she brings to the task. A good example of the effects of
reader characteristics is provided by Anderson, Reynolds, Schallert, and
Goetz (1977). They gave readers an ambiguous passage using words such
as "play," "score," and "arrangement." Music students tended to interpret
the passage as a discussion of a woodwind ensemble, whereas physical education students tended to interpret it as a card game. In addition, 62 percent of the students said that the other interpretation had never occurred
to them.

Research has also provided many examples of how text characteristics
can influence what is comprehended. Readability research has shown that
word familiarity and sentence length can affect comprehensibility. More
recent research has revealed that passage coherence and organization may
also affect comprehensibility. Indeed, Chapter Eight in this text provides a
checklist of thirty-five text factors that may influence the comprehension
process.

Thus, we need a definition of comprehension that mentions both
reader and text influences. An excellent definition that does emphasize
both of these has been suggested by Johnston (1981): "Reading comprehension is viewed as the process of using one's own prior knowledge and

---

[2]Throughout this book, the term "text" will be used to refer to the written passage being read. It is not meant to refer to a textbook, which is only one kind of text. Magazine articles, newspapers, essays, and paragraphs are examples of other types of texts that might be
assigned.

the writer's cues to infer the author's intended meaning" (p. 16). This definition stresses the fact that comprehension is affected by both the reader's background and the text characteristics. It also stresses the active role of the reader who can only infer the complete message from what is explicitly stated. One change in Johnston's wording that might be made is that changing "knowledge" to "experiences." This could be done to emphasize that *both cognitive* prior knowledge and *affective* attitudes and interests influence what is inferred.

On the basis of this definition, we can now predict that two readers will comprehend similarly only when they have very similar interests and backgrounds and are reading the same text; but is it also possible for two very similar readers reading the same passage to comprehend differently? The answer is definitely yes: a high school student reading a magazine article in the dentist's office is likely to comprehend differently from a similar student reading the same article to prepare for a debate. A sixth-grade student reading a book for a book-sharing club at the local library may comprehend differently from a similar student reading the same book for language arts class. You can probably think of other examples in which what is comprehended is affected by the total situation (situational context).

All of the factors influencing what is comprehended, the *comprehension contexts,* have been diagrammed as a "contexts pyramid" (see Figure 1-2) by Mosenthal (1984); this diagram emphasizes the fact that what is

FIGURE 1-2   The Context Pyramid of Reading Comprehension*

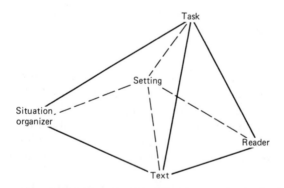

The Context Pyramid of reading comprehension. Following Jenkins (1979, p. 432), each vertex represents a cluster of variables of a given type shown to influence reading comprehension. Each degree represents a two-way interaction between Contexts; each plane calls attention to a three-way interaction, and the entire Figure represents the five-way interaction of all the variables that could possibly influence reading comprehension.

*From Mosenthal, P. (1984). Reading comprehension research from a classroom perspective. In J. Flood (Ed.), *Promoting Reading Comprehension.* Newark, Delaware: International Reading Association. Reprinted with the permission of P. Mosenthal and the International Reading Association.

comprehended is influenced by the individual reader's characteristics, the text's characteristics, and the situation-related factors: the situation organizer, the task, and the total setting. In the classroom, the situation organizer is usually the teacher; the task usually consists of a variety of instructions, questions, and/or activities provided in the teacher's manual or workbook; and the setting is usually the classroom in an individual, a small-group, or a whole-class format.

At this point, then, it would be useful to expand on Johnston's definition to include the situational contexts that influence comprehension. Perhaps the following expanded definition will suffice:

> Comprehension can be seen as the process of using one's own prior experiences and the writer's cues to infer the author's intended meaning. This process varies in ways designed to satisfy the requirements of the total situation in which it is taking place.

Now we have a definition that seems to describe the comprehension process accurately in terms of what influences it, but not in terms of what is actually happening. In what ways does it vary? How does the reader go about inferring the author's intended meaning? To answer these questions, we will need to combine this latest definition with our earlier attempt.

DEFINING COMPREHENSION

Before reading any farther, take out a sheet of paper and try to write out the definition just given above. Then try to expand this definition to include the five comprehension processes discussed earlier. Try to avoid using the new terminology. This will help you to check your comprehension of what you read in this chapter. You may wish to compare your definition with the one given here. The new terminology has been inserted to help you review.

> Comprehension can be seen as the process of using one's own prior experiences (reader context) and the writer's cues (text context) to infer the author's intended meaning. This process can involve understanding and selectively recalling ideas in individual sentences (microprocesses), inferring relationships between clauses and/or sentences (integrative processes), organizing ideas around summarizing ideas (macroprocesses), and making inferences not necessarily intended by the author (elaborative processes). These processes work together (interactive hypothesis) and can be controlled and adjusted by the reader as required by the reader's goals (metacognitive processes) and the total situation in which comprehension is taking place (situational context).

WHEW!

AN EXAMPLE

Suppose that you are teaching current events to a class of fifth-grade students. You ask each student to read a newspaper article and tell the class what it said. Sally, an average reader with a generally good attitude, reads the following article.

> No issue has been more controversial in the political history of the United States than the right of "judicial review." Judicial review takes place when the Federal courts decide whether laws passed by Congress and signed by the President conform to the Constitution. This right is not a right at all, however, at least not like the first ten Amendments to the Constitution which establish a "Bill of Rights" for citizens of the United States. Rather, the right of judicial review is a long-honored tradition that began with the path-breaking decisions of the Marshall Court in the nation's early days.
>
> The opponents of this tradition have been as loud as the tradition has been long. It is not surprising then that once again there are many who wish to restrict or perhaps even abolish judicial review. Especially in the 1980s, after nearly two decades of "liberal" Warren Court decisions, this tradition is being challenged by conservatives who oppose the Supreme Court's decisions on school prayer, busing, abortion, and rights of accused criminals. In fact, Congress is presently considering nearly 40 bills limiting the jurisdiction of the Federal Courts in such matters.
>
> The alarming aspect of all this is that, beyond authorizing Congress to "ordain and establish" such courts as it chooses, the Constitution says nothing about what courts should exist, let alone what power they should have. It is unlikely but not impossible, therefore, that the current congressional attacks on judicial review could result in the complete elimination of the present Federal Court system. Some fiction of a court system might remain, but the remnants would be like the King's clothes.

In class, Sally says,

> It talked about how the courts can say whether a law is okay and some people don't like what the courts have done so the government might just get rid of the courts altogether. They are talking about passing forty laws to keep the courts from doing things about things like busing and school prayer like Sam talked about in his report last week. There was something about the King's clothes but I didn't understand it. I didn't really care because I thought it was a dumb article anyway.

Now, let's look to see what processes Sally used to comprehend this article. Table 1-1 shows our best guess as to the processes evidenced in her recall. Study this chart. Note that even for this simple exercise, Sally seems to have used all five comprehension processes.

Sally's report also provides some examples of how the comprehension processes interact: Sally recalled the details surrounding the issue of school prayer because she elaborated in terms of Sam's report. She recalled the detail of "forty laws" because it was relevant to the main point of limiting

TABLE 1-1 Comprehension Processes Evident in Sally's Report

RECALL	PROCESS
"It talked about how the courts can say whether a law is OK and some people don't like what the courts have done so the government might just get rid of the courts altogether."	Macroprocesses (She has reduced the article to a kind of summary statement.)
"They are talking about passing forty laws to keep the courts from doing things . . . "	Microprocesses (She has remembered specific details that she thought were important.)
" . . . about things like busing and school prayer . . . "	Integrative processes (She has integrated two sentences of the article.)
" . . . like Sam talked about in his report last week."	Elaborative processes (She has linked this article to something she heard before.)
"There was something about the King's clothes but I didn't understand it. I didn't really care because it was a dumb article anyway."	Metacognitive processes (She was aware of what she didn't understand and decided not to do anything about it.)

the courts. Her summary didn't include the point of the last sentence because she failed to understand it at the microlevel.

Moreover, Sally's report also provides us with some examples of the ways in which the text, the reader, and the situation can influence the five processes. For instance, the author's use of a literary reference limited Sally's microcomprehension (text effect). She might have been able to get the information she needed to figure it out, but her lack of interest caused her to choose not to try any metacognitive strategies (reader effect). Finally, it may be the case that her anxiety (reader effect) about the task of reporting to the class (situational effect) was what caused her poor attitude and her somewhat low level of recall or that knowing that she was going to report to the class (situational effect) caused her to focus on the part related to the other report she knew everyone in the class had heard. Indeed, it would be possible to speculate about how each of the comprehension contexts affected the way Sally used each of the five processes. (See Activity 5 at the end of this chapter.)

A FINAL NOTE

You may have noticed that "comprehension" often inherently implies recall, and it may sometimes seem that these words are being used interchangeably. Indeed, in practice, it is virtually impossible to separate them.

We simply cannot tell what a student has comprehended without asking him or her to recognize or recall it in some way. Thus, in this text, if the terms "comprehension" and "recall" are separated, it will be only for the sake of emphasis. Usually this is done to distinguish between what the reader remembers soon after reading (comprehension) and what is remembered after a period of time (recall).

SELF-CHECK TEST

1. Define each of these terms in your own words (If you cannot, refer to the text and review):

   reader context   macroprocesses
   text context   elaborative processes
   situational context   metacognitive processes
   microprocesses   interactive hypothesis
   integrative processes

2. Answer true or false:

   ___ a. Everything to be comprehended is usually explicitly stated by the author.
   ___ b. A reader's affective experiences affect what is comprehended.
   ___ c. In practice, what a student comprehends and what that student recalls are difficult to separate.
   ___ d. Macroprocesses always occur before elaborative processes.
   ___ e. Inferring relationships between sentences is an elaborative process.
   ___ f. Summarizing is classified here as a metacognitive process.
   ___ g. Chunking is a macroprocess.
   ___ h. Elaborations can affect microprocesses.
   ___ i. Good readers remember everything they have read.
   ___ j. Study skills such as note-taking and underlining are integrative processes.

3. Fill in the blanks in the following passage:

   Comprehension can be seen as the process of using one's own prior _____ (reader context) and the writer's cues (_____ context) to _____ the author's intended meaning. This process can involve understanding and selectively recalling ideas in individual _____ (microprocesses), _____ relationships between clauses and/or sentences (_____ processes), organizing ideas around _____ ideas (macroprocesses), and making inferences not necessarily _____ by the author (_____ processes). These processes _____ (interactive hypothesis) and can be controlled and adjusted by the _____ as required by the reader's_____ (metacognitive processes) and the total _____ in which comprehension is taking place (_____ context).

SUGGESTED ACTIVITIES

1. Diagram your definition of comprehension.
2. Ask a student to read and recall a passage. Tape-record the recall and then write it out on paper. Try to mark each phrase or sentence as to the type of process he or she seems to have used. What were the contexts that caused the student to remember this way?
3. Read a magazine article and write down what you remember. What processes did you use? What contexts affected which processes you emphasized?
4. Begin a notebook or card file of teaching activities. Make a divider for each process and for the three major contexts (reader, text, situation). On each divider, define the process or context and explain why it is important.
5. Speculate on how each of the comprehension contexts affected the way Sally used each of the five processes (see page 10).

REFERENCES

ANDERSON, R. C., REYNOLDS, R. E., SCHALLERT, D. L., & GOETZ, E. T. (1977). Frameworks for comprehending discourse. *American Educational Research Journal, 14,* 367–381.

COHEN,G., & FREEMAN, R. (1978). Individual differences in reading strategies in relation to handedness and cerebral asymmetry. In J. Requin (Ed.), *Attention and performance,* Vol. VII. Hillsdale, N.J.: Lawrence Erlbaum.

JENKINS, J. J. (1979). Four points to remember: A tetrahedral model of memory experiments. In L.S. Cermak & F. I. M. Craik (Eds.), *Levels of processing in human memory.* Hillsdale, N.J.: Lawrence Erlbaum.

JOHNSTON, P. (1981). *Implications of basic research for the assessment of reading comprehension* (Technical Report no. 206). Urbana-Champaign: Center for the Study of Reading, University of Illinois.

JUST, M. A., & CARPENTER, P. A. (1980). A theory of reading: From eye fixations to comprehension. *Psychological Review, 87,* 329–354.

KINTSCH, W., & VAN DIJK, T. A. (1978). Toward a model of text comprehension and production. *Psychological Review, 85,* 363–394.

LEVIN, H., & KAPLAN, E. L. (1970). Grammatical structure and reading. In H. Levin and J. P. Williams (Eds.), *Basic studies in reading.* New York: Basic Books.

MEYER, B., BRANDT, D., & BLUTH, G. (1980). Use of top-level structure in text: Key for reading comprehension of ninth-grade students. *Reading Research Quarterly, 16,* 71–103.

MOSENTHAL, P. (1984). Reading comprehension research from a classroom prospective. In J. Flood (Ed.), *Promoting reading comprehension.* Newark, Dela.: International Reading Association.

REDER, L. M. (1980). The role of elaboration in the comprehension and retention of prose: A critical review. *Review of Educational Research, 50,* 5–53.

ROSENSHINE, B. (1980). Skill hierarchies in reading comprehension. In R. J. Spiro, B. C. Bruce, and W. F. Brewer (Eds.), *Theoretical issues in reading comprehension.* Hillsdale, N.J.:Lawrence Erlbaum.

RUMELHART, D. E. (1976). *Toward an interactive model of reading* (Technical Report no. 56). San Diego: Center for Human Information Processing, University of California.

SPIRO, R. J. (1980). Constructive processes in prose comprehension and recall. In R. J. Spiro, B. C. Bruce, and W. F. Brewer (Eds.), *Theoretical issues in reading comprehension.* Hillsdale, N.J.: Lawrence Erlbaum.

THORNDYKE, P. (1976). The role of inference in discourse comprehension. *Journal of Verbal Learning and Verbal Behavior, 15,* 437–446.

TWO
TEACHING
MICROPROCESSES

In the next five chapters, each of the processes involved in comprehension will be examined in more depth, and relevant teaching suggestions for elementary, remedial, and content-area teachers will be presented. This chapter begins with a discussion of general considerations for designing lessons that teach comprehension processes and ends with a discussion of the two specific microprocesses of chunking words into meaningful phrases and selecting what to remember from individual sentences. As you read, think about students you have known who would have benefited from this type of instruction and about specific applications for your teaching situation. Although an attempt has been made to provide activities for a variety of classrooms, providing a direct application of each suggestion to each possible teaching situation is, of course, impossible.

BASICS FOR TEACHING COMPREHENSION

In a recent study of comprehension instruction in elementary basal reading series, Jenkins and Pany (1980) found that instructional procedures are dominated by classroom discussion and question answering. They also found that no correction procedures are generally provided for use when the student answers wrongly. Students are seldom told *what* they are doing right or wrong; they are just told *that* they are right or wrong.

Similarly, in an important article entitled "The Illusion of Instruction," Duffy and Roehler (1982) point out that most reading instruction follows a simple "repeated exposure" model: students are given repeated practice with a variety of activities with little emphasis on telling them how to do it. This seems to be "based on the expectation that all pupils, regardless of background and/or aptitude, will learn to do the selected task if exposed enough . . ." (p. 439).

Comprehension instruction can go beyond simply asking questions and providing repeated exposures to tasks. As Duffy and Roehler point out, we need to add an "*explicative function*" (p. 441), that is, explanations of *how* to do things. Teachers need to tell students why an answer is not the best and how to change approaches to arrive at better answers. Moreover, teachers can model effective strategies for the students by describing their own thinking processes (Collins & Smith, 1980). The instructional suggestions that follow in this text will often include suggestions for directly explaining and modeling strategies and skills. (See Chapter Twelve for a complete model of direct comprehension instruction.)

A second important concept that can be used for designing comprehension lessons is the "*continuum of independence*" (Herber, 1970). For every skill, each student can be placed on a continuum from being very dependent on the teacher or instructional materials for guidance to being capable of performing the skill in a completely independent way. For instance, one student may be able to construct a chapter outline only if provided with a partial outline in which he or she is to fill in a few missing topics. In contrast, another student in the same class may be able to write the outline if given a blank sheet of paper. Both students can do some outlining, but one is more independent than the other. The goal is to provide the guidance students need in such a way that they progress toward increasing independence. Thus, in this text, an attempt has been made to provide activities that are appropriate for students at a variety of locations on the continuum.

The concepts of *vertical* and *horizontal transformation* (Herber, 1970) also have important implications for teaching comprehension. "Transformation" is the process of modifying or transforming skills to apply in situations different from the one in which they were learned. For instance, outlining a social studies chapter following a sequential organizational pattern involves a slightly different skill than does outlining a science chapter organized by classifications. Similarly, finding the main idea in an essay in the *Weekly Reader* is different from finding the main idea of an essay by Francis Bacon. Herber (1970) called the transforming of skills across content areas "horizontal transformation" and the transforming of skills across grade levels "vertical transformation." The important point is that transformations do not necessarily occur without teacher guidance. Thus, the transforming of skills taught in reading or in the younger grades should be addressed in other content areas and in the upper grades, and activities are provided in this book for a variety of situations for just this reason. (When the term "content area" is used, it is referring to content subjects such as social studies and science as taught in the elementary school as well as those content areas taught in the secondary school. The teaching of reading in the content areas is probably needed in grades K–12, not just in grades 9–12 as is sometimes suggested. Many of the content-area suggestions provided in this text are as appropriate for the fourth grade as they are for the twelfth grade.)

A fourth factor to consider when examining the comprehension activities suggested in this text is the *interrelationship of reading and writing*. Teaching outlining as a reading/note-taking skill is certainly related to teaching outlining as a first step in writing an essay. Teaching students to find main ideas in social studies books is related to teaching students to include main ideas in social studies reports. Although reading researchers are now only beginning to investigate this hypothesis systematically (Aulls & Irwin, in preparation), it seems quite possible that writing instruction can be used to reinforce reading skills, and vice versa. Thus, many of the activities in this text will involve writing as well as reading.

Moreover, the most effective comprehension activities will be those that are designed in reference to all the *comprehension contexts*. Good teachers consider the readers, the text, and the total situation when deciding how to structure tasks. For instance, activities for reluctant readers might be different from those used for students who like reading; activities designed to accompany a novel will be very different from those designed to accompany a lab manual; activities for small groups will be different from those for large groups. In other words, although specific activities will be provided in this text, teachers should feel free to adapt them to the total situation in which they are working.

Similarly, comprehension activities are most effective when they are placed in a *meaningful context*. Students are more likely to interact actively with material that they are reading for a meaning-oriented purpose than with paragraphs they are reading as abstract exercises for skill development. Although it is not always possible, the teaching of reading skills within the context of reading for other reasons is ideal, and the activities in this book can be integrated into a variety of meaningful reading situations.

Finally, and perhaps most important, comprehension must always be taught as a fundamentally *holistic process*. Although we may find it necessary to analyze the process into teachable units, it is always true that many processes are occurring simultaneously. An activity stressing summarizing skills will still require the students to use the other processes to some extent. We cannot completely isolate processes that must interact in order to be effective. We can only highlight one, knowing that the others are being used as well. Failure to complete one process may be a result of problems with another, and it seems critical that teachers often provide holistic activities in which no one process is artificially isolated.

STOP! Review the seven points made in this section. Can you define them all? A thorough understanding will be important for effectively using the activities provided in this book.

CHUNKING

Assuming that readers can read individual words (see the Preface), their first task is to *chunk* the words into meaningful syntactic units. Research continues to indicate that the clause is a basic processing unit for good readers (Hurtig, 1978). Because written syntax is somewhat different from that used in oral language (Leu, 1982) and because controlling eye movements is different from listening, the immediate transfer of this skill from listening to reading cannot be assumed.

Researchers have found that poor readers sometimes benefit from chunking assistance. Cromer (1970) defined *difference readers* as those who had adequate word-level skills but inadequate comprehension skills. He found that these difference readers were aided by having the material divided into chunks for them. Mason and Kendall (1978) similarly found that poor readers' comprehension improved when sentences were segmented. Stevens (1981) found that high school sophomores at all ability levels performed better on a standardized comprehension test when the passages had been chunked by drawing slashes between phrasal units.

One possible cause of word-by-word, unchunked reading is the student's initial concept of the reading process itself. Research indicates that students learn what they are taught (Calfee & Piontkowski, 1981). If children are taught that reading is the decoding of individual words rather than the decoding of a meaningful message, they will concentrate their cognitive energies on simply decoding words. Goodman and Burke (1980) have reported that some beginning readers have said that the purpose of reading is "to learn to read words" and that authors write "to teach you letters and words." It can be predicted that these students may become word-by-word readers who do not chunk the words into meaningful phrases.

Another possible cause of chunking difficulty for some readers is word identification difficulty. If students are having trouble reading the individual words fluently, they may have difficulty with chunking. (See Chapter Seven for a discussion of decoding fluency.)

General Teaching Strategies

To some extent, chunking can be facilitated in classrooms at all grade levels and in all content areas. Students can be encouraged to view reading as a meaning-getting process and therefore to read individual words in the context of meaningful phrases: a third-grade student trying to understand a new word in a science class can be told to look at the whole phrase in which it is used; a fifth-grade student having trouble with an unreasonably long sentence in a social studies text can be shown how to break it into phrases and read it in shorter, meaningful parts first; a ninth-grade student reading Shakespeare for the first time can be shown how finding clause boundaries can make it more understandable and how the phrasal context often gives clues to unusual word meanings.

Moreover, chunking fluency probably develops best when students are given numerous opportunities to practice reading fluently. Because texts in different content areas tend to contain slightly different syntactic patterns, wide reading of easy materials in different subjects and genres would probably be useful. All teachers can contribute to this.

Direct Chunking Instruction

In elementary, corrective, and remedial situations, it may be possible for chunking to be taught directly. Students who can read the words but read without intonation or in a jerky, word-by-word fashion may need to learn to chunk words into meaningful phrases. They may also need to learn to view reading as a meaningful activity. Though there has been little research showing the best ways to teach chunking, the following activities may be useful.

Reading "chunked" material. For students at the most dependent end of the continuum of independence, passages can be rewritten in phrases for practice (see Figure 2-1). Reading "machines" can be made to help students to read in phrases (see Figure 2-2). Put comprehension questions at the beginning and end so that they will read the phrases as meaningful units. Students can practice rereading the same series of phrases until they can pull the paper through very quickly and answer all the questions completely. They can also time each other with stopwatches and, if appropriate,

Figure 2-1 Segment of Story Rewritten for Chunking Practice

One day
a little girl
decided
that she wanted
a new doll.

She wanted one
that looked
just like her.

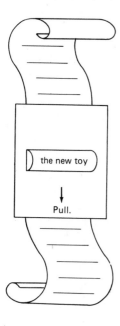

FIGURE 2-2   Reading "Machine" for Chunking Practice.

have contests for speed. (Of course, this is *not* speed-reading—it is not really even reading, at least, natural reading, at all. The main point is to show the students how the words fall into phrases, and the emphasis on rate may encourage them to process the information in phrasal chunks.) Finally, at a more independent level, students can make chunked material and reading "machines" for each other

For older students, teachers can simply mark the phrasal boundaries with slashes on short passages that the students are reading. Eventually, these marks can be used only on the beginning sections of long passages and the students can be asked to try to continue "phrase reading" even after the marks stop. At a more independent level, students can divide passages into phrases themselves. Students can be asked to compare their markings so that they can clarify why they chunk words the way they do. Of course, being able to chunk in this fashion does not guarantee students' ability to chunk automatically as they read. Practice with reading simple but increasingly difficult material that can be processed fluently is still the final step in developing chunking automaticity.

Dramatic reading for chunking practice.   Another activity that may increase students' awareness of the syntactic patterns in written language is reading with expression. A story, play, or poem at the appropriate level and of an appropriate length can be selected on the basis of interest appeal and dramatic dialogue. Different levels of teacher support can be provided as needed. For instance, the teacher can model reading the selection sentence by sentence or section by section with the student imitating the intonation immediately afterward. Similarly, the teacher and student can mark the phrasal units together, and then the student can practice reading the phrases with the teacher or alone. Repeated readings of the same passage will be necessary, and this alone may increase fluency and self-confidence. The end result can be a tape recording for use by other students reading the story or a classroom dramatic presentation as well as an increased awareness of how written language can be divided into meaningful phrases.

Sentence organization instruction.   Practice in synthesizing sentences has been shown to be an effective instructional technique by Weaver (1979). Students can be taught to solve sentence anagrams (sentences in which the words have been scrambled) by using a "word-grouping strategy" (p. 135). In other words, they can be taught first to arrange the words into phrases and then to arrange the phrases into sentences. They should probably first identify the verb phrase and then ask "wh" questions to identify the other phrases. The strategy should be modeled first. Then, students can be given sentences of increasing length. Here is an example of a teacher modeling a sentence anagram task:

GIVEN: boy store the the was to going   [on cards]
TEACHER: Well, the verb is "going," so we'll start with that:

     | GOING | [placed on table]

Are there any helping verbs? Yes, "was" is a helping verb. Let s tape these together.

| WAS | = | GOING | [taped together]

Now, I can ask, *Who* was going? Well, it was either the boy or the store . . . probably BOY, and THE goes with it, so I'll tape THE to BOY and put it in front of my other phrase.

| THE | = | BOY | | WAS | = | GOING | [two taped phrases placed next to each other]

Now, what words are left?

| STORE | | THE | | TO | [left on table]

Can I make a phrase from those? Yes,
and I'll tape those together.

| TO | = | THE | = | STORE | [taped together]

Does this go with the rest? Yes, at the end:

| THE | = | BOY | | WAS | = | GOING | | TO | = | THE | = | STORE |

Result: three taped-together phrases placed in the correct order

Paraphrase instruction.   One way to encourage students to focus on phrase meaning rather than on word identification is to provide tasks that require students to identify or supply a paraphrase of an original statement. Pearson and Johnson (1978) distinguish between semantic paraphrases as in 3a and 3b that follow and syntactic paraphrases as in 3c and 3d. Syntactic paraphrase tasks are probably more useful for chunking instruction than are semantic paraphrase tasks.

A semantic paraphrase is

3a.   Jack jumped over the bushes.
3b.   Jack leaped over the hedge.

A syntactic paraphrase is:

3c.   Jack flew the kite.
3d.   The kite was flown by Jack.

Note that the exact connotations of paraphrases are often somewhat different. For example, 3c emphasizes the person who is doing the action whereas 3d emphasizes the object of the action. Thus, it would be better to ask students to select or write sentences whose meanings are "similar" rather than "the same."

Games in which students match pairs or triples of sentences with similar meanings can be used in the elementary grades. Also, team activities in which the person "up" must create a paraphrase in less time than the corresponding member of the other team can be used with older children. The purpose of these activities is to encourage word-by-word readers to focus on the meaning of the sentences. This requires them to chunk the individual words into meaningful phrases.

MICROSELECTION

As good readers read, they are constantly selecting what details to retain in their memories (see Kintsch & van Dijk, 1978). Even when reading individual sentences, students must be actively involved in selecting the most important ideas in each of those sentences. This can be called *microselection*. This is similar to the traditional skill of "finding the main idea of individual sentences," which has been suggested as a prerequisite skill for finding the central ideas in longer passages (Baumann, 1982).

There is evidence that good readers are likely to recall important rather than unimportant details (Meyer, 1977). "Important" can be informally defined as those details that are most highly related to the central idea of the passage or most necessary for the understanding of subsequent ideas. Thus, even though "microselection" refers to selecting the important details in individual sentences, it seems that successful microselection is dependent on successsful macroprocessing or finding the central idea of the whole selection. This is a good example of how various processes interact.

General Microselection Instruction

Teachers at all levels can directly encourage students to select important details from sentences during class discussions. They can explain the concept of microselection so that students don't get bogged down in trying to remember every word. They can model the process themselves: "Now, what *I* want to remember from this sentence is . . . because . . . ." Examples of teachers teaching microselection range from the kindergarten teacher who, when reading a story to the students, stops and asks, "What was the most important word in that sentence? Why?" to the high school chemistry teacher who, after students read a sentence with a long list of properties for a given substance says, "Which of these properties do you want to remember for our experiment?" (Remember that it is important for all teachers to model and reinforce skills such as microselection so that horizontal and vertical transformation can take place.)

Activities for Microselection Instruction

Selective paraphrase. Paraphrasing activities like those used to stress phrase meaning would probably be useful for teaching microselection. In this case, required or recognized paraphrases should be summary sentences that summarize the first sentence into its main point. For example, sentence 3f is a "selective paraphrase" of sentence 3e.

3e. The boy whom many of us called Gus was caught by the men in blue who had been chasing him.
3f. Gus was caught by the police.

Games in which students compete to supply the shortest selective paraphrase may also be useful. (Of course, activities must reflect the students' level of independence. For students who are at the most dependent level of the continuum of independence for this skill, selective paraphrases from which they can select the best should probably be supplied by the teacher. Students who already have some independence can be asked to supply their own.)

Write your own test.   Students can get involved with meaningful selection by creating their own tests. To focus on microselection, give students worksheets containing important sentences about the material being studied. For each sentence, ask them to write a test question that reflects what is important.

Selecting what to study.   Another meaningful selection task is involving students in deciding what to study. For microselection, the teacher can select or create sentences containing both important and unimportant details from the current unit. List them for the students on an initial study guide. Then, students can make up their own study sheets on which they list only one important detail from each of the sentences listed. They study and then are tested on the important details alone.

SUMMARY

The comprehension activities provided in this book are based on several important considerations. First, explaining the "how" and "why" and modeling the skills are as important as the practice activities themselves. Activities should be appropriate for a student's level of independent functioning with that skill and should be provided in a variety of grade levels and content areas to encourage the appropriate skill transformation. Writing can probably be used to teach comprehension, and vice versa. All comprehension activities must be adjusted to reflect the reader, the text, and the total situation involved, and they are more likely to be effective if they are connected to meaningful reading assignments. Finally, although specific activities can emphasize one process, it must be remembered that the comprehension processes always work together and cannot be completely separated.

Microprocesses are those processes involved in understanding individual sentences. The two microprocesses discussed in this chapter were chunking and microselection. Research has shown that poor readers may have trouble with these skills. Procedures for use in a variety of classrooms were suggested for each.

SELF-CHECK TEST

1. List six characteristics of a good comprehension activity.
2. Define each of these terms:

explicative function

continuum of independence

horizontal transformation

vertical transformation

chunking

difference readers

"reading machine"

sentence anagram task

syntactic paraphrase

microselection

selective paraphrase

3. Answer true or false:

___ a. Once a student can do a skill in the third grade, he or she can do it at every grade level thereafter.

___ b. Students should be expected to perform skills independently from the very beginning.

___ c. It is important to isolate each skill when designing activities.

___ d. A student's intonation often gives a clue about his or her chunking ability.

___ e. Microprocesses should be taught only in the elementary schools.

___ f. If students can read the individual words, they can chunk appropriately.

___ g. A difference reader is one who cannot select what to remember.

___ h. Word identification tasks are useful for teaching chunking.

___ i. Syntactic paraphrase tasks are useful for teaching macroselection.

___ j. The "repeated exposure model" is the approach recommended in this text.

SUGGESTED ACTIVITIES

1. Create a lesson that encourages the students to chunk words into meaningful phrases. Be sure to tell how you would explain and/or model this skill. If possible, try your lesson with an appropriate student. Evaluate its success.

2. Create a lesson that teaches students to select what is important in sentences from a typical reading assignment in your class. Be sure, again, to tell how you would explain and/or model this skill. If possible, try the lesson and evaluate its effectiveness.

3. Continue your notebook of instructional activities by creating materials to teach chunking and selection at a specified grade level. (You need not limit yourself to the activities suggested in this book.)

4. At the beginning of this chapter, some general considerations for teaching comprehension were discussed. What other ones can you suggest? Think of as many as you can and briefly describe each.

REFERENCES

AULLS, M., & IRWIN, J. (in preparation). *Research relating reading and writing processes.* Newark, Dela.: International Reading Association.

BAUMANN, J. (December, 1982). Teaching children to comprehend main ideas. Paper presented at the annual meeting of the National Reading Conference, Clearwater, Fla.

CALFEE, R. C., & PIONTKOWSKI, P. C. (1981). The reading diary: Acquisition of decoding. *Reading Research Quarterly, 16,* 346–373.

COLLINS, A., & SMITH, E. (1980). *Teaching the process of reading comprehension* (Technical Report no. 182). Urbana-Champaign: Center for the Study of Reading, University of Illinois.

CROMER, W. (1970). The difference model: A new explanation for some reading difficulties. *Journal of Educational Psychology, 61,* 471–483.

DUFFY, G. G., & ROEHLER, L. R. (1982). The illusion of instruction. *Reading Research Quarterly, 17,* 438–445.

GOODMAN, V., & BURKE, C. (1980). *Reading Strategies: Focus on comprehension.* New York: Holt, Rinehart and Winston.

HERBER, H. (1970). *Teaching reading in the content areas.* Englewood Cliffs, N.J.: Prentice-Hall.

HURTIG, R. (1978). The validity of clausal processing strategies at the discourse level. *Discourse Processes, 1,* 195–202.

JENKINS, J. R., & PANY, D. (1980). Teaching reading comprehension in the middle grades. In R. J. Spiro, B. C. Bruce, and W. F. Brewer (Eds.), *Theoretical issues in reading comprehension.* Hillsdale, N.J.: Lawrence Erlbaum.

KINTSCH, W., & VAN DIJK, T. A. (1978). Toward a model of text comprehension and production. *Psychological Review, 85,* 363–394.

LEU, D. J. (May, 1982). Written text and oral expectations: Discourse conflicts for beginning readers. Paper presented at the annual meeting of the International Reading Association, Chicago.

MASON, J., & KENDALL, J. (1978). *Facilitating reading comprehension through text-structure manipulation* (Technical Report no. 92). Urbana-Champaign: Center for the Study of Reading, University of Illinois.

MEYER, B. J. F. (1977). What is remembered from prose: A function of passage structure. In R. O. Freedle (Ed.), *Discourse production and comprehension,* Vol. I. Norwood, N.J.: Ablex.

STEVENS, K. (1981). Chunking material as an aid to reading comprehension. *Journal of Reading, 25,* 126–129.

WEAVER, P. A. (1979). Improving reading instruction: Effects of sentence organization instruction. *Reading Research Quarterly, 15,* 129–146.

THREE
TEACHING INTEGRATIVE PROCESSES

One of the most important words in the definition of comprehension that was stated in Chapter One is *infer*. The role of inference in comprehension cannot be overstressed. In fact, it could be said that there can be little or no comprehension without it. Inferring is necessary for understanding the author's message at even a literal level. Consider the following short passage. What inferences are you making as you try to comprehend the author's message?

Sally rode her bike to the store. John followed her. He got a flat tire. He cried.

Well, the most obvious inferences are those involving the pronouns: "her" means "Sally's" and so forth. You also probably inferred that John rode a bike, that the flat tire was on his bike, and that the flat tire caused him to cry. Note that some of these inferences are necessary to understand the meanings of individual words, but, mostly, they are necessary for understanding how the sentences fit together.

This chapter is about integrative processes. They can be defined as the processes involved in understanding and inferring the relationships between clauses and/or between sentences. There are three main types of integrative processes: understanding anaphora, understanding connective relationships, and "slot-filling" inferences.

UNDERSTANDING ANAPHORA

Anaphoric relations are relations between words in which one word or phrase is being used to replace another. For instance, in sentences 4a and 4b that follow, the pronoun "he" is being used to replace "John":

4a. *John* followed Sally.
4b. *He* got a flat tire.

The word being replaced, in this case, "John," is called the *antecedent*.

There are at least three types of anaphoric relations. First, in *pronominal anaphora*, the antecedent is replaced by a personal pronoun, such as *I, me, we, us, you, he, him, they*; a demonstrative pronoun, such as *this, that, these, those*; a proverb, such as *so, does, can, will*, and *have*; or a locative pronoun, such as *here* or *there*. Second, in *substitution*, other synonyms, more inclusive terms such as "these reasons" or "this problem"or "the former," and more specific terms may be used as substitutes. Third, in *ellipsis*, the repeated word or clause may be implied rather than stated directly.

Moreover, these three types of anaphoric relations (pronominal anaphora, substitution, and ellipsis) can also be classified according to what is being replaced. When nouns or noun phrases are being replaced, the relationship exemplifies *nominal anaphora*. In a similar fashion, we can describe *verbal anaphora* and *clausal anaphora*. Table 3-1 gives examples of these two classification systems and how they fit together. Study this table before reading on.

TABLE 3-1   Examples of Anaphoric Relations

	PRONOMIAL	SUBSTITUTION	ELLIPSIS
Nominal	Jack went to the store. He bought candy.	He bought candy. The sugary treats delighted him.	He bought candy. He gave some to Susie.
Verbal	Jack went to the store. So did Sally.	Jack ran to the store. Sally dashed there, too.	I do "care." Do you?
Clausal	Jack went to the store that he always went to. Sally went there, too.	Jack looked as if he had lost his best friend. Sally looked sad, too.	Someone took my candy. I wish I knew who.

Anaphoric relations can be classified in at least two other ways: adjacent versus remote relations and forward versus backward relations. In adjacent relations, the antecedent and the term replacing it are in adjacent clauses or sentences. In remote relations, they are separated by at least one sentence. In forward anaphoric relations, the antecedent comes before the substituting term; in backward anaphoric relations, the antecedent comes second (see Barnitz, 1980). To help clarify these distinctions, Table 3-2 gives examples of anaphoric relations that have been classified according to all these categories. Study this table. Then try to fill in Table 3-3. The answers can be found at the end of the chapter. Of course, it is not critical that you be able to classify all the relations without error. The purpose of this exercise is to familiarize you with the variety of anaphoric relations students encounter as they read. Were you aware of them before reading this chapter?

In general, research seems to indicate that the type of anaphoric relation may make a difference in its comprehensibility. Remote relations may be more difficult to comprehend than adjacent ones (Clark & Sengul, 1979; Moberly, 1978), nominal anaphora may be easier to comprehend than clausal anaphora, and forward relations may be easier than backward ones

TABLE 3-2 Classifying Anaphoric Relations

EXAMPLE	PRONOMIAL, SUBSTITUTION, OR ELLIPSIS?	NOMINAL, VERBAL, OR CLAUSAL?	ADJACENT REMOTE?	FORWARD OR BACKWARD?
Three little pigs went to market. Only two came home.	Ellipsis	Nominal	Adjacent	Forward
The roses and the carnations were beautiful. It was a very hot day. The flowers did not last long.	Substitution	Nominal	Remote	Forward
Tom was hurt at the game. It was really a rough play. He can't play tomorrow.	Pronomial (personal)	Nominal	Remote	Forward
Sally plays tennis. Jack does too.	Pronomial (proverb)	Verbal	Adjacent	Forward
Because he had already been there, he refused to go to the place where he had lost the ring.	Pronomial (locative)	Clausal	Adjacent	Backward

TABLE 3-3   Classifying Anaphoric Relations

EXAMPLE	PRONOMIAL, SUBSTITUTION, OR ELLIPSIS?	NOMINAL, VERBAL, OR CLAUSAL?	ADJACENT OR REMOTE?	FORWARD OR BACKWARD?
Jack is going to run. So will Sally.				
As he has done before, Jack failed the test.				
Jack, Sally, Susie, and Ken had a party. It was on Hallowe'en. A good time was had by all.				
They all passed the test. This pleased me.				
Jack is happy. Sally, too.				

(Barnitz, 1980). Thus, instructional activities might be designed that begin with the simpler adjacent, forward, nominal relations and progress to the more difficult remote, backward, clausal relations. Of course, the conceptual and linguistic difficulty of the material is probably a more important variable than the type of anaphoric relation for determining whether or not it will be comprehended.

Incidental Teaching of Anaphoric Inference

Teachers at all grade levels and in all content areas should be alert to the use of anaphoric references in text assignments. Are there any ambiguous referents? Ask questions that require students to understand referents in their readings. This will give you an idea of whether some direct discussion about finding referents will be necessary. Here are some examples of teachers checking to see if their students are making anaphoric inferences. Note how this skill is important at all grades.

EXAMPLE 1.   THIRD-GRADE AVERAGE READING GROUP

STUDENTS READ:	John went home with Jack. He played his trumpet, and Jack played his drums. Their parents came by to listen. They were amazed by their music.
TEACHER ASKS:	Who was amazed? [why?]

EXAMPLE 2. TENTH-GRADE SOCIAL STUDIES CLASS

STUDENTS READ:	As part of the agreement, Americans gave up their claim to Texas. They were, however, already moving into the region. They were lured by the hope for practically free land.
TEACHER ASKS:	To what region were the Americans moving?

Activities for Direct Instruction in Anaphoric Inference

Many basal series already include some activities for teaching anaphoric inference, although basal activities differ significantly in amount and type. Generally, these activities usually involve students in filling in blanks with pronouns or referents, writing paraphrases, identifying referents for pronouns, or answering questions (Willekens, in press). An excellent discussion of additional activities that can be used as supplements has been provided by Baumann and Stevenson (in press). "Anaphoric cloze," "tying it together," and "making it shorter," described next, are typical examples of possible activities for teaching anaphora.

Anaphoric cloze.   Activities in which students must supply the pronoun or referent can be called *anaphoric cloze* activities. At the most dependent level, students can be given several choices from which they must select the correct word for the blank space in the passage. At a more independent level, students can be asked to supply the correct word themselves. A similar activity might involve students in replacing all pronouns with referents, or vice versa.

"Tying it together."   Students can be shown how sentences are linked by anaphoric reference. Then they can be asked to mark pairs of sentences as follows:

(Jack) went to the store. He bought some candy.

Pairs of sentences can be constructed to give systematic practice with different types of relations. In the beginning, each activity should emphasize one type and direction. As students mature, types, directions, and distances between referents can be mixed. Then, students can work on similarly marking whole passages. Here is an example of a passage from a social studies assignment that students could have marked together using an overhead projector:

By 1859, 100,000 *Easterners* had headed toward *Pikes Peak* in the Rockies. Find (this mountain) on the map at the right. (Many) had left (their) families and (their) sweethearts at home. (Some) wanted to get rich. (Others) just wanted enough money to make a new start in life for (their) families.

"Make it shorter." Students can also be given pairs of sentences in which anaphoric substitution could be used to shorten one of the sentences. For instance, students could be asked to make one of these sentences shorter:

4c. Jack, Sally, and Sue went to the store.
4d. Jack, Sally, and Sue bought some candy.

This is a good example of an exercise in which reading and writing instruction overlap.

Lesson sequence. Again, these exercises can be designed for different types of relations at first, and then they can progressively include more types so students have to choose. Depending on the level of the students , a reasonable progression might be as follows:

1. Personal pronouns only
2. Demonstrative pronouns only
3. Locative pronouns only
4. A mixture of pronouns
5. Proverbs only
6. A mixture of pronouns and proverbs
7. Substitution with synonym
8. Substitution with more general word
9. A mixture of types of substitution
10. A mixture of pronomial and substitution relations, and so on

Of course, you will also find that it is often not the type of relation but rather the difficulty or content area of the material that determines the difficulty of these exercises. Thus, you may wish to design activities with materials from different content areas and difficulty levels.

Warning

None of these activities is a natural reading task. They may supplement understanding anaphora when reading for meaning, but they will not substitute for it.

UNDERSTANDING CONNECTIVES

Anaphoric relations tie separate clauses and sentences together because the antecedent and the replacing term refer to the same thing. Clauses and sentences can also be tied together through *connective concepts*. Connective concepts are the concepts that relate two events to each other. For instance, in sentence 4e (below) one event caused another (a causal connective); in sentence 4f one event happened before another (a time sequence connective); and so forth.

4e. The blossom opened <u>because</u> the sun was shining.
4f. I went to the store, <u>and then</u> I went to the park.

Table 3-4 shows some possible types of connective concepts and the explicit cues often used to express them. Study this table.

Connectives can be expressed explicitly with the use of specific words, as exemplified in Table 3-4, or they can be implicit, that is, implied by the author but not directly stated. For instance, sentences 4g and 4h are related by means of an implicit causal connective, that is, a causal relationship that is *not* directly stated:

4g. Mary had a stomachache.
4h. She ate too much.

A recent study of implicit connectives in children's social studies texts has indicated that these are as common in primary-level texts as they are in high school texts and that the two types most often stated implicitly are causal and time sequence connectives (Irwin, 1982). Moreover, research also indicates that implicitly stated connectives are more difficult to comprehend than are explicitly stated ones (Irwin, 1980; Irwin & Pulver, 1984). Further examples of implicit causal and time sequence relations are provided in Table 3-5. Look through the materials your students read. Can you find other examples of implicit connectives?

Like so many comprehension tasks, inferring implicit connective concepts almost always requires that the reader have specific kinds of prior knowledge. In sentence 4i following, students who know that they are reading about a time in history in which many Americans owned slaves will be more likely to make the correct inference than will students who do not know this. Thus, teaching connective inference will often involve a review of students' prior knowledge. (See Chapter Seven for methods for doing this.)

4i. Mexico allowed slavery. Many Americans moved to Mexico.

TABLE 3-4   Some Common Types of Connective Concepts

TYPES	CUES USED	EXAMPLE
Conjunction	and in addition to also along with	Jack went to the store. Sally went also.
Disjunction	or either . . . or . . .	Either Jack went to the store, or he went home.
Causality	because so consequently	Jack went home because he was sick.
Purpose	in order to for the purpose of so that	Jack went home in order to get his money.
Concession	but although however yet	Jack left for home, but he hasn't gotten there yet.
Contrast	in contrast similarly (also comparative and superlative forms of adjectives)	Jack was very sick. In contrast, I feel better!
Condition	If . . . then . . . unless except	If Jack is sick, then he can't play ball.
Time	before always after while when from now on	Before Jack got sick, he went to the store.
Location	there where	Jack is at home where, he will be able to rest.
Manner	in a similar manner like as	Jack was blue and feverish, as Sally was yesterday.

Source: The list of connectives is derived from a taxonomy presented by Turner, A. & Greene, E. *The construction and ease of a propositional test base.* (Technical report no. 63, Institute for the Study of Intellectual Behavior, University of Colorado, Boulder, 1977).

TABLE 3-5 Typical Implicit Connectives

	CAUSAL	TIME SEQUENCE
Fiction	Johnny loved playing the trumpet. He loved being good at something.	Johnny got first place at the country fair. He got first place at the state fair. He flew to Washington to compete against all the other state fair winners.
Content area	It was easy to go into making iron. Only one machine was needed.	Several Northern recruits overpowered the watchman. They ordered the telegraph wires cut. They freed the slaves. They escaped while it was still dark.

Finally, before you teach students to understand either explicit or implicit connective relations, you must be able to identify them. In Passage 3-1, the connective concepts are marked and available cue words are underlined. Each connective has also been classified according to the following abbreviated key:

C = causality
T = time sequence
P = purpose
Cn = concession
Ct = contrast

Study this passage. How many of these connectives are only implicitly stated? What types are they? Mark Passage 3-2 in a similar fashion. The answers can be found at the end of this chapter.

PASSAGE 3-1[1]

                                           C

People were building homes and stores.   They bought more and more
     C   Cn

wood.   The sawmills were very busy. <u>But</u> soon there was no wood left to cut
   C   C

down.   One after another, the sawmills closed.   Workers had to find some-
                        C   P

thing else to do.   They began to plant wheat <u>so</u> they could sell it.
  C   T

<u>Thus,</u>   farming   became   important <u>after</u> all the trees had
               T   Ct

been cut down. <u>Now, more</u> people were farmers than builders.

[1]Source: Anderson, E. A., *Communities and Their Needs* (Morristown, N.J.: Silver Burdett, 1972), p. 62. Reprinted by permission.

PASSAGE 3-2[2]

Only a few people in the Denver area became rich from mining gold and silver. But many stayed anyway. There were many opportunities to become rich by farming. Many of the wealthy people built large homes in order t o show how rich they were.

But Denver needed a railroad. Denver's citizens organized their own railroad company.

(Clue: There are five connective concepts. Two are only implicitly stated.)

Incidental Teaching of Connective Inference

As with anaphoric relations, teachers in all grade levels and content areas can promote connective inference by asking relevant questions. If they find that students have failed to make the appropriate inferences, they can direct students to the appropriate sentences. They might then discover that the problem involved a lack of background knowledge. Then, students can simply be given the important background information. If the problem seems to be a lack of awareness of the importance of looking for implicit relationships, this can be discussed directly. (Remember the "explicative function" in teaching reading skills. Don't just tell them they are wrong! Tell them why, and show them how to find the answer.)

Direct Connective Instruction

As with many other processes discussed in this book, there is very little research to demonstrate what activities best teach this skill. However, the following activities seem appropriate.

Connective cloze. Pulver (in press) has recommended that after students have had some practice with identifying and interpreting explicit connectives, they can be given sentence sets in which the connectives have been deleted. Begin with easy sentences involving common events, as in sentence 4j, but eventually you can ask students to supply connectives deleted from content-area sentences, as in sentence 4k. Students can be given connectives from which to choose, or, at a more independent level, they can choose their own.

4j. Susie wanted to go to the party, _____ she was too sick.
4k. The homesteaders often wanted Indian land, _____ it was good for raising cattle.

---

[2]Adapted from Dempsey, J. H. *This Is Man* (Morristown, N.J.: Silver Burdett, 1972), p. 185. Reprinted by permission.

The final step would involve asking students to supply implicit connectives deleted from whole passages.

Sentence combining. Activities involving sentence combining effectively integrate the teaching of reading and writing processes. Younger students can be given cards with main clauses and cards with a variety of connective cue words. They can then work to see how many ways the clauses can be put together. This would be a good follow-up activity for the sentence anagram task described in Chapter One. Older students can be asked to fill in missing connectives from a suggested list, to match clauses that can be connected with "because," and so on. One more difficult variation for older students would be to ask them to reverse the order of the clauses by changing the connective. For instance, in the sentences that follow, 4l can be rewritten as 4m and 4n can be rewritten as 4o.

4l. The batter was old, so the cake didn't rise.
4m. The cake didn't rise because the batter was old.
4n. It was raining, but John went to the game.
4o. John went to the game although it was raining.

Finding implicit connectives. Students who are at a more independent level for this skill can be asked to find the explicit and implicit connectives in their reading assignments. Because they are the most commonly implicit, this should probably involve causal and time sequence connectives only. Pulver (in press) has suggested that students be taught the following four-step procedure:

1. Look at where the sentences come together.
2. Think about how they might be related.
3. Use what you already know about the topic to determine if your guess made sense.
4. Try to insert a connective between the two sentences. Does this new sentence make sense?

Warning

Marking up passages, manipulating cards, and filling in words are not reading processes. Extend connective activities back into natural reading tasks with questioning and discussion.

SLOT-FILLING INFERENCES

Let's look again at the inference example given in the introduction to this chapter. This time some of the required inferences have been marked (A = anaphora, C = connective):

>   A   A   A
> Sally   rode   her   bike   to   the   store.   John   followed   her.   He
>   C A
> got a flat tire. He cried.

We can now see at least four uses of pronomial anaphora and one implicit causal relation. You will remember, however, that you also inferred that John rode a bike and that the flat tire was on this bike.

These are called *slot-filling inferences* (Trabasso, 1981). Slot-filling inferences are inferences that fill in important missing aspects of the given situation. In general, the relevant missing "slots" are determined by the situation and may involve answering the following questions (based on Fillmore, 1968, and Kintsch, 1974):

Agent	= who did it?
Object	= to whom or what was it aone?
Instrument	= what was used to do it?
Experiencer	= who experienced the feeling or thought?
Source	= where did it (or they) come from?
Goal	= what was the result or goal?

In the example, it can be inferred that the bike was the instrument of travel and the object of the broken tire. Other slot-filling inferences might involve such things as character motivation, other psychological and physical causes, enabling circumstances, and spatiotemporal relationships (adapted from Warren, Nicholas, & Trabasso, 1979). For instance, in the example, the story content might have resulted in an inference that John followed Sally because he liked her (character motivation) or that he no longer had a broken leg (enabling circumstance).

Our prior knowledge of the situation also determines what might be inferred. For instance, for sentences 4p and 4q following potential slot-filling inferences are given in parentheses. Can you tell what slot-filling inferences might be made for sentences 4r and 4s?

4p. She stirred the coffee. [She used a spoon.] (instrument)
4q. They moved to the South. [They moved from the North.] (source)
4r. She dropped the china plate.[3]
4s. The rain quickly turned to ice on the streets.[4]

Finally, it is the surrounding context that determines what slot-filling inferences are necessary. For instance, for 4p, what if the sentence following it were 4t?

---

[3][The plate broke.] (goal)

[4][It was cold outside.] (enabling circumstance)

4t. The sugar made her sick.

Now, a critical slot-filling inference is that she stirred sugar (object) into the coffee.

Instructional methodology for slot-filling inference will probably be similar to that used for anaphora and connective inference. Students can be asked questions about the slot-filling inferences required in their reading assignments. Prior knowledge should be checked when it is found that students have not made the necessary inferences. Students can discuss the reasoning processes used to make various inferences and, if necessary, the teacher can model these processes. Activities that require students to combine sentences with slot-filling inferences can be used to supplement more natural reading tasks.

A FINAL LOOK AT INTEGRATIVE PROCESSES

When we look at passage coherence in a general way, we can see that there are actually two kinds of relationships that tie sentences and clauses together: (1) "local" connections, or those that link individual sentences and clauses to each other; and (2) "global" connections, or those that link each individual clause and sentence to the main idea or focal event of the passage. In this text, the term "integrative processes" is used to refer to the processes involved in comprehending local connections only. Global connections are understood through macroprocesses, which will be discussed in Chapter Four.

Recent research on the integrative processes used by children in their reading and writing activities suggests that this distinction between local and global connections may have important developmental and instructional implications. Scardamalia and Bereiter (1983) found evidence that elementary school children, when reading for comprehension, tend to rely on global connections rather than on local ones more than did the adults in their study. McCutchen (1982) similarly found that, when writing, older (sixth- and eighth-grade) students used a higher proportion of local connections that did younger (second- and fourth-grade) students. Thus, it may be that direct instruction in integrative processes can improve both the reading and the writing skills of students who do not use these local connections and that this instruction can begin in the intermediate grades.

SUMMARY

To comprehend even the simplest passage, readers make many inferences. Many of these inferences are necessary to integrate the clauses and sentences conceptually. Inferences and direct interpretations that are necessary for such integration can be called "integrative processes."

There are three main types of integrative processes: understanding anaphoric references, understanding explicit and implicit connectives, and making other necessary "slot-filling" inferences. Anaphoric terms can replace nouns or noun phrases (nominal), verbs or verb phrases (verbal), or whole clauses (clausal). The substituting term can be a pronoun or proverb (pronominal), a synonym, a more inclusive or a more specific term (substitution), or an implied repetition (ellipsis). Anaphoric relations can be forward or backward and adjacent or remote.

Connectives are concepts that connect events. There are at least ten kinds of connectives. Examples include conjunction, causality, concession, and time sequence. Many different cue words can be used to state these relationships explicitly; or they can simply be implied by the author. Causal and time sequence relationships are the types most frequently stated implicitly. Implicitly stated connectives are probably more difficult to comprehend than are explicitly stated ones.

Finally, there are many other types of inferences required to integrate sentences. These include filling in necessary information about things such as agents, objects, instruments, character motivation, and enabling factors. They are therefore called "slot-filling inferences."

When working with students in the area of integrative processes, it is important to assess the students' prior knowledge of the passage topic. Integrative references usually require some background information. Activities can be designed to show students the various ways in which sentences are conceptually integrated and to give them practice with the various integrative processes. However, it must be stressed that isolated drill with artificial activities will have only limited utility. Probably the best instructional activity is the natural questioning and discussion that precede and follow meaningful reading tasks. During this time, teachers of all grade levels and content areas can encourage, model, and explain integrative processes.

SELF-CHECK TEST

1. For each of the following anaphoric relations, tell whether it is pronomial, substitution, or ellipsis:
   a. I returned six library books yesterday. I forgot to return these.
   b. Jack chased the spider. The insect was afraid.
   c. Jack likes Jill. So does John.
   d. Can I read this? No, but I can try.
2. For each of the following pairs of sentences, tell what kind of connective could be inferred to connect them:

a. It never rains here. It is raining now.

b. Jack was nervous. He had to give a speech.

c. He went to the store. He went to the party.

d. The dog was small. The cat was smaller.

3. Here are a reading passage and a series of questions asked by Miss Jones, a remedial reading teacher at John Doe High School. The answers are those given by Jack, a tenth-grade student diagnosed as reading at somewhere around the third-grade level. What can Miss Jones guess about Jack's ability to integrate sentences in various ways? Be specific.

It was Bob's first day of school, though it was already December. He was very excited. He didn't know which pair of shoes to wear. Getting dressed always confused him, and choosing footwear was especially puzzling. He had such big feet. He looked outside to check the weather. He wore his boots.

Q: What happened in the story?
A: Someone wore boots.

Q: What day was it?
A: Bob's first day of school in December.

Q: Was someone excited?
A: Yes.

Q: Who?
A: I'm not sure.

Q: What was puzzling?
A: Choosing footwear.

Q: Why was choosing footwear a problem?
A: I don't know.

Q: What was the weather like?
A: It didn't say.

4. Define the following terms:

demonstrative pronoun	implicit connective
clausal ellipsis	slot-filling inference
verbal substitution	local connection
concession connective	global connection

SUGGESTED ACTIVITIES

1. Look through a textbook you do or would use in your teaching. Find three kinds of anaphoric relations. What kinds of explicit connectives are used? Do you see

any implicit connectives? Read through a typical chapter or story. What kinds of slot-filling inferences are required? Write a short description of the integrative processes necessary for comprehending this textbook.

2. Copy a page from a textbook you do or would use in your teaching. Mark all the intersentential connections.

3. For the grade level and content area you do or will teach, design a series of instructional activities to teach a specific type of integrative process. The activities should begin with the simplest level and progress gradually toward the more difficult levels. Try to make the activities as meaningful as possible by using materials the students will be reading for other purposes.

TABLE 3-3   Classifying Anaphoric Relations (Check)

EXAMPLE	PRONOMINAL, SUBSTITUTION, OR ELLIPSIS?	NOMINAL, VERBAL, OR CLAUSAL?	ADJACENT OR REMOTE?	FORWARD OR BACKWARD?
Jack is going to run. So will Sally.	Pronomial (proverb)	Verbal	Adjacent	Forward
As he has done before, Jack failed the test.	Pronomial (personal)	Nominal	Adjacent	Backward
Jack, Sally, Susie, and Ken had a party. It was on Hallowe'en. A good time was had by all.	Substitution	Nominal	Remote	Forward
They all passed the test. This pleased me.	Pronomial (demonstrative)	Clausal	Adjacent	Forward
Jack is happy. Sally, too.	Ellipsis	Verbal	Adjacent	Forward

PASSAGE 3-2   (Check)

On'y a few people in the Denver area became rich from mining gold and silver.
Cn   C
But many stayed anyway.   There were many opportunities to become rich from
                                                          P
farming. Many of the wealthy people built large homes in order to show how rich
they were.
Cn   C
But Denver needed a railroad.   Denver's citizens organized their own railroad
company.

REFERENCES

BARNITZ, J. (1980). Syntactic effects on the reading comprehension of pronoun-referent structures by children in grades two, four and six. *Reading Research Quarterly, 15,* 268–289.

BAUMANN, J., & STEVENSON, J. (in press). Teaching students to comprehend anaphoric relations. In J. W. Irwin (Ed.), *Understanding and teaching cohesion comprehension.* Newark, Dela.: International Reading Association.

CLARK, H. H., & SENGUL, C. J. (1979). In search of referents for nouns and pronouns. *Memory and Cognition, 7,* 35–41.

FILLMORE, C. J. (1968). The case for case. In E. Bach and R. T. Horms (Eds.), *Universals in linguistic theory.* New York: Holt, Rinehart and Winston.

HALLIDAY, M. A. K., & HASAN, R. (1976). *Cohesion in English.* London: Longman Group.

IRWIN, J. W. (1980). The effects of explicitness and clause order on the comprehension of reversible causal relationships. *Reading Research Quarterly, 15,* 477–488.

IRWIN, J. W. (1982). Coherence factors in children's textbooks. *Reading Psychology,* 1983, *4,* 11—23.

IRWIN, J. W., & PULVER, C. (1984). The effects of explicitness, clause order, and reversibility on children's comprehension of causal relationships. *Journal of Educational Psychology, 76,* 399–407.

KINTSCH, W. (1974). *The representation of meaning in memory.* Hillsdale, N.J.: Lawrence Erlbaum.

McCUTCHEN, D. (1982). Development of local coherence in children's writing. Unpublished manuscript, University of Pittsburgh.

MOBERLY, P. (1978). *Elementary children's understanding of anaphoric relationships in connected discourse.* Unpublished doctoral dissertation, Northwestern University, Evanston,Illinois.

PULVER, C. (in press). Teaching students to understand explicit and implicit connectives. In J. W. Irwin (Ed.), *Understanding and teaching cohesion comprehension.* Newark, Dela.: International Reading Association.

SCARDEMALIA, M., & BEREITER, C. (1983). Topical versus propositional approaches to text processing. In H. Mandl, N. Stein, and T. Trabasso (Eds.), *Learning and comprehension of texts.* Hillsdale, N.J.: Lawrence Erlbaum.

TRABASSO, T. (1981). The making of inferences during reading and their assessment. In J. T. Guthrie (Ed.), *Comprehension and teaching.* Newark, Dela.: International Reading Association.

TURNER, A., & GREENE, E. (1977). *The construction and use of a propositional text base.* (Technical report no. 63.) Boulder, Colorado: Institute for the Study of Intellectual Behavior, University of Colorado.

WARREN, W. H., NICHOLAS, D. W., & TRABASSO, T. (1979). Event chains and inferences in understanding narratives. In R. O. Freedle (Ed.), *New directions in discourse processing,* vol. 2. Hillsdale, N.J.: Lawrence Erlbaum.

WILLEKENS, A. (in press). Anaphoric reference instruction: Current instructional practices. In J. W. Irwin (Ed.), *Understanding and teaching cohesion comprehension.* Newark, Dela.: International Reading Association.

FOUR
TEACHING
MACROPROCESSES

You may remember that in Chapter Two it was pointed out that readers cannot usually remember every single idea in a passage. Rather, even at the level of individual sentences (during microprocessing), they are selective about what to remember. One of the influences guiding this selection is macroprocessing. Macroprocessing is the ongoing process of creating or selecting an organized set of summary ideas, presumably for the purpose of organizing recall and reducing the number of ideas to be remembered. Macroprocessing aids in the recall of details by providing "hooks" or general ideas to which those details can be linked. Obviously, macroprocessing also aids in the recall of general ideas. Macroprocessing requires the ability to select what is important and the ability to summarize details. Both of these require an awareness of the overall organizational structure of the passage.

Macroprocessing interacts with microprocessing in that it helps students decide which individual idea units to remember (microselection). It can also be related to integrative processing: just as integrative processes enable readers to see relationships between sentences (local connections) so that they can be remembered as a unified whole, macroprocesses enable readers to tie ideas together by means of an overall summary structure to which every individual idea is related (global connections). Macro- and integrative processes interact in that local connections provide cues as to the global connections, and vice versa. For instance, if a reader decides that the overall structure of the passage is going to be a chronological description of an historical event, then that reader will be likely to look for time sequence connectives at the local level. Similarly, a predominance of local time sequence relations will lead a good reader to see that the global organizational structure is probably a chronological one.

Of course, the way each of these processes is utilized varies according to the reader's purpose. When reading for a test in physics, a student will generally spend a great deal of time understanding and reviewing individual, specific details. When reading several editorials for preparation for a classroom discussion, a student may decide simply to summarize each author's position into one general statement. Similarly, a reader can probably control the amount of material summarized during macroprocessing: finding the main idea is one degree of specificity in which each paragraph is reduced to one summary idea. Other levels are also possible. An entire chapter can be summarized into two or three statements, for instance.

This chapter contains descriptions of the kinds of organizational patterns that readers use to help them select, invent, and organize the summary ideas that they encode into memory. Methods for helping students use these patterns are also presented. Finally, methods for teaching students to select and summarize as they read will be discussed.

STORY GRAMMARS

Good readers remember stories better when they are organized like other stories (Stein & Nezworski, 1978; Mandler & DeForest, 1979). Recently, researchers have tried to characterize a typical story structure. One such *story grammar* has been provided by Stein and Glenn (1977). According to their grammar, the information in a well-formed narrative can be broken into six categories (see Table 4-1). The last five categories form a group called an "episode" and occur in the specified temporal sequence. Sometimes parts of episodes are signaled by words such as "suddenly" or "finally," but usually the division is based on the content. Sometimes the information required by a given category is not stated explicitly but, rather, is to be inferred by the reader. Finally, many stories have several episodes, and these episodes are connected by means of time sequence (*then* . . .), causal (*because* . . .), and simple conjunctive (*and* . . .) relations. Table 4-1 also includes a typical story that has been divided into story grammar categories according to the Stein and Glenn grammar. Study this example.

Figure 4-1 presents another story for you to label. Note that it has more than one episode. Answers can be found at the end of this chapter. If

TABLE 4-1   Categories Included in a Simple Story

1.	Setting	Introduction of the protagonist; can contain information about physical, social, or temporal context in which the remainder of the story occurs.
2.	Initiating event	An action, an internal event, or a natural occurrence which serves to initiate or to cause a response in the protagonist.
3.	Internal response	An emotion, cognition, or goal of the protagonist.
4.	Attempt	An overt attempt to obtain the protagonist's goal.
5.	Consequence	An event, action, or end state which marks the attainment or nonattainment of the protagonist's goal.
6.	Reaction	An emotion, a cognition, an action, or an end state expressing the protagonist's feelings about his or her goal attainment or relating the broader consequential realm of the protagonist's goal attainment.

A Well-Formed Story

1.	Setting	a.	Once there was a big gray fish named Albert.
		b.	He lived in a big icy pond near the edge of the forest.
2.	Initiating event	c.	One day, Albert was swimming around the pond.
		d.	Then he spotted a big juicy worm on top of the water.
3.	Internal response	e.	Albert knew how delicious worms tasted.
		f.	He wanted to eat that one for his dinner.
4.	Attempt	g.	So he swam very close to the worm.
		h.	Then he bit into him.
5.	Consequence	i.	Suddenly, Albert was pulled through the water into a boat.
		j.	He had been caught by a fisherman.
6.	Reaction	k.	Albert felt sad.
		l.	He wished he had been more careful.

Source: N. L. Stein, "How Children Understand Stories: A Developmental Analysis," in L. Katz (ed.), *Current Topics in Early Childhood Education,* Vol. 2 (Hillsdale, N.J.: Ablex, 1979), p. 265.

you are an elementary teacher or a literature teacher, you will also wish to complete Activity 1 at the end of this chapter.

It is probably clear how story structure relates to summarizing. When readers select or construct ideas that represent the "gist" of a story, they often use the ideas that summarize the major informational categories. Thus, a sensitivity to typical story structures probably enables students to summarize the information in a story more efficiently (see Kintsch & Greene, 1978).

Instructional Procedures for Story Grammar Awareness

If you teach with fiction, you may wish to investigate the possibility of improving your students' macroprocessing ability by increasing their awareness of story structure. When appropriate, you can explain this con-

FIGURE 4-1   *A SIMPLE EXERCISE IN ANALYZING STORY STRUCTURE*

Once there was a very tall girl named Alice. Alice was the tallest girl in her class. All of her classmates made fun of her. This made her feel very bad. She even tried walking with her knees bent. That just made her look funny. Looking funny made her feel even worse.

One day Alice's teacher said that they were going to have a guest speaker, and in walked the tallest woman Alice had ever seen. She was the star of the local women's basketball team. She talked to the students about the new league, the games that had been played, and what it was like to be a professional athlete. Everyone admired her. Alice was very excited. She asked if she could, maybe, be a player someday. The woman replied that since she was so tall, she would have a better chance than many. For the first time, Alice was proud of being tall.

cept directly and you can show them how it works using meaningful stories. The following activities have been suggested by Whaley (1981). They can be used as either reading or listening activities and may involve writing responses.

1. *Prediction task.* Have students tell what comes next in an unfinished story. Using a variety of choices, discuss how the same sort of thing tends to come at this point in the story. In this manner, you can gradually call attention to various categories in the story structure.

2. *Macrocloze task.* Have students fill in information omitted from the middle of the story by giving them the story with blank space where a given category of information had been. Discuss why one kind of information is usually supplied. An interesting variation is to have different groups completing this task for different portions of the story. Then, a new story can be created by putting all the new portions together.

3. *Scrambled stories.* Separate the story into categories and then scramble the order of the categories. Students decide on the best order. (If the story categories are on different strips of paper, this would be a useful extension of the sentence anagram and sentence-combining exercises recommended in Chapters Two and Three, respectively.)

Finally, Rubin and Gentner (1979) have developed an instructional technique called "story maker." Students are given choices on cards for each stage of the development of the story. Each choice leads to another specific set of choices. Figure 4-2 diagrams such a storymaker tree. In this case, the setting and the initiating event have been combined on card set 1. Card set 2 contains possible internal responses. Card set 3 contains possible attempts. Card set 4 contains consequences and reactions combined. Of course, combining categories is not necessary and can be done in other

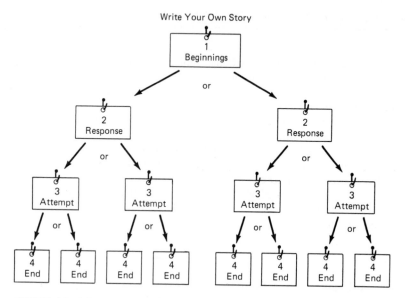

FIGURE 4-2 A Simple Storymaker Tree

ways, or students can write endings themselves. Cards can be hung on hooks on a pegboard or presented to the class by the teacher. Students may even progress to the level of storymaker maker. That is, in groups, they can make up their own storymaker trees; then, they can "write" stories using each other's storymakers. (This is a good example of combining reading and writing instruction.)

ORGANIZATIONAL PATTERNS IN EXPOSITORY MATERIALS

Recent research has repeatedly shown that readers who use the author's organizational pattern to organize their own memory of the passage actually recall more than those who do not (Elliot, 1980; Meyer, Brandt, & Bluth, 1980). Moreover, good readers are more likely to do this than are poor readers (Gabriel, Braun, & Neilsen, 1980; Meyer, Brandt, & Bluth, 1980; Taylor, 1980).

For instance, Example A shows what two students recalled after reading a passage from a sixth-grade science book:[1]

[1]From Mallinson, G. G.; Mallinson, J. B.; Brown, P. G.; Smallwood, W. L.; & Knapp, J., *Understanding Your Environment*, Book 6 (Morristown, N.J.: Silver Burdett, 1981), p. 201

EXAMPLE A

> The atmosphere is made up of gases, liquids, and solids. The atmosphere is like all matter. It has mass and takes up space. It is held around the earth by gravity. You know that gravity is the force of attraction between objects.
>
> You live in the layer of air that is at the bottom of the atmosphere. This layer contains dust, smoke, clouds, and invisible gases. Because of this, the lowest layer of the atmosphere often looks hazy. The upper layers of the atmosphere contain mostly invisible gases. There are few solids or liquids in those layers. They look perfectly clear.
>
> **Here is what Johnny said when asked about what he read:**
>
> It said about gravity being a force and about atmosphere being matter. It also said that there are invisible gases in the atmosphere.
>
> **In contrast, let's look at Sally's recall:**
>
> It was about how the atmosphere is made out of matter like gases and solids and, like matter, is held down by gravity. The lower layer has things like smoke that make it hazy, but the upper layer is clear.

Johnny has recalled little and has failed to grasp the main points in the passage. In contrast, Sally has recognized that the first paragraph was a description of the characteristics of the atmosphere and the second paragraph was based on a comparison of the clarity of the lower and upper layers. Probably because she was sensitive to these organizational patterns, she remembered more, and what she remembered was the more general and, therefore, in this case the most important information.

To illustrate further the importance of organizational awareness, Example B shows the recall of a fourth-grade student who doesn't know what to remember on social studies materials but can easily summarize stories in basal readers. In this case, we might speculate that this student did not grasp the definition/example pattern in the social studies selection but did understand the basic categories to be expected in a well-formed story.

This example is not really unusual. It seems that awareness of organizational patterns in expository materials develops much later than does an awareness of story structure. In the research of Stein and Glenn (1977), even seven-year-old children showed an awareness of story structures. In contrast, Meyer, Brandt, and Bluth (1980) studied the recall protocols of ninth-graders and found that only the good readers in this high school sample used the organizational structure to organize their recall.

EXAMPLE B

SOCIAL STUDIES PASSAGE[2]

One of the most important parts of the Hindu religion was the caste system. This was a way of organizing people into separate groups.

There was a separate caste for almost every occupation. There was a caste for farmers and one for carpenters. There was a caste for leatherworkers, a caste for sweepers, and castes for many others. People in the lower castes were not allowed to be educated. Nor could they take part in religious services. And the poorest people, who did the dirtiest work, were called the untouchables. They did not even dare to let their shadows fall on people of the highest castes.

RECALL

There were farmers and carpenters and people that worked with leather. You couldn't touch some people.

PASSAGE FROM STORY[3]

Wendall lived with Mother, Father, William, Alice, and the baby, Anthony. Everybody was happy—most of the time. There was always work to do.

"William," Mother would say, "would you please put these newspapers outside?"

"I have to play ball," William would say. "Send Wendall."

Or Father might ask Alice to go to the store.

"I have to do my homework," Alice would answer. "Send Wendall."

Wendall loved his mother and father very much. He liked to help them. But sometimes he wished—just a little—that William and Alice liked to help as much as he did.

RECALL

It was about a boy named Wendall who lived with his family. Whenever there were chores to do, his brother and sister were busy with things like playing ball and doing homework, so he had to do them.

[2]From Dempsey, J.H. *This Is Man.* (Morristown, NJ: Silver Burdett, 1972), pp. 102–103.
[3]From "Send Wendall," by Genevieve Gray (New York: McGraw-Hill, 1974), p. 244.

Thus, although many teachers will find that their students have an awareness of the story structures found in basal readers and in literature, fewer will find that their students have mastered the organizational patterns in their content-area materials.

Several categorization systems are available to classify the organizational patterns used in expository materials. It is probable that none is complete and that authors may use variations and combinations, but it is useful to be aware of typical patterns. Table 4-2 shows the classification system given by Armbruster and Anderson (1981) along with the authors' purposes and questions addressed by each. According to this system of classification, content-area materials usually use one of the following organizational patterns: *description, temporal sequence, explanation, compare/ contrast, definitions/examples,* and *problem/solution.* (Note that *cause/effect* is included in *explanation; process descriptions* are included in *temporal sequence;* and *classification* is probably a kind of *definition* pattern.) Study Table 4-2 and then try to fill in Table 4-3. (Answers can be found on page 65.) If you teach in one of the content areas, you will also want to complete Activity 2 at the end of this chapter which asks you to identify the patterns used in your textbook. This can provide much useful information for guiding students' recall (see Instructional Procedures following).

TABLE 4-2 Types of General Author Purposes and the Corresponding Text Structures

EXAMPLES OF AUTHORS' PURPOSES OR QUESTIONS

IMPERATIVE FORM	INTERROGATIVE FORM	STRUCTURE
Define A.	What is A?	
Describe A.	Who is A?	Description
List the features (characteristics, traits) of A.	Where is A?	
Trace the development of A.	When did A occur (in relationship to other events?)	Temporal sequences
Give the steps in A.		
Explain A.	Why did A happen?	
Explain the cause(s) of A.	How did A happen?	
Explain the effect(s) of A.	What are the causes of, reasons for (effects, outcomes, results of) A?	Explanation
Draw a conclusion about A.		
Predict what will happen to A.	What will be the effects, outcomes, results of A?	
Hypothesize about the cause of A.		
Compare and contrast A and B.	How are A and B alike? different?	Comparison/contrast
List the similarities and differences between A and B.		
Define and give examples of A.	What is A, and what are some examples of A?	Definitions, examples
Explain the development of a problem and the solution(s) to the problem.	How did A get to be a problem, and what is (are) its solution(s)?	Problem/solution

Source: Armbruster, B. & Anderson, T. Content Area Textbooks. (Reading Education Report No. 23. Center for the Study of Reading, University of Illinois at Urbana-Champaign, 1981.) pp. 5 and 6.

TABLE 4-3   A Simple Exercise in Identifying Organizational Patterns

SIMPLE PARAGRAPH	PATTERN USED?
The two groups used very different approaches. One group tried to solve the problem alone, while the other group immediately began to look for someone to ask. One group divided the tasks among the individuals, while the other group did everything as a whole.	
There were many reasons for the move from country to city. There were more jobs in the city. There were also more cultural events, more shops, and more educational opportunities.	
A chemical change is a process by which new substances are created. Burning and rusting are examples of chemical changes.	
There were so many people moving into the cities that many had trouble finding places to live. New homes were built at an amazing rate.	

Finally, another way to characterize the organization of content-area texts is through the main idea/detail structure. Research indicates that the presence of main ideas seems to facilitate recall (Christie & Schumacher, 1978; Fishman, 1978; and others). Certainly, students who have mentally arranged ideas according to main topics have organized those ideas in terms of global connections, and thus their recall will be better than that of students who have not mentally organized the material around main topics. Thus, this skill is critical for reading and remembering expository material.

Instructional Procedures

Study guides.   Study guides (activities completed during reading) can be used to focus the students' attention on the appropriate organizational patterns. Tables, charts, and diagrams that students complete while they are reading are especially effective, because they help the students to visualize the organizational patterns. Examples include comparison and cause/effect charts for comparison and cause/effect patterns, tables of attributes for descriptive patterns, tree and flow charts for temporal sequence and classification patterns, diagrams for descriptive patterns, and outlines for main idea/detail structures. Figures 4-3 and 4-4 are examples of study guides that focus the students' attention on organizational patterns.

Hierarchical summary procedure.   Taylor (1982) has suggested the use of a hierarchical summary procedure to direct the students' attention to the organizational pattern. She recommends that this procedure be used with middle-grade students and, when she did this, she found that it improved not only the amount recalled during reading but also the quality of the students' written compositions. The five steps of this procedure are as follows:

1. *Previewing.* Students preview a few pages of the assignment and generate the skeleton outline of numbers and letters for the sections indicated by subheadings. The teacher may want to help them with this at first.
2. *Reading.* Children read in sections, filling in the outline for the section as they proceed.
3. *Outlining.* For each subsection, students write a main idea *in their own words.* Then, they fill in the supporting details *in their own words.* At the end of a major section, they write a main idea for the section *in their own words,* and they summarize the subsection into key phrases in the left margin.
4. *Studying.* After reading is completed, the students review their "hierarchical summaries."
5. *Retelling.* Finally, in partners, students orally retell what they learned from reading the assignment.

FIGURE 4-3 Tree Chart Showing Major Concepts in Fifth-Grade Science Chapter

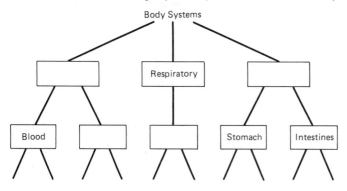

1. Fill in the four missing labels in the boxes in the chart.
2. Add two specific parts for each of the organs.

FIGURE 4-4   Compare the Body Systems of the Frog and the Grasshopper (Ninth-Grade Science)

	FROG	GRASSHOPPER
Digestive System		
Respiratory System		
Nervous System		

1. Fill in this chart with brief descriptions.
2. In terms of which system are the frog and the grasshopper most nearly alike? Tell how they are the same.
3. In terms of which system are the frog and the grasshopper most greatly different? Tell how they are different.

Teacher assistance and class discussion will be necessary as students are learning this procedure, but, gradually, they will be able to do it on their own. Figure 4-5 provides a fictional example of a short section of a student's hierarchical summary.

Mapping.   Another way to encourage students to use global connections is to encourage them to construct a diagram of these relationships (Hanf, 1971). Armbruster and Anderson (1980) found it to be a successful technique for improving middle school students' recall. They taught students specific techniques for diagramming six of the possible types of connections: examples, property, definition, comparison/contrast, temporal, and causal. Davidson (1982) has recommended a less highly structured approach. She suggests that each student be encouraged to diagram the passage structure in his or her own creative way. Then, students can compare their maps and discuss the differences. A map of a main idea/detail structure from a content-area text is given in Figure 4-6. Figure 4-7 shows how another student may have mapped the same chapter. This map stresses the causal relationship between the Puritan religious beliefs and their other activities. The tree chart used in the study guide in Figure 4-2 can also be regarded as a kind of map.

The ConStruct procedure.   Vaughan (1982) has recommended that content-area teachers use the ConStruct procedure to help their students comprehend their texts. Research seems to indicate that this procedure may increase recall (Vaughan, Stillman, & Sabers, 1978). The stages proceed as follows:

FIGURE 4-5 *SECTION OF STUDENT HIERARCHICAL SUMMARY*

I.   Puritan cultural values that still influence our society

    A.   Puritans respected education.

       Most towns built schools.

Puritan values affect us today

       Harvard College was supported by taxes.

       Today, we have public education for all.

    B.   Puritans believed that work was for God and that leisure was bad.

       They disliked games and holidays.

       They associated wealth with work and poverty with illness. Thus, poor people were sinful.

       Today, we still respect people who work and have wealth.

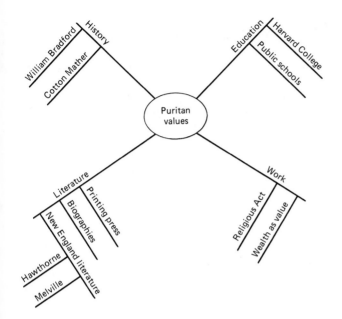

FIGURE 4-6 Mapping Main Idea/Details in Chapter on Puritan Values

FIGURE 4-7
Alternative Map of Chapter on Puritan
Values

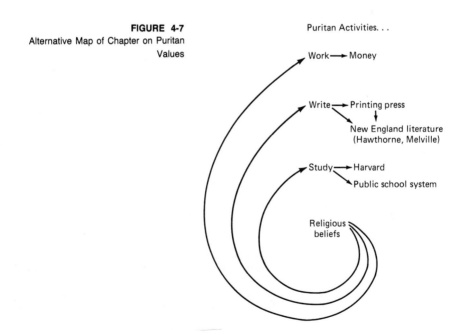

1. *Survey Read.* Read quickly, focusing on such things as introductions and sub-headings. Construct a general framework for a graphic overview, a graphic representation similar to a map. (See Figure 4-8.)
2. *Study Read.* Read to understand all the material. Add details to the graphic overview. (See Figure 4-9.)
3. *Comprehension Check.* Reexamine portions not understood earlier. Insert clarified material into graphic overview. (See Figure 4-10.)
4. *Review Read.* Skim selection and graph to reinforce comprehension.

FIGURE 4-8   Top–level Graphic Overview*

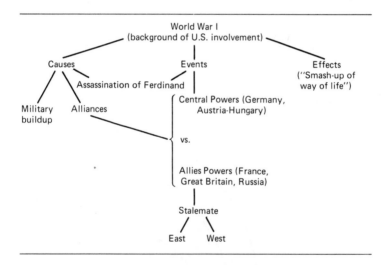

FIGURE 4-9   Second–Stage Graphic Overview†

*Source: Vaughan, J. Use the ConStruct procedure to foster active reading. *Journal of Reading, 25,* 1982, 413. Reprinted with permission of J. Vaughan and the International Reading Association.

†Source: Vaughan, J. Use the ConStruct procedure to foster active reading. *Journal of Reading, 25,* 1982, 414. Reprinted with permission of J. Vaughan and the International Reading Association.

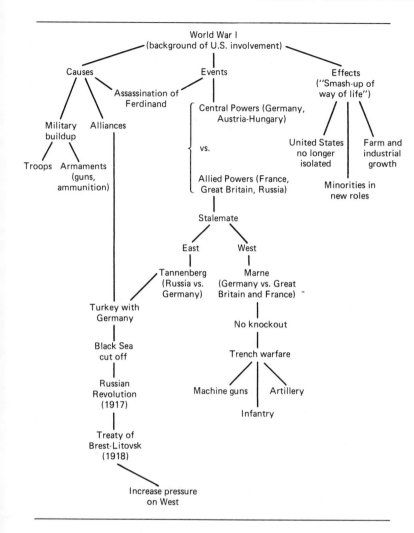

FIGURE 4-10 Completed Graphic Overview[**]

MACROSELECTION

Perhaps the most important step in effective macroprocessing is selecting the most important information to remember from the reading passage. Unless defined otherwise by the teacher or the situation, "more important"

[**]Source: Vaughan, J. Use the ConStruct procedure to foster active reading. *Journal of Reading, 25,* 1982, 415. Reprinted with permission of J. Vaughan and the International Reading Association.

can be defined as that information that is more highly related to the general topics in the organizational structure of the passage. Thus, an understanding of the organizational pattern is essential for *macroselection*.

Good readers tend to remember the more important information more often than they remember less important information (see Meyer, 1975), and there is evidence that younger students may have some trouble picking out what is important (Brown & Smiley, 1978). Students' ability to select what is important may also be related to the difficulty of the material; that is, they can do it well with easy material but have more trouble with more difficult material (see Brown, Smiley, & Lawton, 1977; Danner, 1976).

Direct Macroselection Instruction

Macroselection instruction is a good example of reading skill instruction that can easily be integrated into the curriculum in every content area at every grade level. Students can be told that part of good reading is picking out the important things to remember. After an assignment is read, students can be asked what was important and why. As students work on meaningful materials, comprehension activities can be designed to encourage them to make these choices. Actually, all the organizational activities suggested earlier in this chapter will help students to select what is important. Figure 4-11 provides an example of a similar activity designed to help students select important details to remember from a science chapter. Two other activities that probably encourage active selection follow. Each of these activities can be adapted for a variety of ages and content areas.

Which one?   Divide students into pairs or small groups. Have them read a section of the textbook or story in short segments. While reading each segment, have each student write down the *one* most important thing to remember. Students then compare their choices. As a team, they must choose only one. If appropriate, team answers can be compared for the whole class. Test items can later be selected from class choices. This activity has the advantage of being appropriate for students at various stages of independence on this skill because it allows them to learn from each other.

Write a fair test.   Involving students in writing tests can be a way of asking them to think about what is important. On the most dependent level, you can ask students to make up the test by selecting the most important questions from a list you provide. On a more independent level, they can make up the test from scratch. (Of course, this activity will encourage micro- as well as macroselection. Remember, all these processes interact!)

FIGURE 4-11   *ACTIVITY FOR HELPING TENTH-GRADE SCIENCE STUDENTS*
DETERMINE WHAT DETAILS TO REMEMBER

STUDY GUIDE FOR FIRST SECTION OF PHYSICAL SCIENCE CHAPTER
ON MATTER

As you read, complete the following.
I. Here are the main points of this chapter. For each, list five related details
    that would be important to remember.
    A. Matter can be classified in several ways.
        1.
        2.
        3.
        4.
        5.

    B. In a chemical change, new substances are formed.
        1.
        2.
        3.
        4.
        5.

    C. A chemical equation describes chemical changes.
        1.
        2.
        3.
        4.
        5.
II. On the following list of details, put an asterisk (*) by the four
    most important.

    A. Compressed air below $-201°C$ is a liquid.
    B. An element is a substance that cannot be broken down into sim-
       pler substances.
    C. Seawater is a mixture.
    D. The three forms of matter are solid, liquid, and gas.
    E. Chlorine is a dense, greenish-yellow gas.
    F. Water is the same compound while it is liquid water, vapor, or
       ice.
    G. The formation of dew is a chemical change.
    H. Sodium is soft enough to be cut with a knife.

Tomorrow in class, we will discuss why you thought these were important.

MACRORULES AND SUMMARIZING

Often, selecting what to remember involves more than just lifting facts
from the text. When students are trying to select what to remember, they
will often decide to create a summary statement rather than select a state-

ment from the assignment. Recently, it has become possible to be quite specific about the way students may arrive at summary statements. These statements seem to reflect several processes that can be used in conjunction with macroselection. The four *macrorules* that readers seem to use to create passage summaries can be described as follows (Brown & Day, 1983):

1. *Deletion.* Unimportant and redundant information is deleted.
2. *Superordination.* More general terms are substituted for groups of specifics.
3. *Selection.* General statements (topic sentences) are selected to retain.
4. *Invention.* Explicit topic statements are invented when they are not stated.

Figure 4-12 gives an example of a typical summary and the rules used to derive it. Note how these rules work together to result in concise summary statements.

Research has substantiated the hypothesis that poor readers are less able to use summarization rules efficiently than are good readers (Winograd, 1984). In a study of children's use of these "macrorules," Brown and Day (1983) found that elementary school children (fifth-graders) seemed to know how to delete appropriately, but they did not use the other rules adequately. The invention rule seemed to be the most difficult and was seldom used before the high school level. Even tenth-graders used this rule in only one-third of the appropriate situations. Moreover, it seems that even college students sometimes have trouble summarizing (Taylor, 1983).

Finally, finding the main idea can be seen as the application of these macrorules at the paragraph level. Finding the main idea of a paragraph is simply paragraph summarization. If the main idea is stated explicitly, finding it involves "selection." If it is not stated, finding it requires "invention," a more difficult process. (Remember: finding the main idea is important for all the reasons that macroprocessing is important: helping readers to select what to remember and to organize the information for more efficient recall.)

Incidental Instruction: K–12

Students at all grade levels can be encouraged to do some kind of summarizing. This can be done in a variety of regular classroom activities: book discussion, book reports, study guides, research papers, quizzes, and so on. When students are summarizing for these meaningful tasks, they are deleting unimportant information, selecting important information, and creating general statements not directly given (superordination and invention). When you are giving the assignment, you can model summarizing for them. Activities in which students compare summaries of the same material will result in an increased understanding of the material to be recalled as well as an increased understanding of the skill of summarizing.

FIGURE 4-12 *EXAMPLE OF SUMMARY*

Europe and the United Stated neared a face-saving formula to rescue the World Trade Conference here but made little attempt to hide the fact that they were deeply divided about the future of the trading system.

A conference spokesman said the European Common Market appeared ready to sign a final communique but only after inserting paragraphs underlining their disagreement on fundamental matters.

For instance, one clause will pledge the 88 nations at the conference "to refrain from" new protectionist measures, but the Europeans, beset by recession and unemployment, rejected this pledge and insisted on inserting a milder paragraph stating that the Common Market would "resist" protectionism, the spokesman said. All other nations here, including the United States, planned to endorse the tougher clause.

Another paragraph, also endorsed by the rest of the conference, called for new rules on farm trade. The Common Market, whose subsidized farm exports have been under heavy U.S. attack, refused to go along with this.

The conference, scheduled to end Saturday, stretched over into Sunday in an attempt to avoid a total breakdown.

Summary:

Europe and the United Stated neared agreement on the World Trade Conference, but they are divided about the future of the trading system. Members of the European Common Market were ready to sign an agreement, but only if they could make changes. For instance, they are less opposed to protectionism than are the other countries. They also refuse to go along with new rules on farm trade.

1. Delete information (crossed off with one line).

2. Use superordination (on circled information).

3. Select topic sentence (in gray).

4. Invent summary statements (for information in braces in article; underlined sentences in summary)

Source: "Future of World Trade Dim After Rift at Geneva Parley," by R. C. Longworth, *Chicago Tribune,* Sunday, November 28, 1982.

Source: "Future of World Trade Dim After Rift at Geneva Parley," by R. C. Longworth, *Chicago Tribune,* Sunday, November 28, 1982.

Direct Summarizing Instruction

Direct rule instruction. Although insufficient research has yet been done on this procedure, teachers may wish to try directly teaching summarization rules to older students. Deletion could probably be taught first. Superordination, selection, and invention can be taught using short passages that can be easily summarized in this way. Brown and Day (1981) found that selection seemed harder to learn than superordination and that the poorer writers among the junior college students in their study needed very explicit instruction in rule usage. They also found that with the most disabled students, instruction in invention was not effective. Evidently, a certain level of reading and writing ability is a prerequisite to learning to use this rule.

How short can you make it?   Writing and reading instruction overlap when you ask students to write summaries. One motivational approach might be to have students see how short they can make a summarizing statement. Students can work in pairs and compete or work as a team in competition with another team.

Select the best.   Provide students with alternative summaries of the same passage. At an easy level, have one summary that includes unimportant information and one that includes all the important information. At a more difficult level, have one summary that uses only deletion and selection and one that uses invention. Ask students to select the better summary. Ask them to explain their choice.

Finding the main idea.   There is certainly no shortage of activities for teaching students to find the main idea. Most traditional reading methods texts and classroom reading curricula include many of these. They range from straightforward drill to such activities as writing titles and drawing pictures. The important thing to remember is that the difficulty of the material and the explicitness of the main idea affect the difficulty of the task.

Baumann (1982) has suggested a kind of skill hierarchy for teaching main idea skills that begins with microselection followed by macroselection and then invention at the paragraph level. It ends with macroselection and invention at the passage level (see Table 4-4). Baumann (1984) found a direct teaching strategy using this taxonomy to be effective for teaching sixth-grade students to perform these processes.

It is important to remember that, as with instructional activities suggested in other chapters, isolated drill in finding the main idea is *not* the same thing as using a main idea strategy in a natural reading task. There is no substitute for showing students how and why they can look for main ideas when they are actually reading various types of materials for various assigned and self-selected purposes.

SUMMARY

Macroprocessing is the ongoing process of creating an organized set of summary ideas for the purpose of recall. Awareness of the organizational pattern is critical for effective macroprocessing. For stories, this entails having an awareness of the structure of a typical story; typical stories probably include one or more sets of the following categories: (1) setting, (2) initiating event, (3) internal response, (4) attempt, (5) consequence, and, (6)

TABLE 4-4   Content of Main Idea Instruction for Strategy Group

LESSON NUMBER AND TITLE	DESCRIPTION
1. Main ideas in lists of words	Students are taught how to analyze a list of related words and determine the "main idea" (e.g., shirt, pants, dress, hat, shoes = clothing).
2. Main ideas in sentences	Students are taught how to analyze a sentence and determine its topic and then what is said about the topic, which collectively describes the main idea. For example, in the sentence, Susan, the girl who lives down the street in the blue house, goes to Girl Scouts every Wednesday afternoon, the topic is Susan, what is said about the topic is goes to Girl Scouts, and the main idea is Susan goes to Girl Scouts.
3. Topics and explicit main ideas in paragraphs	Students are taught to generalize the skill of identifying topics and what is said about them to paragraphs. After such a main idea is determined students learn to look for a sentence that states the main idea (topic sentence).
4. Explicit main ideas and supporting details	Students review finding explicit main ideas and are then taught to identify details that support main ideas.
5. Topics and implicit main ideas in paragraphs	Students are taught to identify implicit main ideas by following the procedure learned in Lesson 3, that is, determine the topic and what is said about the topic. Students are then taught to compose a main idea when they are unable to find a topic sentence in a paragraph.
6. Implicit main ideas and supporting details	Modeled after Lesson 4, students are taught to associate details with inferred main ideas.
7. Topics and explicit main ideas in passages	Students are taught to identify the topic of a passage, what is said about the topic (i.e., content of paragraphs that comprise the passage), and then identify a main idea (theme statement) for an entire passage.
8. Topics and implicit main ideas in passages	Students are taught to infer main ideas for passages when no theme statement is present. Lesson is modeled after Lesson 5.

Source: J. Baumann, "Teaching Children to Comprehend Main Ideas," paper presented at the annual meeting of the National Reading Conference, Clearwater, Florida, December 1982.

reaction. Typical expository materials are organized according to one or more of the following patterns: (1) description, (2) temporal sequence, (3) explanation, (4) comparison/contrast, (5) definitions/examples, and (6) problem/solution. They can also be seen as having a main idea/detail organizational pattern.

Based on their awareness of the organization, students summarize by selecting the most important information (the information most related to the general topics in the organizational structure), deleting the unimportant information, substituting general terms for specifics, and inventing topic statements. Finding (or inventing) the main idea can be viewed as summarizing at the paragraph level.

The activities suggested in this chapter are designed to heighten students' awareness of organizational patterns and to increase their ability to select what is important and to summarize what they read. All can be used as part of the instruction in subjects in which students are reading for other purposes. Such integration is critical if students are to learn to use these strategies in natural reading tasks.

SELF-CHECK TEST

1. Define each of these summarization rules:

   deletion
   superordination
   selection (macro-)
   invention

2. Answer true or false:

   ___ a. Macroprocessing is important only when you just want to remember the gist of a passage.
   ___ b. The invention rule is the easiest to use.
   ___ c. Summarizing effectiveness depends on an awareness of the organizational pattern.
   ___ d. Awareness of the organizational pattern can result in more information recalled.
   ___ e. There is no relationship between micro- and macroprocessing.
   ___ f. There is no relationship between integrative and macroprocessing.
   ___ g. Finding the main idea should only be taught in the intermediate grades.
   ___ h. Story grammar awareness should be taught only to older children.

3. List five types of organizational patterns. Write a sample paragraph for each.

4. For each of these activities, tell which skill it was designed to teach.
   Select the best
   Macrocloze
   Mapping
   How short can you make it?
   ConStruct procedure
   Story maker

SUGGESTED ACTIVITIES

1. Select a story that you would assign to students in your class. Make a copy of the story. On the copy, label the story grammar categories. Are there any important story categories to be inferred? Write these inferences in the margin.

Then write a summary of the story by summarizing the information in each story category. Finally, discuss whether this story is well formed according the Stein and Glenn story grammar categories.

2. Select a content-area textbook chapter that you would assign to students in your class. What kinds of organizational patterns are used? What kinds of study guides could be used to focus your students' attention on these patterns? Would a main idea/detail guide be better? Make one of these guides.

3. Write a five-sentence summary of this chapter. What summarization rules have you used?

4. Collect a set of paragraphs designed to assess your students' abilities to find explicit (selection) and implicit (invention) main ideas.

FIGURE 4-1 (Check)   *A SIMPLE EXERCISE IN ANALYZING STORY STRUCTURE*

Setting Initiating event Internal response Attempt Consequence Reaction	{ Once there was a very tall girl named Alice. Alice was the tallest girl in her class. All of her classmates made fun of her. This made her feel very bad. She even tried walking with her knees bent. That just made her look funny. Looking funny made her feel even worse.
Initiating event Internal response Attempt Consequence Reaction	One day Alice's teacher said that they were going to have a guest speaker, and in walked the tallest woman Alice had ever seen. She was the star of the local women's basketball team. She talked to the students about the new league, the games that had been played, and what it was like to be a professional athlete. Everyone admired her. Alice was very excited. She asked if she could, maybe, be a player someday. The woman replied that since she was so tall, she would have a better chance than many. For the first time, Alice was proud of being tall.

TABLE 4-3 (Check)   A Simple Exercise in Identifying Organizational Patterns

SIMPLE PARAGRAPH	PATTERN USED?
The two groups used very different approaches. One group tried to solve the problem alone, while the other group immediately began to look for someone to ask. One group divided the tasks among the individuals, while the other group did everything as a whole	Comparison/contrast
There were many reasons for the move from country to city. There were more jobs in the city. There were also more cultural events, more shops, and more educational opportunities.	Explanation

TABLE 4-3   (cont.)

SIMPLE PARAGRAPH	PATTERN USED?
A chemical change is a process by which new substances are created. Burning and rusting are examples of chemical changes.	Definition/examples
There were so many people moving into the cities that many had trouble finding places to live. New homes were built at an amazing rate.	Problem/solution

REFERENCES

Armbruster, B. B., & Anderson, T. H. (1980). *The effect of mapping on the free recall of expository text* (Technical Report no. 160). Urbana-Champaign: Center for the Study of Reading, University of Illinois.

Armbruster, B., & Anderson, T. (1981). *Content area textbooks* (Reading Education Report no. 23). Urbana-Champaign: Center for the Study of Reading, University of Illinois.

Baumann, J. (December 1982). Teaching children to comprehend main ideas. Paper presented at the annual meeting of the National Reading Conference, Clearwater, Florida.

Baumann, J. (1984). The effectiveness of a direct instruction paradigm for teaching main idea comprehension. *Reading Research Quarterly, 20,* 93–115.

Bean, T. H., Singer, H., Sorter, J., & Frazee, C. (December, 1982). Acquisition of summarization rules as a basis for question generation in learning from expository text. Paper presented at the annual meeting of the National Reading Conference, Clearwater, Florida.

Brown, A. L., & Day, J. D. (1981). Strategies and knowledge for summarizing texts: The development and facilitation of expertise. Unpublished manuscript, University of Illinois.

Brown, A. L., & Day, J. D. (1983). *Macrorules for summarizing texts: The development of expertise.* Urbana-Champaign: Center for the Study of Reading, University of Illinois.

Brown, A., & Smiley, S. (1978). *The development of strategies for studying prose passages* (Technical Report no. 66). Urbana-Champaign: Center for the Study of Reading, University of Illinois.

Brown, A., Smiley, S., & Lawton, S. (1977). *The effects of experience on the selection of suitable retrieval cues for studying from prose passages* (Technical Report no. 53). Urbana-Champaign: Center for the Study of Reading, University of Illinois.

Christie, D. J., & Schumacher, G. M. (1978). Memory for prose: Development of mnemonic strategies and use of higher order relations. *Journal of Reading Behavior, 10,* 337–344.

Danner, F. W. (1976). Children's understanding of intersentence organization in the recall of short descriptive passages. *Journal of Educational Psychology, 68,* 174–183.

Davison, J. (1982). The group mapping activity for instruction in reading and thinking. *Journal of Reading, 26,* 52–56.

Elliot, S. N. (1980). Children's knowledge and use of organizational patterns of prose in recalling what they read. *Journal of Reading Behavior, 12,* 203–212.

FISHMAN, A. S. (1978). The effects of anaphoric reference and noun phrase organizers on paragraph comprehension. *Journal of Reading Behavior, 10,* 159–167.

GABRIEL, H., BRAUN, C., & NEILSEN, A. (December, 1980). An investigation of the effects of textual organization on comprehension of good and poor readers. Paper presented at the annual meeting of the National Reading Conference, San Diego, California.

HANF, M. B. (1971). Mapping: A technique for translating reading into thinking. *Journal of Reading, 14,* 225–270.

KINTSCH, W., & GREENE, E. (1978). The role of culture-specific schemata in the comprehension and recall of stories. *Discourse Processes, 1,* 1–13.

MANDLER, J. M., & DEFOREST, M. (1979). Is there more than one way to recall a story? *Child Development, 50,* 886–889.

MEYER, B. J. F. (1975). *The organization of prose and its effects in memory.* Amsterdam: North-Holland.

MEYER, B., BRANDT, D., & BLUTH, G. (1980). Use of top-level structure in text: Key for reading comprehension of ninth-grade students. *Reading Research Quarterly, 16,* 72–103.

RUBIN, A., & GENTNER, D. (December, 1979). An educational technique to encourage practice with high-level aspects of texts. Paper presented at the annual meeting of the National Reading Conference, San Antonio, Texas.

STEIN, N. (1979). How children understand stories: A developmental analysis. In L. Katz (Ed.), *Current topics in early childhood education,* Vol. 2. Hillsdale, N.J.: Ablex.

STEIN, N. L., & GLENN, C. G. (1977). An analysis of story comprehension in elementary school children. In R. Freedle (Ed.), *Multidisciplinary approaches to discourse comprehension.* Hillsdale, N.J.: Ablex.

STEIN, N. L., & NEZWORSKI, T. (1978). The effects of organization and instructional set on story memory. *Discourse Processes, 1,* 177—193.

TAYLOR, B. M. (1980). Children's memory for expository text after reading. *Reading Research Quarterly, 15,* 399–411.

TAYLOR, B. M. (1982). A summarizing strategy to improve middle grade students' reading and writing skills. *The Reading Teacher, 36,* 202–205.

TAYLOR, K. K. (1983). Can college students summarize? *Journal of Reading, 26,* 524–529.

VAUGHAN, J. L. (1982). Use the conStruct procedure to foster active reading. *Journal of Reading, 25,* 412–422.

VAUGHAN, J. L., STILLMAN, P. L., & SABERS, D. L. (December, 1978). Developing ideational scaffolds during reading. Paper presented at the annual meeting of the National Reading Conference, St. Petersburg, Florida.

WHALEY, J. F. (1981). Story grammars and reading instruction. *The Reading Teacher, 34,* 762–771.

WINOGRAD, P. N. (1984). Strategic difficulties in summarizing texts. *Reading Research Quarterly, 19,* 404–425.

FIVE
TEACHING ELABORATIVE PROCESSES

So far in our examination of the comprehension process, we have described a reader who chunks words into meaningful phrases and selects from those phrases the ideas to be remembered. That reader also ties the individual ideas into a coherent whole by noticing or inferring relationships among individual sentences and by summarizing the passage into general ideas and organizing the ideas around an organizational structure. The questions we must now ask are, Have we described everything a reader "comprehends" when he or she reads? Does this describe everything a reader does when trying to understand a passage? Do students ever report having comprehended anything other than micro, integrative, or macro information?

The answer is, of course, "Yes." Readers will often make inferences that are not necessary for microprocessing, integrative processing or macroprocessing. These can be called "uninvited inferences" or *elaborations*. Readers often elaborate on the author's intended message.

ELABORATIVE PROCESSES

Elaborations can be defined as those inferences that are not necessary for micro-, integrative, or macroprocessing. Readers elaborate for many reasons. Elaborations improve recall (Reder, 1978) and increase enjoyment.

The most typical types of elaborations are (1) making predictions, (2) integrating the information with prior knowledge, (3) forming mental images, (4) responding affectively, and (5) responding with higher-level thinking processes. The amount and type of elaboration used by a particular reader are related to that reader's purpose and prior knowledge.

This can be demonstrated by examining what different readers remember from reading the same passage. The underlined portions are the elaborations in what Susie and Sally have recalled:

SUSIE: It was a story about a little girl who missed her father. She wondered if he loved her. Her mother told her to listen like she listened to other good sounds. I remember especially when she listened to the storm in the mountains. It reminded me of when I was in Colorado last year.

SALLY: It was about a little girl who missed her father. Fathers don't always come home. I had a friend once whose father didn't come home for three years. He was in a war. When he came home, everyone was happy.

As can be seen from Sally's recall, not all elaborations are necessarily facilitative of recall of the passage being read. You may have had experience with children who infer so many extraneous details that their comprehension of the passage is actually reduced. Adams and Bruce (1980) have suggested that decisions about what to infer should be based on "the concept of good structure" (p. 4). Warren, Nicholas, and Trabasso (1979) suggest that good readers infer information that is "relevant to the progress of the narrative" (p. 44). All these authors are trying to suggest that an elaboration is appropriate to the extent to which it is related to the important ideas expressed in the text. Elaborations are also appropriate to the extent that they help the reader achieve his or her purpose. Although no exact rules can be developed to define this for all situations, most teachers are probably able to tell when students are elaborating appropriately and inappropriately.

PREDICTIONS

Many researchers in the field of reading comprehension stress the central role of prediction. (See Collins & Smith, 1980, p. 4.) Collins and Smith define predictions as "hypotheses about what will happen" (1980, p. 14). They suggest that good readers often read with various event and text structure expectations. These predictions probably help these readers to monitor their comprehension and direct their attention to important information.

Some possible types of predictions are given in Figure 5-1. When reading stories, students can make predictions about what will happen, based on such things as what they already know about the character, his or her motivation, or the situation itself. Titles and pictures also often contain

FIGURE 5-1 *POSSIBLE PREDICTIONS MADE BY READERS OF STORIES*

I. Predictions of events based on . . .
  A. Character traits
  B. Character motivation
  C. Situational characteristics
  D. Signals in text
    1. Pictures
    2. Title
II. Structural predictions based on . . .
  A. Prior knowledge of genre
  B. Story grammar awareness

Source: adapted from A. Collins and E. E. Smith, *Teaching the Process of Reading Comprehension,* Technical Report no. 182 (Urbana-Champaign: Center for the Study of Reading, University of Illinois, 1980) p. 16.

hints of what is to come. Students can also infer what kinds of things are likely to come next based on the genre: in a mystery story, one set of events is likely; in a Greek tragedy, another set is more plausible. Moreover, predictions can also be based on the position of the information in the story structure. For instance, if the story has just presented an initiating event, the reader will probably expect an internal response. (See the discussion of story structure in Chapter Four.)

Readers of expository texts also make predictions (see Figure 5-2). These predictions are often based on prior knowledge about the topic. For instance, if one is reading about slavery immediately prior to the Civil War, one might expect that the Underground Railroad will be mentioned. Predictions can also be based on what one knows about certain causal relationships; if one is reading about a series of conflicts between two powerful Western countries in the nineteenth century, one might predict that these conflicts are leading up to a war. (See Chapter Seven for a discussion of the importance of prior knowledge.)

Moreover, content expectations in expository materials are also largely based on structural considerations. If one is reading a long list of details, one might be predicting what the main idea will be, or vice versa. If one has been reading about a problem, one might expect the solution to follow; examples might be expected after a definition; and so on. Thus, an understanding of organizational patterns is probably useful for prediction.

Organizational patterns can be predicted on the basis of at least three aspects of the text: (1) the content area, (2) the prior text, and (3) direct signals. For instance, if one were reading social studies, one would predict that chronology and cause/effect are more likely to be used than definition/

FIGURE 5-2   *POSSIBLE PREDICTIONS MADE BY READERS OF EXPOSITORY TEXTS*

I.   Content predictions based on . . .
   A.   Prior knowledge of the topic
   B.   Prior knowledge of causality
      1.   Physical
      2.   Political
      3.   Psychological
      4.   Other
II. Structural predictions based on . . .
   A.   Prior knowledge of content-area–related organizational patterns
   B.   Organizational patterns in prior text
   C.   Signals in text
      1.   Headings
      2.   Titles
      3.   Introductions
      4.   Transitional statements
      5.   Tables, charts, etc.

example, whereas the opposite might be true for science. If the previous section were entirely chronological, this would strengthen this position. Finally, if the subheading were, "Major Conflicts from 1920 to 1935," the prediction would be further substantiated.

Incidental Instruction in Making Predictions

Students can be encouraged to make predictions at all grade levels and in all subjects. Because predictions are often based on prior knowledge, discussion of predictions should probably be preceded by some discussion of what students already know. Asking students to make predictions when looking over an assignment you are giving can often motivate them at the same time that it increases their comprehension. Group discussion of various student predictions can allow students to be exposed to each other's reasoning processes. Asking students to make predictions while they read may also be useful.

Remedial Instruction in Making Predictions

Some students who are having comprehension problems can be taught to use predictions as a self-help technique. Collins and Smith (1980) suggest that such instruction consist of three stages: (1) teacher modeling, (2) student participation, and (3) silent reading. In the modeling stage, the teacher looks at the title, a picture, or the next section of text and makes a prediction, carefully explaining the reason for this prediction. After this has been done several times, the student can be asked to make the predictions. For the last stage, questions can be inserted in the text and the student can read silently. (See Figure 5-3).

You may also wish to divide your lessons according to the types of predictions you are teaching: prediction in narratives versus prediction in expository materials, content-based versus structurally-based predictions, and so on. This will allow you to do more direct instruction in how to go about making a prediction. Also, it will allow you to give students practice with making the same kinds of predictions for progressively more difficult material.

FIGURE 5-3   *TEXT MARKED TO ENCOURAGE PREDICTION*

GUARDING THEIR PLACE

Besides helping animals build things, instincts help them do other things. An instinct may help animals guard the place that belongs to them.

> What animals guard their place?
> Read to see if you are right.

SINGING GUARD

> What kind of animal is this going to be about?
> What does singing have to do with guarding?
> Read to see if you are right.

Think of the last time you heard a bird sing. You may have thought it was singing because it was happy. But many birds sing to say, "This is *my* place. Stay away, stay away!"

> What other animal makes noise to guard its place?
> Read to see if this is the one talked about.

BARKING POLICE DOG

If you or a friend have a dog, you may have seen how it guards its home. It may bark if someone comes to its home. It may even bark if someone goes by outside. This seems to be its way of saying, "This place belongs to me."

Source: Blecha, M. K., Gega, P. C., & Green, M. *Exploring Science,* Level 3 (River Forest, IL: Laidlaw Brothers, A Division of Doubleday & Company, Inc., 1976), pp. 47–48.

OTHER PRIOR-KNOWLEDGE ELABORATIONS

Reder (1978) has presented a model of elaboration that stresses the role of the reader's prior knowledge. She points out that each word or idea in the passage being read evokes a unique set of associations for each reader. The particular elaboration chosen from this set of associations would be the one most consistent with the passage being read. Moreover, as Reder points out, "How much one elaborates depends upon previous experience with the material, inherent interest in the subject matter, understanding of the text, time allotted to read it, concentration and general tendency to elaborate" (1978, p. 72). Elaboration that integrates new ideas with past experiences clearly affects recall (Reder, 1980).

Let's look at some examples of possible prior-knowledge elaborations other than predictions. Jill, Jack, and John are each commenting on the first four paragraphs of *The Heart of Darkness* by Joseph Conrad. Note how each comment is valid, yet how they differ according to the students' prior experience. Each of these students is actively interacting with the material and will probably remember more than those students who do not use prior-knowledge elaborations. Yet each of these students will probably remember very different things.

JILL: I think the fact that Marlow looks like an idol is an important symbol. It's like when *The Idiot* had so many aspects of a Christ figure. Religious symbolism usually carries deeper meeting.

JACK: This whole scene reminds me of the night I spent on a steamer on the Mississippi. As in this scene, the river seemed to stretch out forever; there was no separation between water and sky. Everything was hazy, and there was a sense of approaching gloom as the sun set. It really gave me the creeps.

JOHN: I like the description of the Director of Companies as looking "nautical." It made me think of an old sea captain I knew as a kid. Like this character, he liked to look out to sea. I picture him with a seaman's cap, a beard, and a pipe. I think it also indicates that he is hardened and is quiet and used to being alone, always dreaming about the old days.

Of course, prior-knowledge elaborations can be inappropriate if they stray too far from the text. (For an example, see Sally's recall at the beginning of this chapter.) In the examples, the students are connecting images in the text with things they have experienced, so we would probably characterize these elaborations as appropriate. If the teacher has given no purpose, we cannot say that one is better than another. If the teacher stressed reading for theme, then Jill's is the most appropriate; if the teacher stressed reading for mood, then Jack's is more appropriate; and so on.

Incidental Instruction in Prior-Knowledge Elaboration

If students are actively interacting with the content they are reading, they will make prior-knowledge elaborations. Good readers will gear these elaborations toward specific purposes. Thus, encouraging students to think about what they already know before reading, giving them a purpose for reading, and getting them actively involved in the material will all be useful for encouraging prior-knowledge elaborations. Prereading purposes such as "Think about how this relates to what we studied in Chapter Three" or "While you are reading, think about other people you know who are like this" will lead to prior-knowledge elaborations. Finally, the teacher's attitude toward elaborations that are shared during class discussions will also make a difference.

Remedial Instruction in Prior-Knowledge Elaborations

In a remedial situation, you may wish to move the student through the same three stages recommended for teaching prediction: (1) teacher modeling, (2) student participation, and (3) silent reading with activities. While you are reading aloud to the student, pause and share appropriate prior-knowledge elaborations. Tell the student that good readers actively think about what they are reading and actively relate it to what they already know or have experienced. Then have the student model the procedure for you. If necessary, discuss the difference between appropriate and inappropriate elaborations. Finally, give the student material to read in which stimulating prior-knowledge questions are inserted and/or possible places for integration with prior knowledge are marked. Figure 5-4 shows how a teacher can follow this procedure with a small group in the fourth grade.

MENTAL IMAGERY

Forming mental images as we read seems to increase the amount we recall. Steingart and Glock (1979), for instance, found that college students instructed to image while they read concrete materials recalled more and made more inferences than did students instructed to repeat the passage to themselves. Whether forming mental images actually increases the amount recalled, however, may also depend on certain characteristics of the reader involved. Research seems to indicate that poor comprehenders are more likely to be helped by imagery instructions than are good comprehenders. (See Golinkoff, 1975–76.) Also, there is evidence that students who can be characterized as "picture learners" are more likely to be helped by imagery

FIGURE 5-4   *TEACHING PRIOR-KNOWLEDGE ELABORATION*

FOURTH–GRADE TEACHER MONOLOGUE

"Now, while you're reading this section, I want you to think constantly about what you already know about what's being said. That will help you understand it better. Let me show you what I mean. Let's look at page 130."
(Teacher reads a few sentences.)

"Well, it says mining helped them have jobs, so it was very important. Why is that important? I have a friend who didn't have a job for a long time. He didn't have any money because of it. He couldn't pay his bills and had to move to a tiny apartment with no windows. He couldn't afford to buy new clothes or good food. The people I know who have jobs have bigger homes, new clothes, and good food. So, if mining helped the people have jobs so they could have these things, I can see why it was so important!

"Let's read on." (Student reads until teacher asks him to stop.)

"So, here it says that life in the city was very different from life in the villages. What do you already know about cities and villages that will help you understand this?"

(Students reply with their prior experiences. Teacher leads them to draw conclusions and summarize differences.)

"So you can see how much what you already know can help you understand what is being said. The worksheet you will be completing while you read will be asking you to do more of this."

---

instruction than those who are not (Levin, Divine-Hawkins, Kurt, & Gutemann, 1974).

Incidental Instruction in Mental Imagery

On a practical level, because it will help some of your students, forming vivid mental images can be encouraged when it is applicable for the material at hand. Various activities can be used: writing elaborative descriptions, describing sounds and smells that are brought to mind during reading, drawing pictures to illustrate the material, and so on. In the content areas, concrete demonstrations of scientific principles, pictures, movies, and cultural artifacts, for example, will also probably facilitate comprehension by making it possible for students to visualize while they are reading. Remember that students will vary in the extent to which mental images are interesting and useful, so you may wish to provide alternative activities for some children.

Remedial Instruction in Mental Imagery

If you feel that a specific student or students might benefit from training in forming mental images, then you can construct specific activities that seem to be useful for this. The first step is making sure that students are prepared. Students can appropriately image only when they have adequate prior experience with the images involved. If you think this might be a problem, bring in some pictures or films with settings or images similar to those involved in the reading selection. If necessary, describe some of the important mental pictures before students actually read the text.

Students can then be asked to draw pictures of critical images in the reading material. Spatial layouts of room, sketches of outdoor settings, and pictures of people can all be assigned as projects to be completed during reading. Students should be encouraged to make their pictures as accurate and detailed as possible. For students who are uncomfortable with drawing, you can construct activities in which students select the best drawing from several that you have constructed.

Aulls (1978) has recommended a four-stage procedure for teaching poor readers to use imagery to facilitate comprehension. The first stage involves having the students draw stick-figure cartoons to illustrate the action in individual sentences. The second step involves having students identify details in increasingly complex pictures and then criticize their own cartoons in terms of completeness. The third step consists of having the students draw cartoons for groups of sentences. And the fourth step involves asking students to use images to aid in answering difficult comprehension questions. The last stage should be extended until students use the procedure without explicit instruction to do so.

AFFECTIVE RESPONSES

An emotional response, especially one intended by the author, is clearly part of the comprehension process. Indeed, Spiro (1984) has suggested that subjective reactions may actually facilitate or interfere with recall. Similarly, the comprehension taxonomy presented by Smith and Barrett (1979) also includes affective responses are part of comprehension. In this taxonomy, the category of "appreciation" includes affective responses related to such things as (1) emotional responses to plot or theme, (2) identification with characters and incidents, and (3) reactions to the author's use of language. In the activities that follow, "reactions to the author's use of language" is interpreted as reactions to connotations and figurative language. Moreover, I have also added "bibliotherapy" or reading for personal growth to this list of possible affective responses.

Again, as with other elaborations, readers who are interacting with the text affectively are being more active than those who are not, and these active, involved readers will probably remember more or different things than will those who are not reacting affectively. One point to remember, however, is that affective reactions are not always appropriate for every purpose. For instance, a literature teacher teaching "The Tell-Tale Heart" by Edgar Allen Poe can encourage an affective response with a dramatic reading with lights off and candles lit. In contrast, a social studies teacher may wish to warn students that an editorial is loaded with emotional language designed to persuade them, thus helping them to resist their affective responses. (The latter instruction would involve higher-level thinking responses, especially analysis; see the description of analysis later in this chapter.)

Incidental Teaching of Affective Response

All teachers should realize that affective responses are a sign of an active approach to reading, though the extent to which they are discussed in normal classroom situations depends on the objectives of the lesson. Perhaps the most common situation for such discussions to occur is one in which students are reading literature. For stories, novels, poems, and plays, the "author's intended meaning" (see the definition of comprehension in Chapter One) almost always includes affective responses.

Activities for Encouraging Affective Responses

Many activities for facilitating emotional responses can be created for specific situations. A few suggestions for each type of affective response are given in the paragraphs that follow.

Emotional response to plot or theme. Emotional responses to plot or theme can be facilitated in prereading discussion by asking students to think about similar events that they have experienced before reading the selection. Similarly, postreading discussions of how similar events or themes apply to their own lives will help them to respond affectively. Finally, role playing critical scenes from the plot may help students to sense the emotional impact of the events.

Identification with characters. Again, discussions in which students think about how they would feel if they were one of the characters will facilitate identification with that character. Also, students can be told that they will be asked to do a postreading writing or speaking activity in which they take on the persona of one of the characters. These may involve writing the character's diary, writing a letter from one character to another, writing the same story from a different character's point of view, or dramatizing part of the story. Finally, students can be asked such questions as "How would you feel if this happened to you?" and "How did X feel?" Then, they can compare their own anticipated reactions with those of the characters.

Connotations and figurative language.   Students should be taught that words have both *denotations*, literal meanings, and *connotations*, implications beyond the literal meanings that are often emotional in character. Students can compare pairs of words or phrases, such as "female biological parent" and "mother," that have the same denotations but very different connotations. They can discuss authors' word choices and suggest other words that would change the story because of their connotations. They can be asked to point out how their reaction to a story or essay was affected by the connotations of specific words. This will lead directly to the higher-level thinking process of analysis.

Figurative language, like connotation, involves meaning that goes beyond the most literal interpretation. The most common types of figurative language are simile, metaphor, and personification (See Table 5-1.) Students should be encouraged to discuss the connotations of such expressions when these expressions occur in their reading assignments.

Bibliotherapy.   Many have suggested that responsive reading can be useful for solving personal problems. This is sometimes called "bibliotherapy." Hafner (1977) suggests that this process takes place through identification with a character, catharsis, and insight (p. 329). (He has also provided an annotated bibliography of books that can be used for such a purpose.) Certainly, teachers should not regard themselves as psychotherapists, but by helping students find books for this purpose, they can help students learn that responsive reading is a useful resource for personal growth.

HIGHER-LEVEL THINKING RESPONSES

When we are speaking of elaborative processes, it is impossible to separate "reading" from "reasoning." When we are reading, we often engage in many types of "higher-level" thinking processes. For instance, transferring information to apply in new situations, analyzing the reasoning used by the author, integrating ideas into a creative idea or product, and making judgments about what is being read are all higher-level thinking responses that

TABLE 5-1   Examples of Types of Figurative Language

DEFINITION	EXAMPLE
Simile: two dissimilar things said to be alike; uses word "like" or "as"	My heart sank like a stone.
Metaphor: same as simile but words "like" and "as" are not used	All the world's a stage.
Personification: representing a thing or animal as a person	His money said it all.

can be a part of a reading act. Bloom (1956) originally called these responses "application," "analysis," "synthesis," and "evaluation," respectively.

Extensive teaching suggestions concerning these processes can be found in Sanders (1966), Burmeister (1978), and others. Though teachers tend to reserve this instruction for older and better readers, students of *all* ages and ability levels should be asked to use these thinking processes during and after reading. Moreover, no one type of thinking should be viewed as inherently more difficult than any other; for instance, some evaluation questions can be easier than some applications questions, and so on. Finally, all these processes can be encouraged in all content areas as well as in reading classes.

Application

Basically, application is the process of deciding what information to apply in a new situation and applying it appropriately. In a true application task, the teacher does not tell the students what they are to apply. Rather, the students realize that a given piece of information is applicable. Many teachers feel that the content they are teaching has not been fully comprehended unless the students can apply it independently.

Examples of application activities can be found in all the content areas. In math and science, word problems often require students to decide which reasoning or mathematical process to use and then to apply it. In social studies, students are applying information if they read a chapter on a given culture and then later accurately predict how someone in that culture will react. You can probably think of numerous other examples. The important thing to remember is that if you must tell the students what information to apply, they have not yet reached the application level of thinking for that piece of content.

Analysis

Analysis can be seen as the process of breaking the information into its component parts and assessing one's own thought processes in relation to those parts. For instance, students are engaged in a analysis when they point out that an author's premises do not lead to the stated conclusion(s) or when they note that the author has used biased language. This is sometimes called "critical reading." Burmeister (1978) lists the following activities as examples:

1. Making judgments related to the authenticity of a source of information
2. Distinguishing between fact and opinion
3. Analyzing propaganda
4. Detecting fallacies of reasoning

Pearson and Johnson (1978) recommend that students be taught to detect bias in writing by recognizing emotionally laden words as well as the use of propaganda techniques, such as implication by association, half-truths, and overgeneralization. The paragraphs that follow contain brief descriptions of these skills and a few possible activities for teaching each of them. Similar activities are often found in basal reader series.

Source credibility.   Students should develop the habit of assessing the possible credibility of each author. For instance, a gardener may be a less credible source than a physician if the article is about treating human bacterial diseases. This is not to say that both points of view shouldn't be considered but, rather, to point out that the reliability of the source must be considered an important piece of information. Activities in which the students read very different types of authors discussing the same topic, and worksheets in which possibly credible authors are to be matched with appropriate statements, are examples of activities that teach students to analyze the credibility of authors.

Fact versus opinion.   Students must be able to distinguish facts, such as "It is 40 degrees today," from opinions, such as "It is cold today." The first of these statements is objectively verifiable. The second is a matter of opinion; the Inuit wouldn't think so! Have students rewrite factual statements as opinions, and vice versa. Have students underline facts and circle opinions in newspaper articles or even in each other's papers. Give students lists of facts and opinions and have them distinguish between them. (See Figure 5-5.)

FIGURE 5-5   *DISTINGUISHING FACT FROM OPINION*

For each of the following statements, tell whether you think it is a fact or an opinion by placing an "F" or an "O" in the blank.

_____   1. Cervantes was a Spanish writer.
_____   2. Spanish writers are better than American ones.
_____   3. Water freezes at 32°F.
_____   4. 60°F is too cold for swimming.
_____   5. El Salvador is a country in Central America.
_____   6. El Salvador is the most important country in Central America.
_____   7. There are fifty states in the United States of America.
_____   8. There are too many states in the United States.
_____   9. Walt Whitman was an American poet.
_____   10. Walt Whitman was the greatest American poet.

TABLE 5-2 Typical Propaganda Techniques

NAME	DEFINITION	EXAMPLE
Name calling	Calling people or things by names with pleasant or unpleasant connotations designed to evoke emotional response	1. Calling local politician a "communist" 2. Calling one politician "skinny" and another "slim"
Implication by association	Using testimonies of trusted people or associating a person or thing with pleasant or unpleasant concepts	1. A distinguished actor tells about how he uses a given product every day. 2. Calling a product something like "The All-American Pen"
Half-truths	Omitting qualifying details or using one truth to imply an opinion	Quoting a noted authority but leaving off the qualification: "If the world were different, this would be great" becomes "This would be great."
Overgeneralizations	Stating sweeping generalizations as if they were facts; failing to give critical details	1. "This vacuum cleaner is the best that has ever been made." 2. "If I am elected, I will work toward ending war and poverty."
Bandwagon	Appealing to the reader's desire to belong: the "everyone does it" approach	"Over two million people have already bought our product."

Propaganda. Typical propaganda techniques are illustrated in Table 5-2. Students can be asked to find examples of these in advertisements, editorials, and political speeches. In school campaigns, they can watch for when they use them themselves!

Fallacies of reasoning. A thorough explanation of possible reasoning fallacies is, of course, beyond the scope of this book. For an excellent discussion of eight common fallacies, see Burmeister (1978). Other discussions can be found in books on critical reasoning.

Emotionally laden words. Perhaps the easiest type of biased writing for students to detect is the use of emotionally laden words. Students can be taught to circle emotionally laden words in newspaper articles and persuasive essays. They can rewrite such passages with the language changed so as to eliminate the bias, or they can compare the words used in articles with opposing points of view.

Synthesis

Synthesis is the process of combining separate pieces of knowledge to come up with knowledge that is new, at least new to the person doing the thinking. It is the process of thinking creatively. In a sense, all elaborations fall into this category, and, as with elaborations, this type of thinking is encouraged only when the teacher abandons the "one right answer" approach and encourages divergent responses. Activities that encourage synthesis often require some sort of creative product, such as a play, a story, or a plan of operation. Examples of activities are rewriting a story as it would occur in a different culture, writing a fictional description of a day in the life of an historical figure, predicting what the world would be like if one natural law were changed, and planning political action after reading about a political issue.

Evaluation

Finally, evaluation involves first deciding on the evaluation criteria and then evaluating the ideas as good or bad, right or wrong, just or unjust, and so on, on the basis of those criteria. For instance, a student who recalls what a critic has said about a play is not evaluating it himself or herself. If, on the other hand, the student decides independently what makes a play good, and then judges the play according to those criteria, that student is evaluating the quality of that play.

Activities in which students assume the role of decision maker can help them to appreciate the importance of this type of thinking. For instance, students can pretend to be members of the Food and Drug Administration setting up criteria to be used for the approval of a new drug; they can be asked to pretend that they are politicians who must vote on pending legislation. Such tasks involve reading for information, setting up criteria, and making difficult evaluative decisions.

FINAL CONSIDERATIONS FOR TEACHING ELABORATION

At least three considerations are relevant to the teaching of all five elaborative processes discussed in this chapter. First, teachers must abandon the "one right answer" approach if they are to encourage elaborations. Elaborations are usually personal responses, which will differ from reader to reader. Students need to feel that their reasoning process will be valued. Because elaborations are divergent responses, they are hard to grade, but this does not mean that they are not an important part of the comprehension process.

Second, elaborative processes are not for only those students who have fully mastered micro-, integrative, and macroprocesses. Students in all grades and all ability levels can elaborate on the meanings they encounter during readings tasks. In fact, the ability to elaborate can facilitate micro-, integrative, and microprocesses as much as the reverse!

Finally, a good general strategy for teaching all elaborative processes is first to model the procedure yourself, then to encourage students to model it for you and for each other, and then to provide tasks that encourage the particular type of elaboration. For instance, if you would like to encourage the formation of vivid mental images, begin by describing your own images to the students after you have all read an image-evoking passage. Then have them read one and tell you about their images. Then have them read silently and then do silent activities that encourage the formation of vivid mental images. A similar series of steps can be used to teach all elaborative processes, including the higher-level thinking responses of application, analysis, synthesis, and evaluation.

SUMMARY

Good readers often go beyond micro-, integrative, and macroprocesses. They elaborate on the text in ways that facilitate recall and make the information more useful to them. Elaborations can be appropriate or inappropriate depending on their effectiveness in facilitating the reader's purpose.

There are many types of elaborations, including (1) making predictions, (2) integrating the information with prior knowledge, (3) forming mental images, (4) responding affectively, and (5) responding with higher-level thinking processes. Predictions are based on the content and the structure of what is being read as well as on the reader's prior knowledge. Affective responses include emotional responses to the plot or theme, identification with characters, and affective reactions to word connotations and figurative language. Finally, higher-level thinking processes include application, analysis, synthesis, and evaluation and can be taught in all content areas as well as in reading classes.

Teachers encourage elaborations when they reject the "one right answer" approach and encourage personal interaction with the material. Elaborations should not be judged on the basis of their "rightness"; rather, they should be judged on the basis of the quality and relevance of the processes involved. Students at all grade and ability levels and in all content areas should be encouraged to elaborate in all of the ways suggested in this chapter. A modeling approach is recommended.

SELF-CHECK TEST

1. Choose either expository or narrative material and list the factors on which readers base their predictions.

2. List five types of elaborative processes.

3. Define the following:
   structurally-based prediction   analysis
   connotation   synthesis
   application   evaluation

4. Fill in the blanks:
   a. High-picture learners should be encouraged to _____.
   b. The first step in teaching prediction is _____.
   c. Appropriate elaborations are _____.
   d. A student may be unwilling to make a prediction because _____ .

5. Answer true or false:

   ___ a. First-grade students should not be expected to elaborate.
   ___ b. Elaboration processes interact with micro-, integrative, and macro processes.
   ___ c. All elaborations facilitate recall.
   ___ d. Affective responses should always be encouraged.
   ___ e. All students will make the same prior-knowledge elaborations.
   ___ f. Thinking and reading are two separate things.
   ___ g. The "one right answer" approach encourages elaborations.
   ___ h. Detecting propaganda is an example of synthesis.
   ___ i. Judging quality is an example of analysis.
   ___ j. Evaluation is harder than application.

SUGGESTED ACTIVITIES

1. Ask some students to make predictions after reading the introduction to a reading assignment. For each response, tell what information the student is using as a basis for the prediction.
2. Practice making predictions yourself. For one day, write down a prediction each time you begin to read something. On what basis are you making these predictions?
3. Design a series of instructional activities that you can use to encourage your students to use one of the elaboration processes.

4. Which elaborative processes are most important in your teaching situation? Why? What can you do to promote them?
5. During a reasonably long reading task, monitor your own elaborative processes. To what extent do you use each type? To what extent is this a result of your purpose for reading? How much is your prior knowledge affecting these elaborations? In what specific ways are your purpose, your prior knowledge, and your preferred method of reading interacting?

REFERENCES

ADAMS, M., & BRUCE, B. (1980). *Background Knowledge and Reading Comprehension* (Reading Education Report no. 13). Urbana-Champaign: Center for the Study of Reading, University of Illinois.

AULLS, M. (1978). *Developmental and Remedial Reading in the Middle Grades.* Boston: Allyn & Bacon.

BLOOM, B. (1956). *Taxonomy of Educational Objectives. Handbook* I: *Cognitive Domain.* New York: David McKay.

BURMEISTER, L. E. (1978). *Reading Strategies for Middle and Secondary School Teachers.* Reading, Mass.: Addison-Wesley.

COLLINS, A., & SMITH, E. E. (1980). *Teaching the Process of Reading Comprehension* (Technical Report no. 182). Urbana-Champaign: Center for the Study of Reading, University of Illinois.

GOLINKOFF, R. M. (1975-1976). A comparison of reading comprehension processes in good and poor comprehenders. *Reading Research Quarterly, 4,* 623–659.

HAFNER, L. E. (1977). *Developmental reading in middle and secondary schools.* New York: Macmillan.

LEVIN, J. R., DIVINE-HAWKINS, P., KERST, S. M., & GUTEMANN, J. (1974). Individual differences in learning from pictures and words: The development and application of an instrument. *Journal of Educational Psychology, 68,* 296–303.

PEARSON, P. D., & JOHNSON, D. D. (1978). *Teaching Reading Comprehension.* New York: Holt, Rinehart and Winston.

REDER, L. M. (1978). *Comprehension and retention of prose: A literature review* (Technical report no. 108). Urbana-Champaign: Center for the Study of Reading, University of Illinois.

REDER, L. M. (1980). The role of elaboration in the comprehension and retention of prose: A critical review. *Review of Educational Research, 15,* 5–53.

SANDERS, N. (1966). *Classroom questions: What kinds?* New York: Harper & Row.

SMITH, R. J., & BARRETT, T. C. (1979). *Teaching reading in the middle grades.* Reading, Mass.: Addison-Wesley.

SPIRO, R. J. (1984). Consciousness and reading comprehension. In J. Flood (Ed.), *Understanding Reading Comprehension.* Newark, Del.: International Reading Association.

STEINGART, S. K., & GLOCK, M. A. (1979). Imagery and the recall of connected discourse. *Reading Research Quarterly, 15,* 66–83.

WARREN, W. H., NICHOLAS, D. W., & TRABASSO, T. (1979). Event chains and inference in understanding narratives. In R. O. Freedle (ed.), *New Directions in Discourse Processing* (Vol. 2). Hillsdale, N.J.: Erlbaum.

SIX
TEACHING
METACOGNITIVE
PROCESSES

Baker and Brown (1980) define a student's *metacognitive skills* as "the knowledge and control he has over his own thinking and learning activities" (p. 2). A good reader is aware of how to adjust his or her reading strategies to achieve his or her purpose and can do so effectively.

This chapter will use the Baker and Brown (1980) division of metacognitive processes into those that are necessary for "reading for meaning" and those that are necessary for "reading for remembering" (p. 5). The most important metacognitive process used by readers to get meaning is monitoring their own comprehension for success or failure. Good readers know when they have or have not understood something, and they know what to do when their comprehension breaks down. Reading for remembering involves the application of many processes that have traditionally been called "study skills": underlining, note-taking, previewing, rehearsing, reviewing, and so on. Moreover, the conscious selection of the recall-facilitating basic processes discussed earlier in this text can also be seen as a metacognitive activity. The important thing is that students are actively selecting their reading strategies so as best to achieve a particular goal.

READING FOR MEANING: COMPREHENSION MONITORING

Good readers are more able to detect passage inconsistencies and to search previous and subsequent text to check for information than are poor readers (DiVesta, Hayward, & Orlando, 1979; Garner, 1980; Garner & Reis, 1981). Collins and Smith (1980) define *comprehension monitoring* as "the student's ability both to evaluate his or her ongoing comprehension processes while reading through a text, and to take some sort of remedial action when these processes bog down" (p. 3). They recommend teaching students what difficulties might occur and what good readers do when these difficulties do occur. Their taxonomy of comprehension failures is given in Figure 6-1. Note that the first two main categories—failure to understand a word and failure to understand a sentence—describe microprocessing failures; the third category—failure to understand how one sentence relates to another—describes integrative processing failures; and the last category— failure to understand how the whole text fits together—roughly corresponds to macroprocessing failures.

Figure 6-2 gives the remedies that Collins and Smith (1980) suggest

FIGURE 6-1 *TAXONOMY OF COMPREHENSION FAILURES*

1. Failure to understand a word
   a. Novel word
   b. Known word that doesn't make sense in the context
2. Failure to understand a sentence
   a. Can find no interpretation
   b. Can find only vague, abstract interpretation
   c. Can find several possible interpretations (ambiguous sentence)
   d. Interpretation conflicts with prior knowledge
3. Failure to understand how one sentence relates to another
   a. Interpretation of one sentence conflicts with another
   b. Can find no connection between the sentences
   c. Can find several possible connections between the sentences
4. Failure to understand how the whole text fits together
   a. Can find no point to whole or part of the text
   b. Cannot understand why certain episodes or sections occurred
   c. Cannot understand the motivations of certain characters

Source: Collins, A. & Smith, E. *Teaching the process of reading comprehension.* (Technical report no. 182). Urbana-Champaign: Center for the Study of Reading, University of Illinois, p. 8.

FIGURE 6-2 *POSSIBLE REMEDIES FOR COMPREHENSION FAILURES*

1. *Ignore and read on,* because this information is relatively unimportant.
2. *Suspend judgment,* because it is likely to be cleared up later.
3. *Form a tentative hypothesis* to be tested as reading continues.
4. *Reread the current sentence(s)* or look for a tentative hypothesis.
5. *Reread the previous context* to resolve the contradiction.
6. *Go to an expert source,* because it simply doesn't make sense.

Source: Collins, A. & Smith, E. *Teaching the process of reading comprehension.* (Technical report no. 182). Urbana-Champaign: Center for the Study of Reading, University of Illinois.

be taught to students. Note that these remedies are presented in order from the least disruptive to the most disruptive, and they should probably be tried in this order. For instance, ignoring and reading on and suspending judgment are less disruptive than stopping to form a tentative hypothesis, so such strategies should be tried first. Formation of a hypothesis would be used when ignoring or suspending judgment were inadequate. Thus, it is also important to teach students how to decide when to give up on one strategy and move on to another.

Teaching students how their comprehension can break down, developing their awareness of when these breakdowns occur, and giving them some strategies to use for remedying the situation will help them to become more active, confident readers. Of course, good readers are not consciously aware of comprehension monitoring until a "triggering event" signals a failure (Baker and Brown, 1980, p. 9). Students simply need to learn what to do when that triggering event (see Figure 6-1) occurs.

Incidental Monitoring Instruction

Comprehension monitoring can be encouraged in a variety of situations, including content-area classes. Whenever students do not understand what they are reading, they should be encouraged to clarify the source of the breakdown. For instance, if students say that they did not understand a newspaper article on a current event, ask them why. They may discover that specific vocabulary words were causing them problems or that they didn't have adequate prior knowledge, or that the main point was unclear. Then, they can be shown how to take the appropriate remedial steps to facilitate their own comprehension. Thus, they can learn to be active, independent readers who are not dependent on having teachers and experts available to help them.

Direct Monitoring Instruction

Assessment.   One way to assess your students' abilities in the area of comprehension monitoring is to provide them with paragraphs in which the information is inconsistent. Which students notice? What do they do about it? Another procedure is to ask students if they have comprehended something they have read. Then, give a test of their comprehension. Have they predicted accurately? Finally, ask poor comprehenders what they do when they come to something they don't understand. If they say, "I don't know," or "I ask someone," then they may lack effective strategies for comprehension monitoring.

Comprehension-rating procedure.   The following instructional procedure has been developed by Davey and Porter (1982) and has been used successfully with middle school poor comprehenders. This "comprehension-rating procedure" involves four steps as follows.

Step 1 was designed to encourage the students to have a "meaning orientation to print" (Davey & Porter, 1982, p. 199). The teacher modeled this orientation by talking about the centrality of comprehension and her own comprehension breakdowns and remedial strategies. Then, she modeled these strategies while reading aloud, using materials with words omitted or with nonsense words substituted for some of the real ones.

Step 2 was designed to help the students focus on meaning. Students read materials using real or nonsense words and indicated whether or not they understood. This activity moved from sentences to paragraphs and from oral to silent work, as the students progressed.

In step 3, a third possible response was included. Students indicated whether they understood well, whether they sort of understood, or whether they didn't understand at all. They also indicated the source of their comprehension failures.

Finally, in step 4, students were directly taught various fix-up strategies. These were divided into word-level and idea-level strategies. Each was demonstrated and practiced. The obvious follow-up procedure is to encourage students to use these monitoring strategies throughout the year on various types of materials.

READING FOR REMEMBERING: STUDY SKILLS

As has been discussed, good readers stop and adopt a remedial strategy when they realize that microprocesses, integrative processes, or macroprocesses have broken down. Good readers also adjust their strategies when they want to remember certain parts of what they are reading.

Comprehension Processes as Directed Study Skills

Of course, many of the processes discussed earlier in this book affect how much and what is remembered after reading. Any time a student makes a choice to use a specific process to increase recall, that student is making a metacognitive decision.

Macro- and elaborative processes provide the most obvious examples of processes that might be chosen to increase recall. For instance, summarizing and noting the author's organization should be recommended as study skills. Indeed, many of the activities suggested in Chapter Four, such as the hierarchical summary procedure and the ConStruct procedure, can be used as study strategies (see pp. 52–57). Finally, elaborations such as imaging and integrating with prior knowledge have very clear effects on recall and can also be taught as self-selected study strategies. (See Chapter Five.)

Self-questioning for Remembering

One newly researched study strategy that has not been previously mentioned is self-questioning. Initial experimentation with this technique has indicated that it may be even more effective for low-ability students than for high-ability students (André & Anderson, 1978–79). Moreover, the technique is probably more effective if students are trained to do it correctly. André and Anderson point out that students should probably be trained first to identify the main idea (on which they will base their question) and then to form a question that either asks for new examples of the ideas presented (preferable) or asks directly about the concept resented, using a paraphrased format.

Figure 6-3 shows a fifth-grade student effectively using a self-questioning technique to guide her own studying. Note the amount of "metacognitive" thinking that is going on.

Before students will be willing to do self-questioning, you will have to convince them that the technique works. One way to do this is by having a classroom demonstration. When they have all read a passage, give a difficult "pop quiz." Then, they can see how much they don't remember. For the next section of the text, give them sample self-questions to answer while they read. Then, give another quiz. They will probably all do much better. This may motivate them to want to learn the technique.

Self-questioning can also be taught by moving students slowly from dependence on the teacher to independent application. On the most dependent level, you will need to supply the questions for the students to an-

FIGURE 6-3   USING SELF-QUESTIONING

TEXT READ	STUDENT THOUGHTS
LESSON 3. MINERS AND RANCHERS The hope of finding gold or silver brought many settlers to the last West. Large numbers of people had moved to California during the gold rush of 1849. More followed in gold, silver, and copper rushes in the 1860s and 1870s.	OK; now, why did people move to the West in the late 1800s? To find gold, silver, and copper, of course. That was easy.
"Boom towns" grew up almost overnight where metals were found. When one person made a strike, more rushed in to search for ore. A few struck it rich. Most did not. Many of them stopped searching and went to work for companies that made a business of mining. Some opened stores or businesses to serve the miners. But most of them became ranchers or farmers.	What was a "boom town"? Well, I guess it was a town that grew up around where people found gold. When people didn't find any, they became the other things for the town, like store owners. I wonder where they got the word "boom." I'll ask the teacher tomorrow.
Many western people, especially on Mexican land, had ranched for years before the Civil War. After the war, the ranching business got a big boost. This happened for two reasons. One, railroads were built across the country to the West Coast. Two, the killing of the buffalo opened new lands for cattle.	Why did all these new Westerners go into ranching? I guess because there was plenty of land and because they could ship the meat by train. They must have run out of gold. I don't know what it had to do with the Civil War. I'll read on to see if it comes up again.
The cattle were raised on the grassy plains.When they were big enough, they were shipped east by train. However, first they had to get to the railroads. This was done by means of a cattle drive. A cattle drive was not a drive at all. It was a very long walk. Cowboys on horses forced the cattle to walk hundreds of miles over dusty trails. Their goal was to reach the cattle pens next to the railroad tracks in Sedalia, Missouri, or Abilene, Kansas, or some other cow town.	What was a "cattle drive"? Well, it was when they had to walk the cattle to the railroad stations. I guess they sent the cattle on the trains while they were still alive. Then, they killed them in the East . . .

Source: From AMERICA PAST AND PRESENT by Joan Schreiber, et al. Copyright © 1983 by Scott, Foresman and Company. Reprinted by permission.

swer. Student answers can be compared and discussed, so that they can learn to recognize an answer that is clear, complete, and in their own words. Then, students can practice writing their own "self-questions." Again, students can compare questions, so that they learn to recognize and write questions that focus on the most important points and ask for examples whenever possible. Finally, students will be able to use this study technique independently, although you should probably collect some written evidence for a while.

Traditional Study Skills

If you have ever been exposed to study strategies, then self-questioning probably reminded you of the second step of a traditional study system.[1] All these systems recommend that students (1) preview the material, (2) focus their attention on key concepts, (3) rehearse the material at intervals, preferably in their own words, and (4) review the material as a whole after reading. Some also recommend taking notes and reflecting (or elaborating) on the material during or after reading. Self-questioning probably helps the student with the second and third strategies: that is, it helps them to focus their attention and rehearse the material at intervals. Let's examine each of these strategies in terms of alternative ways of doing them and ways that you can teach them to your students.

Previewing. Previewing a reading passage usually involves reading the introduction and summary and looking at the titles, subheadings, and pictures. During this process, the reader should be thinking about what he or she already knows about the topic and about what the organizational structure is going to be. He or she may also want to make predictions. If using something like the hierarchical summarization strategy suggested by Taylor (1982) (see Chapter Four), he or she will also write down a skeletal outline during previewing. Thus, previewing allows the reader to begin to mobilize prior knowledge, macroprocessing, and prediction abilities to facilitate comprehension and recall.

Previewing can be taught by guiding students through the process whenever you want them to study/read. Simply allow enough time to do this when you give the assignment. At first, you may need to model the thinking process. Then, they can model it back to you. Eventually, they will be able to do it silently, and, finally, they can be asked to do it as part of the reading assignment. For these last two stages, you may wish to require some sort of written product, such as a skeletal outline or a set of predictions.

Focusing attention. Many study systems recommend turning each subheading into a question to be answered while reading. Others recommend simply looking for the key idea of each paragraph. Self-questioning is a version of this. The point is that the reader should be aware of what information is important for his or her purpose and then focus attention on that information.

Of course, you can help to focus the students' attention by giving

---

[1]Examples include SQ3R (Survey, Question, Read, Recite, Review), PQ4R (Preview, Question, Read, Recite, Review, Reflect), and OK5R (Overview, Key idea, Read, Record, Recite, Review, Reflect) (Robinson, 1961; Thomas & Robinson, 1977; Pauk, 1974, respectively). For a description of at least one system, see almost any text on study skills or secondary reading methods.

them a purpose for reading or a study guide (see Chapter Nine). Eventually, however, students need to learn a focusing strategy they can use on their own. Thus, it would probably be useful for you to guide students through initial content-area chapters, asking them to tell how they will focus their attention for each section.

Rehearsing during reading. Every educational psychology text tells you about the importance of rehearsal for recall. It is important to note, however, the difference between superficial and meaningful rehearsal. (See Bransford, 1979.) Although simply repeating something to be remembered may help retain it for short-term recall, long-term recall requires a more meaningful rehearsal. Thus, it is very important to teach students to rehearse information by using their own words, thinking about how it conceptually relates to other information, and so on.

Rehearsal occurs when students mentally or orally answer the questions they have formed to focus their attention, when they write those answers into their hierarchical summaries, when they summarize paragraphs in the margin, when they underline or take notes, and when they answer the questions on your study guide. Rehearsing should be done at the end of *each section* of the chapter. Some students find that making a tape recording of their summaries of each section is useful. (Though the tape can be used for review, it is probably useful because it required them, while they were reading, to rehearse important information periodically in their own words.)

Rehearsal can be taught as part of the self-questioning study technique. If you would like to teach it as a single technique, you may wish to do a demonstration similar to that suggested for self-questioning in which students are dramatically shown its effectiveness. You may also wish to require that rehearsal be done in writing, so that you can monitor progress.

Underlining and note-taking. Unfortunately, the research that has been done on the effectiveness of underlining and note-taking as compared to just rereading the material has not been very positive. (See Anderson, 1980.) The real benefit of these strategies may simply be that they reduce the material to a manageable size for future study. In some classes, this can be very important, especially at the college level. Several of the macroprocessing procedures recommended in Chapter Four of this text also require note-taking and would probably help guide the more dependent students to take more meaningful notes.

The things to remember if you decide to teach underlining or note-taking are that the reader should (1) actively mark or transform the material into his or her own words, (2) be selective, and (3) look for the organizational pattern. Also, as you know, simply telling the students to do these things will not be sufficient for most students. You need to provide them with good models and then collect their work and give them feedback as they progress.

An excellent description of ways to underline and take notes is available in Pauk (1974). Briefly, for underlining and text marking, Pauk urges students to consider the following (pp. 153–154):

1. Finish reading before marking.
2. Be extremely selective.
3. Use your own words.
4. Be swift.
5. Be neat.

He also suggests that students use a systematic symbol system. Suggestions for this are given in Table 6-1.

For note-taking, Pauk similarly urges students to finish reading each section before writing, to be selective, to use their own words, and to work quickly. He also recommends that they write in full sentences and that they summarize the notes with key words written in the left-hand margin. The key words in margins could be used for review and recitation while the right-hand side is covered.

Reviewing.   Rehearsing after the entire reading assignment has been completed will also promote recall. Students can be encouraged to go back over the same things examined during previewing; the introduction, summary, graphic aids, and subheadings. For each subheading, they should summarize the related section in their own words. If they marked the text or took notes, then putting summary terms in the margins and reciting from those might provide a useful review. The important thing is that they look away from the page to recite the information rather than simply reading things over without meaningfully rehearsing them.

You will probably want to model this procedure first. You may want to walk them through a review on the day each assignment is due. However, reviewing the next day is not the same thing as reviewing at the end of reading when the information is still fresh. Try a classroom experiment. For two weeks, have half the students review at home while the other half doesn't. (Make sure that ability levels are the same in each half.) As often as possible, show how the review group has superior recall.

A total study approach.   Even after students understand all of the aforementioned strategies, they may need a way to put them all together into a systematic approach. One way is to have students think in terms of what they want to do (1) before (previewing), (2) during (focusing and rehearsing), and (3) after reading (reviewing). (See Anderson, 1980.) Indeed, students should be taught that the difference between study reading

TABLE 6-1 Suggestions for Marking Textbooks

EXPLANATION AND DESCRIPTION	SYMBOLS, MARKINGS, AND NOTATIONS
1. Double lines under words or phrases signify the main ideas.	Radiation can produce mutations . . .
2. Single lines under words or phrases signify supporting material.	comes from cosmic rays . . .
3. Small circled numbers above the initial word of an underlined group of words indicate a series of arguments, facts, ideas, either main or supporting.	Conditions change . . . ① rocks rise . . . ② some sink . . . ③ the sea dashes . . . ④ strong winds . . .
4. Rather than underlining a group of three or more important lines, you may use a vertical bracket in the outer margin.	⎡ had known . . . ⎢ who gave . . . ⎢ the time . . . ⎣ of time . . .
5. One asterisk in the margin indicates ideas of special importance; two, ideas of unusual importance; and three, ideas of outstanding importance: reserved for principles and high level generalizations.	*When a nuclear blast is . . . **people quite close to the . . . ***The main cause of mutations . . .
6. Circle key words and terms.	The ⟨genes⟩ are the . . .
7. Box in the words of enumeration and transitions.	┃fourth,┃ the lack of supplies . . . ┃furthermore,┃ the shortage . . .
8. A question mark in the margin, opposite lines you do not understand, is an excellent reminder to ask the instructor for clarification.	❓ ┃The latest . . . ┃cold period . . . ┃about 1,000,000 . . . ┃Even today . . .
9. If you disagree with a statement, indicate that in the margin.	*disagree* ┃Life became . . . ┃on land only . . . ┃340 million years . . .
10. Use the top and bottom margins of a page to record any ideas of your own that are prompted by what you have read.	*Why not use carbon dating?* *Check on reference of fossils found in Tennessee stone quarry.*
11. On sheets of paper that are smaller than the pages of the book, write longer thoughts or summaries, then insert them between the pages.	*Fossils* *Plants =* 500,000,000 *years old* *Insects =* 250,000,000 *" "* *Bees =* 100,000,000 *" "* *June fish =* 350,000,000 *" "* *Amphibians =* 300,000,000 *" "* *Reptiles =* 300,000,000 *" "* *Birds =* 150,000,000 *" "*
12. Even though you have underlined the important ideas and supporting materials, still jot brief summaries in the side margins.	*adapt -* ____ *spacial* *layer -* ____

Source: Walter Pauk, *How to Study in College* Third Edition, p. 155. Copyright © 1974 by Houghton Mifflin Company. Used by permission.

and leisure reading is that, for the former, additional activities at all three of these stages are needed.

Finally, for most students, trying to learn all of these stages at once is discouraging. It just looks like too much work. Thus, you will probably want to introduce these stages one at a time, making sure that each has become habitual and "easy" before moving on to the next.

Teaching Study Skills: K–12

Although the procedures described in the foregoing paragraphs are primarily geared for older students, it would probably be useful to begin to encourage these habits as soon as students are engaged in trying to remember material. Elementary students can be asked to write summaries of reading assignments, which can be kept in a loose-leaf notebook and studied before the test. Before reading, students can be directed to preview the material and to decide what should be remembered. After reading, students can divide into pairs to "test" each other. This would require them to rehearse aloud. Finally, just teaching younger students to preview, read, and then review will probably lay a foundation for more sophisticated strategies to be used later.

BASIC PROCESSES, COMPREHENSION CONTEXTS AND METACOGNITIVE DECISIONS

In addition to monitoring comprehension for meaning and selecting study strategies for recall, good readers often adjust their use of comprehension processes according to the three comprehension contexts. (You will remember from Chapter One that these included the reader, textual, and situational characteristics.) Each time a reader decides to use a specific process in a specific way because of a specific context, he or she is making a metacognitive decision. (Note that using elaboration to facilitate recall is still elaborative processing, but *making the conscious choice* to emphasize it is a metacognitive process.)

For instance, the reader must take into account his or her own prior knowledge: If he or she lacks the necessary background information he or she may choose to read slowly, resolving problems by referring to another source (comprehension monitoring). Very easy material with which he or she is familiar can be read more quickly with an emphasis on summarizing the important points (macroprocessing).

Similarly, different types of texts will require different processes. A poem may require affective response, whereas an essay may require analysis to be understood fully. A clearly organized text will require less macroprocessing effort than will one whose main points are obscure and unrelated.

Finally, the total situation, including the purpose for reading, will also affect metacognitive choices about basic processes. If the purpose for reading the poem mentioned above were to understand imagery, then imaging while reading might be more important than affective response. If the purpose were to understand rhythm and meter, then slow oral reading, with an emphasis on chunking, would be essential. (See Chapter Nine for a complete discussion of reading purposes and methods.)

It would be impossible to delineate completely all the possible ways that good readers may choose to vary their use of basic processes in response to various comprehension contexts. The next three chapters contain more extensive descriptions of each of these contexts. After reading these chapters, you may be able to give even more examples of metacognitive strategy decisions possible for flexible comprehenders.

SUMMARY

Metacognitive processes are those processes by which students are consciously aware of and selectively apply various reading strategies. They include monitoring one's own comprehension for success or failure, taking remedial action when necessary, and selecting comprehension processes and study strategies when recall is important. Study strategies include such things as self-questioning, previewing, focusing attention, rehearsing, underlining, note–taking, and reviewing. Students also adjust their approaches according to their own abilities, the characteristics of the material, and the specific task involved. For a more thorough discussion of these factors, see Part Two of this text (Chapters Seven, Eight, and Nine).

SELF-CHECK TEST

1. Fill in the following list of metacognitive skills:
    I. Reading for meaning
        A.
        B.

      II.   Reading for remembering
          A.
          B.
          C.
          D.
          E.
      III.   Adjust strategies according to . . .
          A.
          B.
          C.

2. Define the following terms:

metacognitive processes	previewing
comprehension monitoring	focusing
comprehension-rating procedure	rehearsal
self-questioning	

3. Fill in the missing comprehension failures:
    a. Failure to understand a word
        i. Novel word.
        ii.
    b. Failure to understand a sentence
        i. Can find no interpretation.
        ii.
        iii. Can find several possible interpretations (ambiguous sentence).
        iv.
    c. Failure to understand how one sentence relates to another
        i. Interpretation of one sentence conflicts with another.
        ii.
        iii. Can find several possible connections between the sentences.
    d. Failure to understand how the whole text fits together
        i.
        ii. Cannot understand why certain episodes or sentences occurred.
        iii.

4. List six possible comprehension remedies.

5. Answer true or false:

____   a. The comprehension rating procedure is a way the teacher can assess the students' comprehension.

____   b. Ignoring a comprehension breakdown is always an ineffective thing to do.

____   c. Self-questioning is only for college students.

____   d. Students must be taught to rehearse verbatim from the book.

____   e. Many students need to be convinced that study strategies are worth the time.

___ f. All students know when they have failed to understand.

___ g. Instruction in study habits should begin in the elementary school.

SUGGESTED ACTIVITIES

___ 1. Read something that is difficult for you to understand. For each break-down, identify the source from Figure 6-1 and a remedy from Figure 6-2.

___ 2. Examine your own study reading. Can it be improved? If not, tell what you do and why it works. If so, develop a new procedure and practice it for two weeks.

___ 3. Design a set of materials to use in diagnosing your students' comprehension monitoring abilities.

___ 4. Design a set of lessons to teach your students one of the skills described in this chapter.

___ 5. Study Figure 1-1 (p. 4). For each subprocess, describe a situation in which a reader might choose to utilize that subprocess more than the others.

REFERENCES

ANDERSON, T. H. (1978). *Another look at the self-questioning study technique* (Reading Education Report no. 6). Urbana-Champaign: Center for the Study of Reading, University of Illinois.

ANDERSON, T. H. (1980). Study strategies and adjunct aids. In R. J. Spiro, B. C. Bruce, and W. F. Brewer (Eds.), *Theoretical issues in reading comprehension.* Hillsdale, N.J.: Lawrence Erlbaum.

ANDRE´, M. E. D., & ANDERSON, T. H. (1978–79). The development and evaluation of a self-questioning study technique. *Reading Research Quarterly, 14,* 605–623.

BAKER, L., & BROWN, A. L. (1980). *Metacognitive skill and reading.* (Technical report no. 188). Urbana-Champaign: Center for the Study of Reading, University of Illinois.

BRADFORD, J. D. (1979). *Human cognition: Learning, understanding, and remembering.* Belmont, Calif.: Wadsworth.

COLLINS, A., & SMITH, E. E. (1980). *Teaching the process of reading comprehension* (Technical Report no. 182). Urbana-Champaign: Center for the Study of Reading, University of Illinois.

DAVEY, B., & PORTER, S. M. (1982). Comprehension-rating: A procedure to assist poor comprehenders. *Journal of Reading, 26,* 197–202.

DiVESTA, F. J., HAYWARD, K. G., & ORLANDO, V. P. (1979). Developmental trends in monitoring text for comprehension. *Child Development, 50,* 97–105.

GARNER, R. (1980). Monitoring of understanding: An investigation of good and poor readers' awareness of induced miscomprehension of text. *Journal of Reading Behavior, 12,* 55–63.

GARNER, R., & REIS, R. (1981). Monitoring and resolving comprehension obstacles: An investigation of spontaneous lookbacks among upper-grade good and poor comprehenders. *Reading Research Quarterly, 16,* 569–582.

PAUK, W. (1974). *How to Study in College*. Boston: Houghton Mifflin.
ROBINSON, F. P. (1961). Study skills for superior students in the secondary school. *The Reading Teacher, 25*, 29–33.
TAYLOR, B. M. (1982). A summarizing strategy to improve middle grade students' reading and writing skills. *The Reading Teacher, 36*, 202–205.
TAYLOR, K. K. (1983). Can college students summarize? *Journal of Reading, 26*, 524–529.
THOMAS, E. L., & ROBINSON, H. A. (1977). *Improving Reading in Every Class* (2nd Ed.). Boston: Allyn and Bacon.

SEVEN
INDIVIDUAL READER
CONTEXTS:
Who Is Reading?

You will remember from Chapter One that the "comprehension context" can be divided into three sets of influences: the reader-related context, the text-related context, and the situational context. An easy way to remember these contexts is always to think in terms of the five W's: who, what, where, when, and why. The "who" is the reader and his and her individual characteristics that affect what he or she will comprehend; the "what" is the reading material itself and its individual characteristics that will affect what is comprehended; the "where," "when," and "why" are the situational characteristics that affect what is comprehended. The next three chapters include discussions of each of these contexts. Because they all affect what is comprehended, they have important implications for how you teach.

You may also remember from Chapter One that the characteristics of the individual reader affect what is comprehended, because the reader actively interprets the cues on the printed pages in the light of what he or she brings to it. This includes his or her prior knowledge about the topic, emotional attitudes relative to the topic and the assignment, and reading skills. Thus, all comprehension instruction must begin with an assessment of *who* will be "inferring the author's intended meaning" (see Chapter One, page 9) in terms of these individual characteristics.

PRIOR KNOWLEDGE

Comprehension has been defined as "building bridges between the new and the known" (Pearson & Johnson, 1978, p. 24). This definition, like the one used in this book, stresses the active nature of the process and the importance of prior knowledge. Comprehension simply cannot take place when nothing is already "known" because then there is nothing to which the reader can link the "new." That readers remember more when they are familiar with the topic has been extensively substantiated by recent research (Chiesi, Spilich, & Voss, 1978; Spilich, Vesonder, Chiesi, & Voss, 1979; and others). Presumably, this is because the knowledgeable readers can link the incoming information to what they already know.

Indeed, prior knowledge is so necessary for comprehension that some speculate that it can often account for a large portion of the difference between successful and unsuccessful comprehenders. Taylor (1979) found that poor readers seem to be more vulnerable to the effects of topic familiarity in terms of the amount recalled than are good readers. Johnston and Pearson (1982) found that manipulating topic familiarity affected comprehension even when differences associated with standardized test scores were partialed out. Moreover, in their study, scores on prior knowledge questions were significant predictors of scores on all the other types of questions!

One can easily trace how prior knowledge influences all of the comprehension processes discussed in Chapters Two through Six in this book. One example of the effects of prior knowledge on microprocessing is provided by Anderson, Reynolds, Schallert, and Goetz (1977) (see Chapter One, page 7). This was the study in which the music students thought a passage was about a rehearsal whereas the physical education students thought it was about a card game. The reader's prior knowledge also affects the ability to make integrative inferences (Pearson, Hansen, & Gordon, 1979; Wilson & Hammill, 1982). Hildyard (1979) found that although such inferential ability seems to develop with age, younger students do make these inferences when they have adequate prior knowledge. Similarly, macroprocessing ability seems to depend on prior knowledge of the content area: good readers recall more when the passage is organized according to expected patterns. Obviously, elaborative processing, which includes integration with prior knowledge, predictions based on prior knowledge, and so on, clearly requires that the reader have some prior knowledge. Finally, remedying comprehension failures and selecting material for rehearsal require that students have prior knowledge about alternative sources of information and about what information is most likely to be important.

Facilitating Prior-Knowledge Usage

Students can directly be told to use their prior knowledge when necessary for various comprehension processes. For instance, when teaching students to make connective inferences, teachers will want to remind students to think of what they already know about the events and then to determine how they might be related. As part of comprehension monitoring, students can learn to identify the comprehension failures that result from not having the background knowledge assumed by the author.

Another excellent way to teach students to use their prior knowledge actively while reading is to use the modeling approach suggested for many other skills in this text. As you read to students, pause and share your thinking processes. Show them how you are using your prior knowledge for all the processes needed for comprehending. Ask them to do the same. Figure 5-4 (Chapter Five) gives an example of a teacher doing this to teach prior-knowledge elaboration. A similar procedure could be used to show students how prior knowledge helps with the other processes.

Finally, previewing an assignment provides an excellent opportunity to review prior knowledge. As students preview, have them discuss what they already know. Write key concepts on the board and have students speculate about what they expect in the reading, given what they already know about the topic. The process of prethinking about prior knowledge when previewing an assignment at home can also be modeled for the students by the teacher or by one of the other students.

Schema Theory

Many recent researchers discuss "prior knowledge" as being organized into "schemata" (singular, "schema"), so it is probably important for you to have a basic understanding of this term (Anderson, Spiro, & Anderson, 1977; Rumelhart, 1981; and others). Put simply, a schema is a knowledge structure. It can be a concept or it can be a set of related concepts and it can be about objects, ideas, or phenomena (see Pearson & Spiro, 1980). For instance, you probably have a schema for a desk that includes the characteristics of desks and a mental image of a typical desk. Similarly, you also probably have a schema for going to a movie that includes such things as buying a ticket, smelling popcorn, and so on.

Based on cues in the text, we select the schema to be used for comprehension. Then, as we read, we fill in the details required by that schema, sometimes from explicit information and sometimes with slot-filling inferences. For instance, suppose we are reading about Johnny going to a movie and mention is made of something white and crunchy on the floor. Our movie schema would probably enable us to determine the source of this unknown substance. If the story mentioned that he tripped when looking for a seat, most readers would infer that this was because it was dark in the theatre. Popcorn and darkness in the theatre are probably parts of a typical movie schema, and such inferences would also help to explain the upcoming facts about his going to buy something and then accidentally returning to the wrong seat. Note, however, that a student who has no movie schema might not know what he bought, why he bought it, or why he couldn't find his seat. Moreover, a student who was using a classroom schema might have inferred that there was paper on the floor, that someone tripped him, that he went to buy a pencil, and so on.

A schema can also determine what prior knowledge elaborations are made. If nothing to the contrary is said in the text, good readers using a movie schema will probably infer that Johnny enjoyed the movie. This is because the movie schema says that this is true by "default" (Rumelhart, 1981), that is, if nothing is said to the contrary. Again, students without a developed schema might not elaborate in this way, and students using a classroom schema might elaborate with totally different assumptions about the purpose of the movie.

Finally, schemata also help students to select important information. Anderson, Spiro, and Anderson (1977) wrote two similar passages containing mention of the same eighteen foods. One was about a restaurant visit and the other was about a grocery trip. They found that readers of the restaurant version were more likely to remember who got what food than were readers of the grocery version. This was, presumably, because "who gets what food has significance within a restaurant schema whereas it matters not in a supermarket who throws the brussel sprouts in the shopping cart" (Anderson, 1977, p. 12). Thus, the schema selected can determine what students choose to remember as well as what slot-filling inferences and prior-knowledge elaborations they make as they read.

In terms of schema theory, then, teachers need to make sure that students have the appropriate schema, that they select the appropriate schema to use for interpreting while reading, that they maintain an awareness of the relevant schema for as long as is necessary, and that they not over- or underrely on their schema for interpretation. These skills have been called "schema availability," "schema selection," "schema maintenance," and "control mode reliance" (Pearson & Spiro, 1980).

Facilitating Schema Usage

Pearson and Spiro (1980) have made several instructional suggestions for the teacher attempting to teach students to use schemata effectively. These can be listed according to the separate schema-related skills:

Schema availability.   Before reading, give students a pretest or, on the board, have them list words that they associate with key concepts. This will give you an idea of what information you need to fill in, and it will help them to review what they already know.

Schema selection.   To some extent, the assessment technique used to test the schema availability will have already helped the students to know what schema to select. Also, you can begin by asking students to write down everything they know about a topic (Pearson & Johnson, 1978) or, as a class, do a map (see Chapter Four in this text and pages 108–109 in this chapter).

Schema maintenance.   According to Pearson and Spiro (1980), "some students begin appropriately but somewhere along the way forget what they are reading about" (p. 82). Again, creating an ongoing visual representation such as a map or other organizational chart (see Chapter Four) while reading may help with this.

Control mode reliance.   Students who overrely on text cues need to be encouraged to see reading as a meaning-oriented activity. Using listening and reading tasks, embed anomalous statements and have the students find the statements that don't make sense. You can also try this: provide students with multiple answers to questions. One answer can be text based, another schema based, and the rest wrong. Have them select the two best answers and tell which is from the text and which is from what they know.

The opposite and somewhat less common problem is the problem of the student who overrelies on schemata. For these students, the multiple-answer activity may help. Also, activities that focus on details and precise meaning may be necessary.

The question of the flexible use of schema-based and text-based processing strategies has also been addressed by Tierney and Pearson (1981): In different situations, different patterns are appropriate. For instance, when reading lab directions, one would need to be more text based than when reading a novel for pleasure. Teachers can alert students to these approaches especially when text-based interpretations are necessary. Also teachers can provide study guides that encourage text- or schema-based approaches when necessary.

It also seems that the tendency to rely on schema- or text-based processes may be related to individual characteristics of the reader. Spiro and Tirre (1979) found that college students who were more "stimulus bound" on an embedded figures task were also more "text bound" on a reading comprehension task. As Spiro (1979) points out, however, for good readers, this tendency to rely on one or the other is used only when the situation permits, whereas poor readers may overrely on one even when it has negative effects on comprehension. Also, for poor readers, an overreliance on one style can be an attempt to compensate for a weakness: using prior knowledge to avoid decoding, and vice versa. Remediation must be based on a clear assessment of the cause of the inappropriate style.

Finally, it has also been suggested that schema theory gives us a useful way to understand students' wrong answers. In examining these answers, one might discover that they have been caused by one of the following (Strange, 1980):

1. No schema exists.
2. Schema is naîve.
3. No new information exists in story, so details are forgotten.
4. Story has insufficient cues for schema development.
5. Inappropriate schema is used.
6. Schema-based response is not sufficiently related to the text.
7. Text-based response is not sufficiently related to schema.

If you are able to determine that one student habitually falls into one or two of these errors, then the problem can be remedied by addressing the cause.

Building Prior Knowledge

Perhaps the major teaching implication of prior–knowledge and schema theory is that teachers must make sure that students have the necessary background knowledge before reading. If a schema pretest or prereading discussion reveals that students have insufficient background knowledge, then comprehension will be poor unless the teacher or the students find some way to fill in the important gaps in their background. Lectures and activities that build background may be useful. Such things as field trips, movies, and guest speakers build motivation as well as background knowledge. Using reading to build background is a strategy that is often overlooked, although Crafton (1983) found that students who read two passages on the same topic made more inferences, used more prior knowledge, became more personally involved, and recalled more than did students reading passages on different topics. Library books, magazines, and even lower-level textbooks can be used to help students acquire the necessary background knowledge. This will also give them a strategy for acquiring background information on their own when there is no teacher there to provide it for them. Finally, many of the prereading activities mentioned earlier for encouraging prior-knowledge usage and schema availability will also naturally lead to building students' background through discussion.

Developing Meaning Vocabulary

In practice, it is difficult to separate a knowledge of relevant background information from a knowledge of relevant word meanings. Expanding students' meaning vocabulary is a critical part of making sure that they have adequate background knowledge, and because word meanings are learned best when learned in terms of their associations with other concepts, it is probably best to think of expanding prior knowledge and building vocabulary simultaneously. Indeed, McNeil (1984) has suggested that one hypothesis explaining the strong correlation between vocabulary knowledge and comprehension ability is that "a person who knows a word well knows other words and ideas related to it. It is this network of ideas that enhances comprehension" (pp. 96–97). Thus, methods for teaching word meanings that link concepts together are probably more useful than the traditional approach of asking students to supply definitions of individual words.

Another problem with the way vocabulary is often taught has been pointed out by Herber (1970). There is evidence that words must be used "many times in many situations" (p. 160) before they are really known. Memorization of definitions and brief prereading discussions are insufficient. "Students develop vocabulary when they use words in situations that have meaning, in conversations and animated discussion" (p.162). Similarly, Shank (1982) hypothesizes that "to teach new words one must allow them to be used immediately and orally" (p. 164). Thus, vocabularly teaching methods that require students to use the words in meaningful ways, orally and in writing, are more likely to result in learning than is decontextualized memorization.

Finally, as Pearson and Johnson (1978) point out, "One of the axioms of instruction for concept development is that there is no substitute for direct experience" (p. 34). If there is no way to relate the new word meaning to the direct experience of the students, then it should be associated with something they have experienced. Concrete examples, role-playing simulations, pictures, and other aids that provide some direct experience are likely to be more useful than abstract definitions.

To summarize, teachers may wish to (1) teach vocabulary word meanings in terms of their connections to the other key background concepts needed for comprehension of the material, (2) encourage and facilitate repeated use of these words in meaningful oral and written situations before and after reading, and (3) find links between the meanings of the new words and the prior experience of the students. (Clearly, if these are to be done well, the teacher will have to limit the number of words to be introduced. Herber (1970) recommends that teachers consider choosing only key terms and that the number of these to be taught reflect the relative importance of the unit and the background and abilities of the students.)

Some specific vocabulary activities that lend themselves to the foregoing guidelines are (1) semantic mapping, (2) the Frayer model, and (3) the Possible Sentence Lesson. Of course, the creative teacher will be able to think of other methods for specific groups of words in specific situations; other vocabulary teaching suggestions can be found in Johnson and Pearson (1978), McNiel (1984), and other reading methods texts.

Semantic mapping.   To teach students to see how new concepts can be defined and related to other concepts, a class-constructed semantic map may be useful (see Hanf, 1971; McNiel, 1984; Pearson & Johnson, 1978; and others). For mapping the meaning of an individual concept, you may wish to include words telling properties, categories, and examples. Begin by having students list any related terms that come to mind. Then, assemble them into a diagram in which the relations of property, category, or example are indicated. Figure 7-1 shows a possible prereading map for the concept "natural resource." A similar procedure can be used to link together all the new words in a unit. Simply lead the students through a map of the whole assignment, inserting the new words where they belong. Fig-

FIGURE 7-1   Class-Constructed Semantic Map for "Natural Resource"

Brainstormed terms: Valuable
                                   Rocks
                                   Trees
                                   Nature
                                   Water

Map:

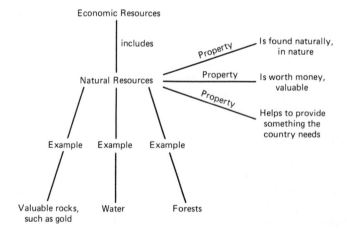

ure 7-2 shows a postreading map that places the new concept of natural resources in a general network with the other new concepts in the chapter.

The Frayer model. The Frayer model of concept development (Frayer, Frederick, & Klausmeir, 1969) provides an outline for defining words so that students understand the concepts rather than memorizing the definitions. This model suggests that defining words should proceed through these steps:

1. Naming relevant attributes
2. Eliminating irrelevant attributes
3. Giving examples
4. Giving nonexamples (examples of what it is not)
5. Giving subordinate terms
6. Giving superordinate terms
7. Giving coordinate terms

For instance, to define the term "natural resource," a teacher might say,

1. A natural resource is anything occurring naturally in the environment that has monetary value.
2. It doesn't matter whether it is liquid, gas, or solid.
3. Gold, oil, forests, rich soil, and coal are examples.
4. In contrast, cars and wheat crops are *not* natural resources. They do not occur naturally, but require human intervention.

FIGURE 7-2 Post-Reading Semantic Map for Social Studies Chapter

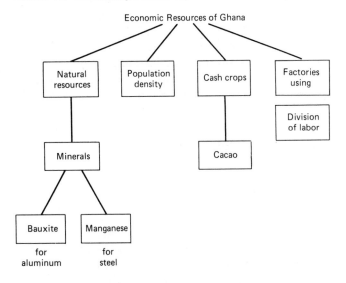

5. Natural energy resources such as coal are one type of natural resource.
6. Natural resources are part of a country's economic resources.
7. Crops and factories are other economic resources.

Of course, involving the students in each of these steps would probably be better than having the teacher supply all the information. Indeed, it might be useful to make sure that students always define words in these ways.

Possible sentence lesson.   Finally, a useful technique for introducing new content-area vocabulary has been suggested by Moore and Arthur (1981), although this technique is useful only for words that are defined in the context of the assignment. The four steps proceed as follows.

Step 1: Teacher identifies target words, lists them on the board, and reads them to the class.

Step 2: Students pair words on the list and dictate sentences using both members of the pair.

Step 3: Students read to determine the accuracy of their statements.

Step 4: Students use the passage to evaluate their statements. Statements are modified or new ones are supplied and copied into students' notes.

MOTIVATION AND INTEREST

Students can read with greater comprehension when they are motivated (see Fass & Schumacher, 1979). Interest in the material leads to more motivation, and students read interesting material with greater comprehension than uninteresting material, even when the readability level is the same for each (Asher, Hymel & Wigfield, 1978; Bernstein, 1955). Moreover, when investigating metacognitive approaches used by remedial high school students, Ngandu (1977) found that "motivation provided by interesting material usually led to the use of appropriate behaviors" (p. 233). Clearly, teachers can improve their students' comprehension by making sure that they are motivated and interested.

One very good model for the teacher concerned with promoting motivation has been suggested by Dulin (1978). This model can be stated as follows:

$$\text{Motivation} = \frac{\text{expected reward}}{\text{expected effort}}$$

According to this ratio, motivation can be increased by increasing the expected reward *or* by decreasing the expected effort. The greatest amount of motivation would result from doing both of these things. You can probably think of many ways to do this. Some example suggestions are provided in Table 7-1. Space is left so that you can include some of your own. (Of course, not all possible motivational techniques are given in Table 7-1. There are many ways to motivate students, so many that they are beyond the scope of this book.)

One thing you should notice in studying Table 7-1 is that the teacher behaviors listed as decreasing effort are strategies suggested in other parts of this book. When you are adequately preparing students to read for comprehension, you are decreasing the amount of effort needed to comprehend. An automatic side result is that you will also be increasing motivation.

CULTURAL DIFFERENCES

Students in the public schools in the United States come from a variety of cultural backgrounds. These differences are likely to have a strong influence on comprehension, though, in this author's opinion, remarkably little research has been done in this area. Perhaps it is because these differences can be largely subsumed under the previous two categories, prior knowledge and motivation and interest.

For instance, students from divergent subcultures may have a different vocabulary and different schemata, and this is likely to interfere with comprehension (see Obah, 1983). In the movie example on page 104, a migrant worker who had never seen a movie theatre would be unable to make any of the necessary slot-filling inferences or prior-knowledge elaborations. Moreover, culturally different students may also have different text structure expectations (Kintsch & Greene, 1978). They may have different approaches to school tasks, and they may find it difficult to be interested in materials that appear to exclude their cultural group. Ignoring these dif-

TABLE 7-1 Selected Sample Procedures for Increasing Motivation

Increasing Expected Reward

- Provide regular praise.
- Provide interesting activities.
- Write fair tests.
- Provide high-success tasks.
- Involve students in purpose setting.
- Involve students in questioning.
- Use meaningful reading tasks.

Decreasing Expected Effort

- Provide background information.
- Give specific purpose.
- Preview assignment.
- Preview vocabulary.
- Discuss reading strategies and skills.
- Use high-success materials
- Divide long chapter into shorter assignments.

ferences perpetuates low achievement for these divergent cultural groups. Teachers wishing to teach comprehension to all children must assess how cultural differences are influencing the prior knowledge, motivation, and interest level of the children in their classrooms.

Moreover, when we remember that our society is composed of a dominant and various subordinate cultures when viewed from a standpoint of power and access to resources, we can see that in the schools, we are trying to teach the linguistic practices of the dominant culture (Giroux, 1981). (Indeed, this book is about the cognitive practices of the dominant culture.) Needless to say, this pedagogy can be very alienating to children whose ways of thinking are being labeled "incorrect." Of course, taking the opposite position and saying that it is cultural imperialism to teach these processes would have an effect similar to that found by educators in the 1970s who abandoned teaching standard English; it didn't get anybody anywhere. Being able to comprehend in these ways is useful in a society in which this is the dominant mode. Teachers must help culturally divergent students see that their own thinking patterns have value and are not necessarily inferior. Simultaneously, they can teach the students these new ways of comprehending as a means of social mobility and self-understanding. Researchers should begin to examine the cognitive processes of divergent cultural groups so that "incorrect" answers can be viewed in terms of the cultural values and schemata they may reflect.

DECODING FLUENCY

Finally, although word identification is not the topic at hand, a chapter on individual differences in comprehension would be seriously remiss if decoding (word identification) were not mentioned. Just as the comprehension processes all interact with each other, they also interact with word identificaton processes.

Readers who are having to devote attention to identifying words will not simultaneously have attention available for comprehension processes (LaBerge & Samuels, 1974; and others). Imagine yourself having to read a passage in which many of the key words were written backward. Each time you had to stop to figure out the word, you would forget what the sentence was about. This is similar to what happens when students try to read materials with too many words they must work to identify. Indeed, in their theory of automaticity in reading, LaBerge and Samuels (1974) suggest that word identification processes must be *automatic* for comprehension processes to proceed fluently. The implication of this theory is that intensive reading with easy materials or repeated reading of the same material to develop decoding automaticity may also have a facilitative effect on comprehension skills (see Samuels & LaBerge, 1983; and others). Even if you do not choose to develop students' decoding automaticity, it will be useful to remember that decoding automaticity may be an individual difference affecting how well your students comprehend, and all students will be more successful comprehenders when they are given materials they can decode fluently. Although this is often done with grouping for reading instruction, teachers need to consider matching students to materials in the content areas as well (see Chapter Eight).

SUMMARY

All of the comprehension processes require that the students have the requisite prior knowledge (schemata). Teachers must begin by assessing whether or not this is true, by providing background information and vocabulary instruction when necessary, and by helping students to select what information they will need to apply and when to apply it. Some students over- or underrely on schema-based processes and need to be shown how to use an appropriately balanced approach. Moreover, inaccurate student answers can often be interpreted in light of what they reveal about defects in the students' prior knowledge and their ability to use it.

Comprehension is also improved when students are motivated and interested. To some extent, teachers facilitate motivation each time they make the task easier by making sure that students have the requisite skills and schemata.

Teachers should be aware of how cultural differences influence the comprehension of individual students. Cultural differences can clearly be related to differences in prior knowledge, vocabulary, and interest. Moreover, teachers must be careful to recognize the validity of the thinking strategies of culturally different students, even when trying to teach standard ones.

Finally, students cannot be expected to comprehend passages when they are devoting large amounts of attention to identifying individual words. They must be given material they can decode fluently if they are to develop their comprehension skills.

SELF-CHECK TEST

1.Define the following terms:

schema

schema availability

schema selection

schema maintenance

control mode reliance

Schram's motivation ratio

decoding automaticity

semantic mapping

Frayer model

Possible Sentence Lesson

2. Answer true or false:
___ a. Prior knowledge is not important for microprocessing.
___ b. Providing background knowledge is not worth the time.
___ c. Once you give the students the prior knowledge, they will know how to apply it.
___ d. All readers use the same combination of schema- and text-based processes.
___ e. $$M = \frac{\text{expected effort}}{\text{expected reward}}$$
___ f. Comprehension and decoding processes operate independently.
3. List five procedures for assessing and building prior knowledge.
4. List the seven comprehension problems related to schema usage.
5. List the four major reader-related comprehension contexts.

SUGGESTED ACTIVITIES

1. Add twenty items to Table 7-1.
2. While carefully reading a content-area or reading assignment, write down what prior knowledge is necessary. Can you assume that all students have this prior knowledge?
3. For a new unit, define what background knowledge you are expecting students to have. Write a test to assess whether or not they have knowledge you are assuming they have. What will you do to fill in the gaps?
4. Design a lesson for preteaching the new vocabulary in a specific reading assignment. Be sure to link concepts, provide opportunities for use, and relate the concepts to students' direct experience.

REFERENCES

ANDERSON, R. C. (1977). *Schema-directed processes in language comprehension.* (Technical Report no. 50). Urbana-Champaign: Center for the Study of Reading, University of Illinois.

ANDERSON, R. C., REYNOLDS, R. E., SCHALLERT, D. L., & GOETZ, E. T. (1977). Framework for comprehending discourse. *American Educational Research Journal, 14,* 367–381.

Anderson, R. C., Spiro, R. J., & Anderson, M. C. (1977). *Schemata as scaffolding for the representation of information in connected discourse* (Technical Report no. 21). Urbana-Champaign: Center for the Study of Reading, University of Illinois.

ASHER, S. R., HYMEL, S., & WIGFIELD, A. (1978). Influence of topic interest on children's reading comprehension. *Journal of Reading Behavior, 10,* 35–47.

BERNSTEIN, M. R. (1955). Relationship between interest and reading comprehension. *Journal of Educational Research, 49,* 283–288.

CHIESI, H. L., SPILICH, G. J., & VOSS, J. F. (1979). Acquisition of domain-related information in relation to high and low domain knowledge. *Journal of Verbal Learning and Verbal Behavior, 18,* 257–273.

CRAFTON, L. K. (1983). Learning from reading: What happens when students generate their own background information? *Journal of Reading, 26,* 586–593.

DULIN, K. (1978). Reading and the affective domain. In S. Pflaum-Connor (Ed.), *Aspects of Reading Education.* Berkeley, CA: McCutcheon Publishing Co.

FASS, W., & SCHUMACHER, G. M. (1978). Effects of motivation, subject activity, and readability on the retention of prose materials. *Journal of Educational Psychology, 70,* 803–807.

FRAYER, D. A., FREDERICK, W. C., & KLAUSMEIR, H. J. (1969). *A schema for testing the level of concept mastery* (Working Paper no. 16). Madison: Wisconsin Research and Development Center for Cognitive Learning, University of Wisconsin.

GIROUX, H. (1981). Literacy, ideology, and the politics of schooling. *Humanities in Society, 4,* 335–361.

HANF, M. B. (1971). Mapping: A technique for translating reading into thinking. *Journal of Reading, 14,* 225–230, 270.

HERBER, H. (1970). *Teaching reading in the content areas.* Englewood Cliffs, N.J.: Prentice-Hall.

HILDYARD, A. (1979). Children's production of inferences from oral texts. *Discourse Processes, 2,* 33–56.

JOHNSON, D. D., & PEARSON, P. D. (1978). *Teaching reading vocabulary.* New York: Holt, Rinehart and Winston.

JOHNSTON, P., & PEARSON, P. D. (1982). *Prior knowledge, connectivity, and the assessment of reading comprehension* (Technical Report no. 245). Urbana-Champaign: Center for the Study of Reading, University of Illinois.

KINTSCH, W., & GREENE, E. (1978). The role of culture-specific schemata in the comprehension and recall of stories. *Discourse Processes, 1,* 1–13.

LABERGE, D., & SAMUELS, S. J. (1974). Toward a theory of automatic information processing in reading. *Cognitive Psychology, 6,* 293–323.

MACNIEL, J. (1984). *Reading comprehension: New directions for classroom practice.* Glenview, Ill.: Scott, Foresman.

MOORE, D. W., & ARTHUR, S. V. (1981). Possible sentences. In E. K. Dishner, T. W. Bean, and J. E. Readence (Eds.), *Reading in the content areas: Improving classroom instruction.* Dubuque: Kendall/Hunt.

NGANDU, K. (1977). What do remedial high school students do when they read? *Journal of Reading, 21,* 231–234.

OBAH, T. V. (1983). Prior knowledge and the quest for new knowledge: The Third World dilemma. *Journal of Reading, 27,* 129–133.

PEARSON, P. D., & JOHNSON, D. D. (1978). *Teaching reading comprehension.* New York: Holt, Rinehart and Winston.

PEARSON, P. D., & SPIRO, R. J. (1980). Toward a theory of reading comprehension instruction. *Topics of Language Disorders, 1,* 71–88.

PEARSON, P. D., HANSEN, J., & GORDON, C. (1979). The effect of background knowledge on young children's comprehension of explicit and implicit information. *Journal of Reading Behavior, 11,* 201–210.

RUMELHART, D. E. (1981). Schemata: The building blocks of cognition. In J. T. Guthrie (Ed.), *Comprehension and teaching: Research reviews.* Newark, Del.: International Reading Association.

SAMUELS, S. J., & LABERGE, D. (1983). Critique of a theory of automaticity in reading: Looking back. A retrospective analysis of the LaBerge-Samuels reading model. In L. Gentile, M. Kamil, and J. Blanchard (Eds.), *Reading research revisited.* Columbus: Charles E. Merrill.

SCHANK, R. C. (1982). *Reading and understanding: Teaching from the perspective of artificial intelligence.* Hillsdale, N.J.: Lawrence Erlbaum.

SPILICH, G. J., VESONDER, G. T., CHIESI, H. L., & VOSS, J. F. (1979). Text processing of domain-related information for individuals with high and low domain knowledge. *Journal of Verbal Learning and Verbal Behavior, 18,* 275–290.

SPIRO, R. J. (1979). *Etiology of reading comprehension style* (Technical Report no. 124). Urbana-Champaign: Center for the Study of Reading, University of Illinois.

SPIRO, R. J., & TIRRE, W. C. (1979). *Individual differences in schema utilization during discourse processing* (Technical Report no. 111). Urbana-Champaign: Center for the Study of Reading, University of Illinois.

STRANGE, M. (1980). Instructional implications of a conceptual theory of reading instruction. *The Reading Teacher, 33,* 391–397.

TAYLOR, B. M. (1979). Good and poor readers' recall of familiar and unfamiliar text. *Journal of Reading Behavior, 11,* 375–380.

TIERNEY, R. J., & PEARSON, P. D. (1981). *Learning to learn from text: A framework for improving classroom practice* (Reading Education Report no. 30). Urbana-Champaign: Center for the Study of Reading, University of Illinois.

WILSON, C. R., & HAMMILL, C. (1982). Inferencing and comprehension in ninth graders reading geography textbooks. *Journal of Reading, 25,* 424–427.

EIGHT
TEXT CONTEXTS:
What Is Being Read?

In Chapter Seven it was suggested that it is important to prepare students for reading comprehension by assessing and developing their schemata related to the topic. It was also suggested that motivation and interest should be developed prior to reading. Is there anything else you will need to do to ensure that students will understand their reading assignments?

Just as comprehension depends on a match between your students' prior knowledge and the prior knowledge required by the assignment, successful comprehension also depends on a match between your students' reading skills and the skills required to read the assignment. If the material is reasonably "readable" for this group of students, then you can preteach one or two skills that you think need emphasis.

Traditionally, "readability" has been measured by formulas that attempt to determine the grade level for which a piece of reading material is appropriate. Unfortunately, these formulas, though useful, are not 100 percent accurate, cannot be used to rewrite materials, fail to consider many important factors, and give the teacher little information about what skills to preteach to promote comprehension with difficult materials.

The purpose of this chapter, therefore, is to help you become more skillful at detecting possible sources of difficulty in reading materials. Then, you can make effective choices about what materials to use, and even if you find yourself limited to a difficult text, you can provide prereading skill instruction to help the students deal with potential text difficulties.

READABILITY FORMULAS

There are many readability formulas available, and the results often vary from one to the next (see Daines, 1982, pp. 48, 50). (For descriptions of frequently used formulas, see any general reading methods text.) Most of these formulas attempt to measure semantic ("meaning") complexity by assessing the number or percentage of "hard words." ("Hard words" are usually defined as unfamiliar words or words with several syllables.) The other factor that most formulas measure is syntactic complexity. This is usually measured by counting the average number of words per sentence. These measures are then correlated with comprehension scores of students of varying ability levels to determine a predictive formula.

As you know, correlations do *not* indicate causality. This means, then, that although readability scores tend to correlate with successful or unsuccessful comprehension scores, the factors that they measure are not necessarily the *causes* of those scores. Thus, simply rewriting materials by taking out unfamiliar and long words and shortening sentences will *not* necessarily make the material easier to comprehend. Unfortunately, it seems that textbook writers sometimes do this to make their textbooks fit into the desired readability levels. Thus, teachers cannot be content with simply accepting the readability scores given for their textbooks. It may be that the text was too difficult and was poorly adapted to fit formula restrictions that are not causally related to comprehension anyway.

Another problem you have probably already noticed is that there are many important factors these formulas have not considered. Stop and think about the processes described in Part One of this book. What are some other text factors that might affect how easily your students can understand something? Write down as many as you can and then go on to the next section.

ASSESSING "PROCESSABILITY"

As you probably already figured out, to assess the "processability" of your reading assignment, you need to examine what cues are available to the reader for micro-, integrative, macro-, elaborative, and metacognitive processing, as well as what reader-related characteristics are assumed. Let's look at each of these separately.

Microprocessing Factors

Microprocessing factors are the ones best assessed by readability formulas. (Indeed, readability formulas measure only microprocessing factors!) Word familiarity, concept difficulty, and within-sentence syntactic complexity all affect the students' comprehension (see Chall, 1984). Sentence length may affect the students' ability to connect those phrases and to extract the most important facts. If the sentences are too long, unskilled readers who can't select as they go along may be unable to deal with the sentences as unified wholes.

Integrative Processing Factors

Integrative processing considerations provide an interesting example of how readability formulas can be misused to rewrite materials. When sentences are rewritten to make them shorter, important information is often made implicit. For instance, a typical readability adjustment is illustrated in the change from 8a to 8b:

8a. Because Mexico allowed slavery, many Americans and their slaves moved there.
8b. Mexico allowed slavery. Many Americans moved there.

Clearly, the sentences in 8b are shorter, but important intersentential information has been deleted. Now, the reader must infer that the Americans had slaves and that, because they wanted to keep them, they had to move to Mexico.

With all the integrative inferences required by 8b, we would probably predict that it would be more difficult to understand than 8a, even though it is at a lower readability level. In a study examining original and revised versions of school materials, Davison, Kantor, Hannah, Hermon, Lutz, and Salzillo (1980) found that the revised versions were less coherent, especially in the area of intersentential connectives. Similar results were found by Anderson, Armbruster, and Kantor (1980).

Thus, a low "readability" score does not mean that the integrative processing load has been controlled. Indeed, a recent study has found that intersentential coherence breaks seem to be as common in lower-level books as they are in higher-level books (Irwin, 1983). In Chapter Three of this book, you had some practice with identifying explicit and implicit integrative information. Just remember that implicit integrative information requires the reader to make inferences; and, in general, the more inferences required, the more difficult comprehension will be (Irwin & Pulver, 1984; Kintsch & Vipond, 1977; and others).

Macroprocessing Factors

A similar principle applies to macroprocessing. If main ideas are implicit or difficult to find, processing will be inhibited (Christie & Schumacher, 1978; Fishman, 1978; and others). At larger levels, if the main points of whole sections and chapters are unclear, or if the organizational pattern is unfamiliar, macrocomprehension will be more difficult to achieve (Kintsch, 1977; Stein & Nezworski, 1978; and others). Also, the presence of too many irrelevant details can make it difficult for students to perform summarizing processes, probably because the details obscure the main points (Bruning, 1970; Thorndyke, 1979).

Many factors in school materials can contribute to making the organizational pattern clear. Introductions, subheadings, and summaries can stress the overall organization, and the organizational pattern used should be one with which the readers are familiar. Also, activities that help students to organize the materials are helpful. Finally, charts and tables can be provided to help students see how the main points fit together.

Elaborative Factors

A text can encourage prior-knowledge elaboration by explicitly linking new material to what the students already know. The text itself can provide elaboration in the form of numerous examples of new concepts (Klausmeir & Feldman, 1975). If the examples and definitions are concrete, then mental imagery can be encouraged. Finally, prereading questions can encourage prediction and postreading questions can encourage elaborations of all types, including higher-level thinking responses, and elaborations facilitate recall (Reder, 1978).

Metacognitive Factors

For metacognitive factors, you will probably want to examine your materials in terms of how easy they are to study. Do they provide opportunities for practice and review? Is the material broken into manageable units for note-taking? How easy is it to preview? Are there opportunities for students to check their own comprehension (see Anderson, 1980)?

Reader-Related Factors

An analysis of reading material would be incomplete without an assessment of the match with the students in terms of their conceptual, vocabulary, and experiential backgrounds (see Kintsch & Miller, 1984). Also, you will probably want to assess how motivational the material is (Klare, 1976). Such things as format, pictures, print size, and style will affect comprehension if they affect motivation.

THE READABILITY CHECKLIST

The point of all of this is that if you can assess the strengths and weaknesses of your reading materials, you can provide prereading activities, study guides, and other activities that take advantage of the strengths and compensate for the weaknesses. You can assess the readability in such a way that you have information about how best to facilitate comprehension for that assignment. Of course, you can also use your knowledge of comprehensibility factors to select readable materials and to create readable materials of your own.

In Figure 8-1, a checklist is provided to help you structure your analy-

FIGURE 8-1 *READABILITY CHECKLIST*

This checklist is designed to help you evaluate the readability of your classroom texts. It can be used best if you rate your text while you are thinking of a specific class. Be sure to compare the textbook to a fictional ideal rather than to another text. Your goal is to find out what aspects of the text are or are not less than ideal. Finally, consider supplementary workbooks part of the textbook and rate them together. Have fun!

Rate the questions below using the following rating system:

5	Excellent
4	Good
3	Adequate
2	Poor
1	Unacceptable
NA	Not applicable

Textbook title: _____

Publisher: _____

Copyright date: _____

UNDERSTANDABILITY

A. ____ Are the assumptions about students' vocabulary knowledge appropriate?

B. ____ Are the assumptions about students' prior knowledge of this content area appropriate?

C. ____ Are the assumptions about students' general experiential backgrounds appropriate?

D. ____ Does the teacher's manual provide the teacher with ways to develop and review the students' conceptual and experiential backgrounds?

E. ____ Are new concepts explicitly linked to the students' prior knowledge or to their experiential backgrounds?

F. ____ Does the text introduce abstract concepts by accompanying them with many concrete examples?

G. ____ Does the text introduce new concepts one at a time with a sufficient number of examples for each one?

H. ____ Is each definition understandable and at a lower level of abstraction than the concept being defined?

I. ____ Is the level of sentence complexity appropriate for the students?

J. ____ Are the main ideas of paragraphs, chapters, and subsections clearly stated?

K. ____ Does the text avoid irrelevant details?

L. ____ Does the text explicitly state important complex relationships (e.g., causality and conditionality) rather than always expecting the reader to infer them from the context?

M. ____ Does the teacher's manual provide lists of accessible resources containing alternative readings for the very poor and the very advanced readers?

N. ____ Is the readability level appropriate (according to a readability formula)?

LEARNABILITY
Organization

A. ____ Is an introduction provided for each chapter?

B. ____ Is there a clear and simple organizational pattern relating the chapters to each other?

C. ____ Does each chapter have a clear, explicit, and simple organizational structure?

D. ____ Does the text include such resources as an index, a glossary, and a table of contents?

E. ____ Do questions and activities draw attention to the organizational pattern of the material (e.g., chronological, cause and effect, spatial, and topical)?

F. ____ Do consumable materials interrelate well with the textbook?

Reinforcement

A. ____ Does the text provide opportunities for students to practice using new concepts?

B. ____ Are there summaries at appropriate intervals in the text?

C. ____ Does the text provide adequate iconic aids, such as maps, graphs, and illustrations, to reinforce concepts?

D. ____ Are there adequate suggestions for usable supplementary activities?

E. ____ Do these activities provide for a broad range of ability levels?

F. ____ Are there literal recall questions provided for the students' self-review?

G. ____ Do some of the questions encourage the students to draw inferences?

H. ____ Are there discussions that encourage creative thinking?

I. ____ Are questions clearly worded?

Motivation

A. ____ Does the teacher's manual provide introductory activities that will capture students' interest?

B. ____ Are chapter titles and subheadings concrete, meaningful, or interesting?

C. ____ Is the written style of the text appealing to the students?

D. ____ Are the activities motivating? Will they make the student want to pursue the topic further?

E. ____ Does the book show clearly how the knowledge being learned might be used by the learner in the future?

F. ____ Are the cover, format, print size, and pictures appealing to the students?

G. ____ Does the text provide positive and motivating models for both sexes as well as for many racial, ethnic, and socioeconomic groups?

READABILITY ANALYSIS
Weaknesses

A. On which items was the book rated the lowest?

B. Did these items tend to fall in certain categories? Which?

C. Summarize the weaknesses of this text.

D. What can you do in class to compensate for the weaknesses of this text?

Assets

A. On which items was the book rated the highest?

B. Did these items fall in certain categories? Which?

C. Summarize the assets of this text.

D. What can you do in class to take advantage of the assets of this text?

Source: J. W. Irwin and C. J. Davis, "Assessing Readability: The Checklist Approach," *Journal of Reading, 24,* (1980), pp. 124–130.

sis of materials that you want to examine in depth. Take a moment to look it over. You should note that you are asked to rate your material in relation to an ideal, not in relation to the "even worse" book you used last year. Also, note that the checklist is provided in its original format, in which these factors were divided into those that affect "understandability" (immediate recall) and those that affect "learnability" (long-term recall). As you look over the checklist, you will probably see how these factors all are related to the processes and contexts presented in this book.

The biggest advantage of using this checklist is that once you have used it to analyze your materials, you can provide instruction that helps students to comprehend. For instance, if the main ideas or organizational patterns are found to be unclear, they can be given to students in the form of a study guide. If the vocabulary is difficult, it can be presented first. If there are many implicit connectives, this skill can be discussed as part of the assignment. If no introduction is given, you can provide one. You can also teach students to use the assets of the material. For instance, you can show the students how an author has made the organization clear. You can encourage them to use graphic aids, subheadings, and study questions for self-review. You can make sure they know how to use appendices, glossaries, indexes, and so on. A careful analysis of the materials can clearly help you to select useful instructional strategies.

MATCHING STUDENTS WITH MATERIALS

Of course, there is still a limit to what students can read, even with good teaching assistance. It is common practice to divide students into reading groups in which students are given materials at their reading levels. It is much less common, however, for students to be given material at their level in the content areas, especially at the secondary level. Perhaps that is because teachers feel that the large-group, lecture-discussion, one-textbook approach is the only way to teach those subjects.

That is, of course, untrue. When there is an extreme gap between the level of the material and the ability level of a student or students, a multitext approach can be used. Simply find textbooks on the same subject from two or three different levels. You can do this by salvaging old texts from other grade levels when those classes move into a new text, and you may find that you can order a few multilevel books when the ones you normally use need to be replaced. The numbers and levels you need will be determined by the needs of children in your classroom and will vary from school to school.

Once you have some multilevel textbooks, you will need to make up assignments for each topic in each text. This need not take large amounts of time, especially if you phase in only one textbook a year and do it for just a few units at a time. The reward in terms of giving every student something that he or she can read and comprehend will be well worth it!

For example, suppose you are teaching a unit on weather in a seventh-grade classroom. Several of your students are unable to read the text. You suggest that they read a different assignment from the text you have stored at the back of the room. (It happens to be at the fourth-grade level.) It contains information about types of clouds not contained in the regular seventh-grade text. Their responsibility will be to read this section, answer the questions in the text, and report the information back to the whole class, which will be held responsible for knowing it. You can use a similar procedure for your gifted students, who read a special assignment on acid rain and give a report to the class. The "average" students read the regular text and report the informaton to the whole class, thereby reviewing and simultaneously teaching the other students any information they missed by reading the alternative assignments. All students are held responsible for reporting something to the class. All students have been given assignments at which they can succeed. This should increase motivation because there is an expected reward (successful classroom recitation) and the expected effort is realistic (the material is at their level). Finally, all students are held responsible for all the material discussed in class, so no student misses important content because of having done an alternative assignment.

A short-term alternative is to use multilevel reference books for a specific unit. You can have students write individual or small-group reports using reference books that are at their level. The librarian can be a valuable aide in gathering books at a variety of reading levels, and you may be able to store the multilevel reference books in your room while the students are working on their reports. Finally, you may wish to use a contract system rather than specific reports when your students are working in multilevel reference books.

Giving students reading material they can comprehend is absolutely fundamental for developing comprehension skills. Each teacher must carefully consider the advantages and disadvantages of providing alternative materials in his or her classroom.

ACADEMIC LEARNING TIME

Berliner (1981) has defined "academic learning time" (ALT) as "the time a student is engaged with academic materials or activities that yield a high success rate" (p. 211). In the Beginning Teacher Evaluation Study he reports, academic learning time was found to be consistently associated with student achievement, but considerable variance across classrooms in terms of this variable (from 4 to 52 minutes per day) was also found. Teachers can increase the amount of academic learning time related to comprehension by preparing students to read in terms of the reader-related variables discussed in Chapter Seven and by providing them with materials at an acceptable difficulty level.

SUMMARY

The "readability" of the reading material affects whether or not it will be comprehended. Formulas that assess readability give the teacher one clue about the possible level of the material, but there are many factors that they do not consider. A good teacher will assess the "processability" of the material by critically examining the microprocessing, integrative processing, macroprocessing, elaborative processing and metacognitive processing cues provided by the author. Also, prior-knowledge and motivational factors must be examined. A "readability checklist" is provided in this chapter to help the teacher assess these factors. Then, the teacher can prepare prereading presentations and study guides that encourage students to use the cues that are present and help them to compensate for the cues that are missing. When there is an extreme mismatch between the levels of the students and the materials, the teacher can provide alternative materials for the students to read. The goal is to increase the amount of time students spend engaged in successful comprehension tasks.

SELF-CHECK TEST

1. Define the following terms:

   academic learning time   multilevel textbook approach
   readability formulas   multilevel references
   readability checklist

2. List twenty-five things you would look for when assessing the "processability" of your materials.

3. True or False?

   ___ a. Readability formulas assess only microprocessing and integrative factors.
   ___ b. The readability checklist should be used instead of a formula.
   ___ c. If you find difficulties in a text, don't use it!
   ___ d. You would rate a text the same regardless of what group of students is going to use it.
   ___ e. The readability checklist is primarily designed to help teachers know how to teach with the reading materials at hand.
   ___ f. All students should read the same text.

SUGGESTED ACTIVITIES

1. Assess a textbook using the readability checklist.
2. Rewrite the checklist, grouping the factors according to the processing model stated in this book. Reword the items so that they are entirely clear to you.
3. After using the checklist, write a prereading lesson in which you teach the students about using those materials.
4. Find alternative materials for a specific unit in your regular content-area textbook. Make up parallel assignments and a list of concepts to be emphasized in the class discussion.
5. Keep a journal for one week of teaching. Record exact amounts of ALT that go on in your classroom each day for each student. How can this be increased?

REFERENCES

ANDERSON, T. H. (1980). Student strategies and adjunct aids. In R. J. Spiro, B. C. Bruce, and W. F. Brewer (Eds.), *Theoretical issues in reading comprehension.* Hillsdale, N.J.: Lawrence Erlbaum.

ANDERSON, T. H., ARMBRUSTER, B. B., & KANTOR, R. N. (1980). *How clearly written are children's textbooks? Or, of bladderworts and alfa* (Reading Education Report no. 16). Urbana-Champaign: Center for the Study of Reading, University of Illinois.

BERLINER, D. C. (1981). Academic learning time and reading achievement. In J. T. Guthrie (Ed.), *Comprehension and teaching: Research reviews.* Newark, Dela.: International Reading Association.

BRUNING, R. H. (1970). Short-term retention of specific factual information in prior contexts of varying organization and relevance. *Journal of Educational Psychology, 61,* 186–192.

CHALL, J. S. (1984). Readability and prose comprehension: Continuities and discontinuities. In J. Flood (Ed.), *Understanding reading comprehension.* Newark, Dela.: International Reading Association.

CHRISTIE, D. G., & SCHUMACHER, G. M. (1978). Memory for prose: Development of mnemonic strategies and use of higher order relations. *Journal of Reading Behavior, 10,* 337–344.

DAINES, D. (1982). *Reading in the Content Areas: Strategies for Teachers.* Glenview, Illinois: Scott, Foresman.

DAVISON, A., KANTOR, R. N., HANNAH, J., HERMON, G., LUTZ, R., & SALZILLO, R. (1980). *Limitations of readability formulas in guiding adaptations of texts* (Technical Report no. 162). Urbana-Champaign: Center for the Study of Reading, University of Illinois.

FISHMAN, A. S. (1978). The effect of anaphoric references and noun phrase organization on paragraph comprehension. *Journal of Reading Behavior, 10,* 159–170.

IRWIN, J. W. (1983). Coherence factors in children's textbooks. *Reading Psychology, 4,* 11–23.

IRWIN, J. W., & DAVIS, C. (1980). Assessing readability: The checklist approach. *Journal of Reading, 24,* 124–130.

IRWIN, J. W., & PULVER, C. (1984). The effects of explicitness, clause order, and reversibility on children's comprehension of causal relationships. *Journal of Educational Psychology, 76,* 399–407.

KINTSCH, W. (1977). On comprehending stories. In M. A. Just and P. A. Carpenters (Eds.), *Cognitive processes in comprehension.* Hillsdale, N.J.: Lawrence Erlbaum.

KINTSCH, W., & MILLER, J. R. (1984). Readability: A view from cognitive psychology. In J. Flood (Ed.), *Understanding reading comprehension.* Newark, Dela.: International Reading Association.

KINTSCH, W., & VIPOND, D. (June, 1977). Reading comprehension and readability in educational practice and psychological theory. Paper presented at the Conference on Memory, University of Uppsala, Sweden.

KLARE, G. R. (1976). A second look at the validity of readability formulas. *Journal of Reading Behavior, 8,* 129–252.

KLAUSMEIR, H., & FELDMAN, K. (1975). The effects of a definition and a varying number of examples and nonexamples on concept attainment. *Journal of Educational Psychology, 67,* 174–178.

REDER, L. (1978). *Comprehension and retention of prose: A literature review* (Technical Report no. 108). Urbana-Champaign: Center for the Study of Reading, University of Illinois.

STEIN, N. L., & NEZWORSKI, T. (1978). The effects of organization and instructional set on story memory. *Discourse Processes, 1,* 177–193.

THORNDYKE, P. W. (1979). Knowledge acquisition from newspaper stories. *Discourse Processes, 2,* 95–112.

NINE
SITUATIONAL CONTEXTS:
*Why, When, and Where Are
They Reading?*

Suppose you have prepared students to read in terms of skills, prior knowledge, and motivation. You have examined the assignment and feel confident that there are no serious difficulties with its processability. Yet your students still can't answer any of your questions. What has gone wrong?

The answer is that there are still many other aspects of the situation to be considered. Did the students understand the purpose of the assignment, and did they know how to read for that purpose? Did your questions reflect the purpose? Were the questions understandable? Were the social, emotional, and physical environments during reading and during testing ones in which they could perform their best? All of these "situational contexts" affect student performance and should be considered when giving assignments and when assessing comprehension.

THE COMPREHENSION TASK

As discussed in Chapter Six, students can adjust their reading strategies according to the purpose for reading. Research seems to indicate that when students know the objectives of their assignment, they do better

(Duchastel,1979). Many students seem to read differently when they are expecting a test (Christie & Schumacher, 1978; Graesser, Higgenbotham, Robertson, & Smith, 1978), and they may process differently according to what type of test or task they are expecting (Fredericksen, 1975; Mayer, 1975). All this indicates that having a clear purpose and an appropriate method are important components of successful comprehension tasks.

Reading Purposes and Methods

A reading "purpose" can be defined as the new behavior the student is to exhibit as a result of reading. Examples include the following:

1. After reading, students should be able to describe the major parts of a cell.
2. After reading, students should be able to discuss their opinions of the morality of the issue being discussed.
3. After reading, the students should understand why Johnny decided to steal the bread.

There are many ways in which you can clarify the purpose of the task. You can give students behavioral objectives that state exactly what they will be asked to do after reading. You can give prereading questions with the direction to "read to find the answers to these questions." (You will want to make sure that these questions require processing the information rather than just rote recall. See Chapter Ten.) You can preview with them, telling them what they should learn from each section. Finally, you can involve the students in setting the purpose for reading. If it is a story, have them make predictions and then read to see if their predictions were accurate. For nonfiction, ask them what they think they should learn from reading the material, whether they should read for main points or details, and so on.

The next step, of course, is finding a reading method appropriate for the intended purpose. Indeed, a reading "method" can be defined as the strategy selected to achieve the intended goal. Choosing an appropriate method is a metacognitive process. (See Chapter One for the definition of metacognitive processes.) This includes choices about reading rate (which may vary throughout the selection), study strategies (see Chapter Six), and the flexible use of various comprehension processes (for instance, if the purpose was to be able to diagram a cell, a student might wish to be sure to use mental imagery while reading, whereas if the purpose was to summarize an editorial, a student might make extra use of macroprocesses). Examples of methods specific students might select for specific purposes are given in Table 9-1. Study this chart and try to fill in three more of your own.

TABLE 9-1 Examples of Typical School Reading Situations and Effective Reading Strategies

TYPE OF READER	TYPE OF READING MATERIAL	PURPOSE	STRATEGY
Kindergarten student	Picture book	For enjoyment	Look at the best picture. Make up a fun story.
First-grade student, average reading group, wants to succeed	Basal reader	To please teacher; to read aloud with perfect accuracy	Read slowly and carefully. Focus on every word; sound out unknown words.
Second-grade student, good reader, knows a lot about horses	Trade book about horses from school library; looks like easy reading	To give an oral report to the class about the book	Skip the boring parts. Read especially about the pictures so they can be shown. Read quickly, since most information is known already.
Third-grade student, interested only in baseball	First science textbook, section on the planets	To answer questions in the textbook	Look over the questions first. Read the section slowly, noting the subheadings. Use those to help locate the answers.
Fourth-grade student, average reader, generally does all right in math	Math text, section on multiplying fractions	Missed school; must read to do the homework problems	Read very slowly, making sure each sentence is completely understood. Study the examples in the text, step by step. Try practice problems when they are suggested.
Fifth-grade student, below average reader, little interest in history	Social studies textbook on American history, chapter on Constitutional Congress	To pass test	Take each section separately. Use the context to figure out the vocabulary. For each section, write down the key idea. Find someone to listen while you tell him or her what the chapter was about.

TABLE 9-1   (cont.)

TYPE OF READER	TYPE OF READING MATERIAL	PURPOSE	STRATEGY
Sixth-grade student, above-average reader, loves science, has chemistry set at home	Laboratory activity in science text on melting	To do lab the next day	Read each step while visualizing the activity. Make note of special warnings. Try to predict places where things could go wrong. Try to predict the results of each step.
Seventh-grade student, poor reader but very interested in this book	Adolescent novel	For enjoyment and for book report	Read straight through at your own pace in fairly long sittings. Let yourself "get into it"; worry about book report later.
Eighth-grade student, average reader but has little background in current events	Newspaper	To be able to discuss current events in social studies class the next day	Make a list of names, places, and vocabulary words that are causing you trouble. Get help with them from parents, friends, or the teacher the next day. For each major news item, make sure you understand the title and the first two paragraphs. Make a list of these as well. When possible, get background information from adults or older siblings.
Ninth-grade student, upper-level track, college-bound	*Moby Dick,* Chapter 1	To be able to discuss possible symbolism and potential themes	Read slowly circling figurative language and recurring images. Think about common themes in the images. What do they have to do with the action?

TABLE 9-1 (cont.)

TYPE OF READER	TYPE OF READING MATERIAL	PURPOSE	STRATEGY
Tenth-grade student, lower-level track	*Auto Mechanics* magazine	To find new things to do with recently purchased "antique" car	Look at the ads and the titles of the articles. If anything seems "do–able," read carefully, picturing yourself doing it.
Eleventh-grade student, average reader, "C" student, not motivated in general	Chemistry textbook, a whole chapter	To understand what's going on in class	Use a systematic study system. Take notes, at least general ones. Keep a list of new vocabulary words. Find a friend to review the chapter with you. This may keep your interest up.
Twelfth-grade student, average reader, *no* interest in Shakespeare	Shakespearean play, one scene	For quiz	Read aloud, trying to use intonation. Try to visualize the action. If you can't tell what they are saying, think about what they might be saying and *then* see if that is right. Try to make it interesting by thinking about how it would be today.

In studying Table 9-1, you probably noticed that, as mentioned in Chapter Six, to select an appropriate reading method, students must also consider the difficulty of the material in relation to their own skills and prior knowledge. The eighth-grade student with no background in current events had to study vocabulary and background with the help of resource people. A good reader with extensive background in current events could probably read quickly, jotting down a few key ideas for discussion.

Moreover, students vary in terms of their ability to be flexible in their approach to reading tasks. Thus, it would probably be useful to explain the concept of varying methods for varying purposes. Model your own procedure for choosing strategies. Eventually encourage them to choose their own strategies before reading.

The Reading Comprehension Interview

Wixson, Bosky, Yochum, and Alvermann (1984) have developed an interview procedure for assessing intermediate- and middle- school–level children's awareness of the demands of different reading tasks (see Figure 9-1). This interview includes questions about student strategies for actual classroom materials, including a basal reader, a content-area textbook, and comprehension worksheets (see directions on interview). The whole procedure takes about 30 minutes, and the teacher is free to ask other questions. A summary sheet can be completed to analyze student responses (see Figure 9-2). Through the use of an interview such as this, the teacher can gain valuable information about a student's awareness of appropriate reading methods and purposes.

The Assessment Task

Finally, another component of many comprehension tasks in your classroom is the assessment method itself. Sometimes students understand the assignment but not the test. The method you choose to assess whether students have understood what they read should not introduce extraneous skills that do not have anything to do with comprehension. Make sure questions and directions are clear. For instance, if you are asking students to fill in a chart and they can't do it, there are two possible reasons: (1) they didn't understand the material, or (2) they don't understand the chart.

Moreover, your assessment task should reflect the stated purpose. If you tell students to read for details and then give an essay test, they will be justifiably frustrated! The best procedure is to be consistent among purpose setting, discussion, and testing in terms of the mix of types of information requested. (See Chapter Ten for a taxonomy of questions based on the type of information requested.)

THE SOCIAL CONTEXT

Mosenthal (1984) has suggested that

> while reading researchers have tended to define reading comprehension primarily in terms of text, task, and subject contexts, the most important context influencing reading comprehension in classroom lessons may be the interaction between the teacher and the students. (p. 17)

An example is provided by Mosenthal (1979). He found that the way stu-

FIGURE 9-1 Reading Comprehension Interview

Name: Date:
Classroom teacher: Reading level:
                                   Grade:

Directions: Introduce the procedure by explaining that you are interested in finding out what children think about various reading activities. Tell the student that he or she will be asked questions about his/her reading, that there are no right or wrong answers, and that you are only interested in knowing what s/he thinks. Tell the student that if s/he does not know how to answer a question s/he should say so and you will go on to the next one.

General probes such as "Can you tell me more about that?" or "Anything else?" may be used. Keep in mind that the interview is an informal diagnostic measure and you should feel free to probe to elicit useful information.

1. What hobbies or interests do you have that your like to read about?
2. a. How often do you read in school?
   b. How often do you read at home?
3. What school subjects do you like to read about?

Introduce reading and social studies books.

Directions: For this section use the child's classroom basal reader and a content area textbook (social studies, science, etc.). Place these texts in front of the student. Ask each question twice, once with reference to the basal reader and once with reference to the content area textbook. Randomly vary the order of presentation (basal, content). As each question is asked, open the appropriate text in front of the student to help provide a point of reference for the question.

4. What is the most important reason for reading this kind of material?
   Why does your teacher want you to read this book?
5. a. Who's the best reader you know in _____?
   b. What does he/she do that makes him/her such a good reader?
6. a. How good are *you* at reading this kind of material?
   b. How do you know?
7. What do you have to do to get a good grade in _____ in your class?
8. a. If the teacher told you to remember the information in this story/chapter, what would be the best way to do this?
   b. Have you ever tried _____?
9. a. If your teacher told you to find the answers to the questions in this book what would be the best way to do this? Why?
   b. Have you ever tried _____?
10. a. What is the hardest part about answering questions like the ones in this book?
    b. Does that make you do anything differently?

Introduce at least two comprehension worksheets.

Directions: Present the worksheets to the child and ask questions 11 and 12. Ask the child to complete portions of each worksheet. Then ask questions 13 and 14. Next, show the child a worksheet designed to simulate the work of another child. Then ask question 15.

11. Why would your teacher want you to do worksheets like these (for what purpose)?
12. What would your teacher say you must do to get a good mark on worksheets like these? (What does your teacher look for?)

Ask the child to complete portions of at least two worksheets.

13. Did you do this one differently from the way you did that one? How or in what way?
14. Did you have to work harder on one of these worksheets than the other? (Does one make you think more?)

Present the simulated worksheet.

15. a. *Look over this worksheet. If you were the teacher, what kind of mark would you give the worksheet? Why?*
    b. If you were the teacher, what would you ask this person to do differently next time?

Source: K. Wixson, A. Bosky, M. Yochum, & D. Alvermann, An interview for assessing students' perceptions of classroom reading tasks. *The Reading Teacher,* 1984, *37,* p. 348. Reprinted with permission of the authors and the International Reading Association.

FIGURE 9-2

Summary sheet
Reading Comprehension Interview

Name: Date:
Classroom teacher: Reading level:
                                             Grade:

1. What does the child perceive as the goal or purpose of classroom reading activities? (see questions 4 and 11)

    Basal reader:
    Content textbook:
    Reading worksheets:

2. What criteria does the child use to evaluate his/her reading performance? (questions: 5, 6, 7, 12, and 15)

    Basal reader:
    Content textbook:
    Reading worksheets:

3. What strategies does the child indicate s/he uses when engaging in different comprehension activities? (questions: 8, 9, 10, 13, and 14)

    Remembering information
      Basal reader:
      Content textbook:
    Answering questions
      Basal reader:
      Content textbook:
      Reading worksheets:

Source: K. Wixson, A. Bosky, M. Yochum, & D. Alvermann, An interview for assessing students' perceptions of classroom reading tasks. *The Reading Teacher,* 1984, 37, p. 350. Reprinted with permission of the authors and the International Reading Association.

dents resolved contradictions in the text was different when the audience was second-graders from when it was the teacher. Moreover, this difference was different for third-grade readers and sixth-grade readers. Third-graders minimized text restructuring for the teacher as contrasted to when their audience consisted of second-graders; sixth-graders maximized it for the teacher as contrasted to when their audience consisted of second-graders.

Mosenthal and Na (1980b) divided students into three groups in terms of how they verbally interacted with the teacher: (1) imitative—students who generally added no information to teacher's utterances—(2) noncontingent response—students who would identify a new topic, often having little relation to the topic discussed by the teacher—and (3) contingent response—students who added new information that clarified or added to what the teacher said. The interesting finding was that there were also differences among these groups in terms of their recall in a normal reading lesson. The imitative group tended to recall stories literally; the noncontingent response group tended to elaborate and sometimes even to distort; and the contingent response group tended to include text-based inferences. Mosenthal (1984) concludes that "these findings emphasize the importance the interaction between the Audience and Reader Contexts plays in how students comprehend during reading lessons" (p. 23).

Finally, in a study comparing student recall in normal reading lessons, assumed to be low-risk situations, and testing situations, assumed to be high-risk situations, Mosenthal and Na (1980a) found that though responses in the low-risk situation tended to be related to the social interaction patterns described earlier, differences in performance in the testing situation appeared to be related to ability: average- and low-ability students tended simply to reproduce the text, whereas high-ability students used both reproductions and elaborations. Mosenthal and Na speculate that these differences reflect the poor- and average-ability students' desire to minimize risk in the testing situation and the high-ability students' desire to process the text fully.

The point of all this is that student comprehension will be affected by the social context in which it is occurring. This context includes such things as the audience, the teacher-student relationship, and the purpose of the assessment task: Recall will be different with you from what it is with peers. For each individual, recall for you may be related to the way he or she usually relates to you. Moreover, students will recall differently in formal and informal situations.

Finally, another social context to consider is the reading group. There is evidence that teachers interact differently with different reading groups. Cazden (1981) reviews research that indicates that there may be a contrast between the foci of high and low reading groups: for the poorer readers, the focus is on decoding, whereas for the high group, the focus is on meaning. For instance, Allington (1978) found that the cues provided by the teacher to help students decode were different according to group. For the poorer readers, these tended to be letter-sound relationships, but for the better readers, these tended to be semantic and/or syntactic cues. All this is cause for concern when viewed in light of the recent study by Anderson, Mason, and Shirey (1983) that found that a focus on meaning was more effective: their data support the conclusion "that a meaning emphasis gets better results than a word identification emphasis with poor readers as well as good readers" (p. 71). Each teacher must monitor his or her attitudes toward individual groups. Do you expect these students to be able to comprehend? Are you encouraging it? Are you teaching with a meaning emphasis with all groups?

CLASSROOM ENVIRONMENT

In the larger sense, the entire classroom environment can be considered part of the situational context. Recent research on environments conducive to learning indicates that such things as academic learning time (see Chapter Eight), academic focus, and teacher encouragement and direction seem to be related to achievement gains on tests (see Rosenshine, 1978, and Chapter Twelve of this text). Even time of day has been shown to affect comprehension styles (Folkard, 1979). Although a thorough discussion of effective classroom environments is not possible here, it is important to note that the quality of the classroom environment in all of its academic, emotional, physical, and social aspects is likely to affect a student's comprehension performance. For further information, the reader is referred to general texts on pedagogy and the recent research on effective classrooms (See Rosenshine, 1978).

SUMMARY

Even if your students have the necessary skills, schemata, and motivation for the assignment, there may be comprehension problems. These may arise if the purpose for reading is unclear, if students don't know how to read for the intended purpose, if the assessment introduces extraneous factors, if the assessment is unrelated to the original purpose, or if students are unable to perform well because of problems in the classroom environment. Moreover, the entire social context must be considered: the student's usual social patterns will affect what he or she will report in terms of recall, and this can be be affected by whether it is a formal (testing) or an informal setting. Finally, the students will comprehend better if there is some emphasis on meaning, and teachers may wish to make this emphasis similar for all reading-ability groups.

SELF-CHECK TEST

1. List the three major situational contexts described in this chapter. Define each.
2. List four social contexts that may affect comprehension.
3. List three task contexts that may affect comprehension.
4. Answer true or false:

    ___   a.   Most teachers treat all reading groups the same.
    ___   b.   Poor readers should be taught decoding, not comprehension.
    ___   c.   Testing brings out poor readers' ability to elaborate.
    ___   d.   Purposes should be reflected in assessment tasks.
    ___   e.   There are only three or four different ways to read.
    ___   f.   Most students already know how to read for the stated purpose.

5. To review Part Two, fill in the following outline.

I. READER CONTEXTS

    A.
    B.
    C.
    D.

II. TEXT CONTEXTS

    A.
    B.
    C.
    D.
    E.
    F.

III. SITUATIONAL CONTEXTS

    A.
        1.
        2.
        3.
    B.
        1.
        2.
        3.
        4.
    C.

SUGGESTED ACTIVITIES

1. Observe a teacher working with high- and low-ability reading groups. What are the differences between these groups in terms of what goes on in these sessions? How should these differences be minimized?
2. Observe a classroom teacher for an extended period of time. For each assignment, answer the following questions: Was the purpose made clear? Did the assessment match the purpose?
3. If you are a classroom teacher, do activity 1 by observing yourself.
4. If you are a classroom teacher, do Activity 2 by observing yourself.

REFERENCES

ALLINGTON, E. L. (March, 1978). Are good and poor readers taught differently? Is that why poor readers are poor readers? Paper presented at the annual meeting of the American Education Research Association, Toronto.

ANDERSON, R. C., MASON, J., & SHIREY, L. (1983). *The reading group: An experimental investigation of a labyrinth* (Technical Report no. 271). Urbana-Champaign: Center for the Study of Reading, University of Illinois.

CAZDEN, C. B. (1981). Social context of learning to read. In J. T. Guthrie (Ed.),*Comprehension and teaching: Research reviews.* Newark, Dela.: International Reading Association.

CHRISTIE, DANIEL J., & SCHUMACHER, GARY M. (1978). Memory for prose: Development of mnemonic strategies and use of higher order relations. *Journal of Reading Behavior, 10,* 337–344.

DUCHASTEL, P. (1979). Learning objectives and the organization of prose. *Journal of Educational Psychology, 71,* 100–106.

FOLKARD, S. (1979). Time of day and level of processing. *Memory and Cognition, 7,* 247–252.

FREDERIKSEN, C. H. (1975). Effects of context-induced processing operations on semantic information acquired from discourse. *Cognitive Psychology, 7,* 139–166.

GRAESSER, A. C., HIGGENBOTHAM, M. W., ROBERTSON, S. P., & SMITH, W. R. (1978). A natural inquiry into the national enquirer: Self-induced versus task-induced reading comprehension. *Discourse Processes, 1,* 355–372.

MAYER, R. E. (1975). Forward transfer of different reading strategies evoked by testlike events in mathematics text. *Journal of Educational Psychology, 67,* 165–169.

MOSENTHAL, P. (1979). Children's strategy preference for resolving contradictory story information under two social conditions. *Journal of Experimental Child Psychology, 28,* 323–443.

MOSENTHAL, P. (1984). Reading comprehension research from a classroom perspective. In J. Flood (Ed.), *Promoting reading comprehension.* Newark, Dela.: International Reading Association.

MOSENTHAL, P., & NA, T. J. (1980a). Quality of children's recall under two classroom testing tasks: Toward a socio-psycholinguistic model of reading comprehension. *Reading Research Quarterly, 15,* 501–528.

MOSENTHAL, P., & NA, T. J. (1980b). Quality of text recall as a function of children's classroom competence. *Journal of Experimental Child Psychology, 30,* 1–21.

ROSENSHINE, B. V. (1978). Academic engaged time, content covered, and direct instruction. *Journal of Education, 160,* 38–66.

WIXSON, K., BOSKY, A. B., YOCHUM, M. N., & ALVERMANN, D. (1984). An interview for assessing students' perceptions of classroom reading tasks. *The Reading Teacher, 37,* 346–352.

TEN
ASKING QUESTIONS

In Part One of this book, you learned about specific processes involved in comprehension and some ways to teach students to use those processes more effectively. In Part Two, the factors that influence how students will comprehend a specific assignment, and some related teacher behaviors that can promote successful comprehension, were presented. Now it is time to "put it all together" into general teaching suggestions.

One of the most common ways to teach comprehension has been to ask questions before, during, or after reading. Although the use of questions as the only way to teach comprehension is currently being criticized, the use of questions as one part of teaching comprehension still seems viable. As Pearson and Johnson (1978) have said, "The issue is not whether or not to use questions, but how, when, and where they ought to be used" (p. 154).

One of the problems with teacher questioning in the past is that many teachers tended to ask trivial, literal recall questions most of the time (Guszak, 1967). Because many students tend to display the level of thinking required by the questions asked (Hunkins, 1970), this is a questionable procedure at best. The purpose of this chapter is to suggest ways for teachers to ask questions that facilitate all comprehension processes.

QUESTIONING TAXONOMIES

To improve teacher-made questions, several questioning taxonomies have been designed (Barrett, 1979; Sanders, 1968; and others). These taxonomies are very useful for helping teachers to ask a variety of types of questions. The categories listed in these taxonomies include such things as literal recognition or recall, inference, evaluation, and appreciation (Barrett, 1979) and memory, translation, interpretation, application, analysis, synthesis, and evaluation (Sanders, 1968). Note how these include higher-level thinking processes (see Chapter Five), though they are not strictly based on a complete cognitive model of the comprehension process itself.

A QAR Taxonomy

One possible exception to this is the taxonomy suggested by Pearson and Johnson (1978). In this taxonomy, questions are classified according to the relationship between the question and the source of the answer given, thus reflecting the process involved in going from text to response. This "question-answer relationship" (QAR) taxonomy classifies questions according to whether the answer is taken from

1. textually explicit information (TE), that is, information that was directly stated in the text, or
2. textually implicit information (TI), that is, information that was implied in the text, or
3. scriptally implicit information (SI), that is, information already in the mind of the reader. (A script in this case is roughly equivalent to a schema, i.e., prior knowledge of the reader.)

Examples of these types of QARs are provided in Figure 10-1. Study this example before reading further. Try classifying the last three QARs. The answers are at the end of the chapter. Note that you must know the answer before you can classify the question!

This taxonomy is easy to use and helps teachers remember that many questions that appear to be at a fairly low level still require inferences of textually implicit information. For instance, questions that require students to infer implicit connective concepts (such as question 2 in Figure 10-1) require a different process from those requesting explanations of explicitly stated connectives.

Unfortunately, though this taxonomy is appealing in its simplicity, this simplicity may limit its utility in helping you to write more diversified questions. For instance, this taxonomy makes no distinction between such things as connectives and main ideas. Thus, you might forget to ask about one or the other.

FIGURE 10-1 *EXAMPLES OF QUESTIONS CLASSIFIED
ACCORDING TO THE QAR TAXONOMY*

Sally was very eager to get her birthday present. It was going to change her life. The present was 26″ high and went very fast. It meant she could get to school and to baseball practice in half the time. It was not an ugly red like John's. It was a beautiful yellow like daffodils and sunlight, which she loved. Yes, yellow was her favorite color anyway. It made her feel happy.

QUESTION	ANSWER	CATEGORY
1. How high was her present?	26″	TE
2. Why was she eager to get her present?	Because it was going to change her life	TI
	Because it was a bike and everyone loves bikes	SI
3. What is her present?	A bike	SI
4. Does John have a bike?	Yes, an ugly red one	TI
5. What was her favorite color?	Yellow	
6. Do you think Sally would like buttercups?	Yes, because they are yellow	
7. Why was yellow her favorite color?	Because it made her feel happy	

An Expanded QAR Taxonomy

A similar but more specific way to structure your questions is suggested by the subprocess model described in this book. A taxonomy based on both this model and the explicit-implicit distinction of Pearson and Johnson (1978) is provided in Figure 10-2. If you have read Chapters One through Six of this book, you would probably have written the same taxonomy yourself. It simply encourages you to ask questions that require all of the comprehension processes. It has been entitled the "expanded question-answer relationship taxonomy" (Ex-QAR) because, like the Pearson and Johnson (1978) taxonomy, it considers the relationship between the question and the source of the answer but it is also expanded to delineate the types of information involved.

Examples of the kind of information that might be requested in each of the categories in this taxonomy are given in Table 10–1. Again, there are no surprises here, if you have read Part One of this book. Questions asking students about *prereading prior knowledge* are the most removed from the text and would probably review important vocabulary and background information. Questions that ask for *explicit micro*information ask for specific facts from individual sentences and therefore require students to chunk and recognize syntactic relations. Questions that ask for *implicit*

FIGURE 10-2   *THE EX-QAR TAXONOMY*

Questions can be divided into those that request . . .

   I.   Prereading prior knowledge
  II. Microinformation that is
      A. explicitly stated or
      B. implicitly stated
 III. Integrative information that is
      A. explicitly stated or
      B. implicitly stated
 IV. Macroinformation that is
      A. explicitly stated or
      B. implicitly stated
  V. Elaborative information
 VI. Metacognitive strategies used

---

*micro*information probably deal with resolving word and phrase ambiguity and selecting what is important from all the details in individual sentences.

Similarly, questions about *explicit integrative* information ask about anaphoric references and explicit connectives that are stated directly. In contrast, *implicit integrative* questions require the students to use integrative inferences to infer unstated connectives, unstated anaphora (ellipses), and unstated slot-filling information.

At the macro level, questions asking students to restate explicit main ideas, subheads, and summaries are categorized as *explicit macro*questions. Questions that require students to generate unstated main ideas, summaries, or outlines are categorized as *implicit macro*questions.

For elaborative and metacognitive questions, there can be no distinction between explicit and implicit categories, because all of these require that the student use schema-based processes to expand on the text. *Elaborative* questions can require that students use any of the elaborative processes described in Chapter Five herein. *Metacognitive* questions can require the students to identify and resolve textual inconsistencies, to remedy comprehension failures, or to choose an appropriate reading method.

Take a minute to study Table 10-1. Don't try to memorize! Think in terms of how directly this reflects the processing model. On a blank sheet of paper, write out the taxonomy on the left. Then, for a specific assignment, give a few examples of what you might ask to encourage responses in each category. (Remember, your question can't be finally categorized until you see the student's answers.)

Of course, it would be unreasonable for you to ask all kinds of questions all the time. Just try to make sure that you ask those important for the specific reading situation and that, overall, you achieve a balance among

TABLE 10-1   Examples of Information Types Included in the Ex-QAR Taxonomy

Prereading Prior Knowledge	Vocabulary Background Concepts	
Micro	Explicit	Within-sentence syntactic relations Chunks Specific details
	Implicit	Meanings of ambiguous words in context Meanings of ambiguous phrases Important ideas in individual sentences
Integrative Implicit	Explicit	Anaphoric references (except ellipsis) Explicit connectives
	Implicit	Implicit connectives Ellipsis Slot-filling inferences
Macro	Explicit	Explicit main ideas Explicit summaries Organization as stated in subheads
	Implicit	Implicit main ideas Student-generated summaries Outlines or other diagrams of the organizational pattern
Elaborative	Predictions Prior-knowledge elaborations Mental images Higher-level thinking responses Affective responses	$\left\{\begin{array}{l}\text{Application}\\\text{Analysis}\\\text{Synthesis}\\\text{Evaluation}\end{array}\right.$
Metacognitive	Textual inconsistencies Sources of comprehension failure Reading method used	

the categories and between explicit and implicit categories. In other words, you need ask none of the types all of the time, but you must ask all the types some of the time!

The question also often arises as to which of the QARs are easier or for younger students and which are more difficult or are to be reserved for older students. Comprehension processes interact! All students can be asked all types of questions. Relative difficulty is more likely to be related to the actual content of the question and difficulty of the reading material than it is to question category. The important thing is to have prereading, study guide, postreading, and testing questions, when used, cover the same kinds of categories. If you ask microquestions in class and macroquestions on the test, you will be preparing your students for failure. (See Chapter Nine for a discussion of matching purpose and assessment.)

Now let's look at a seventh-grade teacher's actual questions planned according to the Ex-QAR taxonomy. (See Figure 10-3.) (Yes, you would need the answers to verify the predicted classifications.) For the purposes of this example, more questions have been included than would probably be asked for such a short passage. Can you think of others? (You will note that this particular passage lent itself particularly well to integrative-implicit QARs. Of course, another passage might require more QARs in another category. This varies from passage to passage and from subject to subject.) Try to classify the last four questions yourself. The answers are provided at the end of the chapter.

When reading through these questions you probably got a sense of what it means to require students to use their "prior experience and the writer's cues to infer the author's intended meaning" (see Chapter One)! Certainly, students will have to be active comprehenders to answer these questions. But there is still something that could be added to this lesson. The teacher has effectively assessed the product of the students' comprehension processes, but has comprehension been taught? What will the teacher do if the students get the wrong answers? Do the students know what processes to use to get from text and prior knowledge to the right answer?

A Taxonomy for Process Questions

Durkin (1981) has made a distinction between product and process questions. This distinction provides an important criticism of the Ex-QAR taxonomy and others like it. Product questions ask students to report the product of their comprehension process, for example, "Why didn't he cross the Delaware?" In contrast, process questions direct attention to the process used to answer the question, for example, "What do you need to know to understand how these sentences fit together?"

FIGURE 10-3 *POSSIBLE EX-QAR QUESTIONS FOR A BRIEF HISTORY PASSAGE*

This is what the students read:

England's religious problems. The people of England had long been members of the Roman Catholic Church, which was the only Christian church in western Europe. Englishmen, like other Roman Catholics, recognized the Pope as head of the church.

Then, in the 1530s, King Henry VIII led the people of England to break away from the Roman Catholic Church. He set up a church for England completely separate from the Roman Catholic Church. The church founded by King Henry VIII was called the Church of England, or the Anglican Church. The king was the head of the Church of England, as well as the head of the government of England.

Englishmen were not required to belong to the Church of England. But every Englishman had to pay taxes to help support it. And the government did not allow Englishmen to be members of any other church.

Yet many Englishmen did not like the Church of England. One group—the group that angered King James I—wanted to change the Church of England. These people were called *Puritans* because they wanted to "purify" the church. They wanted to change the way the church was organized under bishops. They also thought that certain church customs, such as kneeling, were wrong.

Another group did not stop at asking for changes. Unlike the Puritans, they wanted to separate from the Church of England and set up their own churches. These people were called *Separatists.*

The Pilgrims. Among the Separatists was a small group of people who lived in the English village of Scrooby. It was a pleasant little village where everyone knew everyone else. On Sunday, most of the villagers met at church to worship together. But the Separatists met by themselves and had their own kind of service.

The other people of Scrooby did not like this. Neither did the English government. Time and again, officials tried to make the Separatists of Scrooby worship according to the rules of the Church of England. The Separatists always refused. Finally, the officials acted. Some of the Separatists were put in prison and others had "their houses beset [surrounded] and watched day and night."

The Separatists of Scrooby made plans to leave England and go to the Netherlands. There the government was more tolerant, and the people could worship more freely. So in 1607–1608—just about the time the settlement of Jamestown was getting started—small groups from Scrooby left for the Netherlands.

Religious life in the Netherlands was better. But there were still problems. It was hard to live among foreign people and learn foreign ways. The Separatists were still Englishmen. It worried them to see their children growing up among the people of the Netherlands (called Dutchmen or the Dutch) and speaking the Dutch language.

The Pilgrims crossed the Atlantic. After 12 years in the Netherlands, the Separatists decided to go to America. There they could have their own church and still be Englishmen. They had to borrow money to buy supplies and get a ship. They got permission from the London Company to settle in its territories north of Jamestown.

A number of Englishmen who were not Separatists asked if they, too, might go along to start a new life in America. The leaders agreed. Since so many of the group were willing to go on a long journey for religious reasons—like a pilgrimage to a holy place—the whole group became known as the Pilgrims.

FIGURE 10-3 *CONCLUDED*

QUESTION	CATEGORY
Who led the break from the Roman Catholic Church?	Micro-explicit
Why do you think he wanted to start his own church?	Elaboration, prior knowledge
What groups didn't like the Church of England and what did they want?	Macro-implicit
Why didn't the people of Scrooby like the Separatists' meetings?	Integrative-implicit
Why were some Separatists put in jail?	Integrative-implicit
Why did the Separatists go to the Netherlands?	Integrative-implicit
What does it mean to say that the government was more "tolerant"?	Micro-implicit
Why did they leave the Netherlands for America?	Integrative-implicit
Why were they called "Pilgrims"?	Integrative-explicit
Summarize the story of why the Pilgrims came to America.	
What can you do to make sure you remember this for the test?	
What kind of people do you think the Pilgrims were?	
Do you think there will be any more religious persecution when they get to America?	

There may be situations in which you would like to focus the students' attention on the processes they are using to arrive at their answers. This will especially be the case when they don't know the answers. A simple Process Questioning Taxonomy can be used for these situations (see Figure 10-4). Table 10-2 provides examples of process questions for each category. Study this table. Can you think of others?

In studying Table 10-2, you may have noticed that process questions require students to be consciously aware of their cognitive processes. Thus, all process questions are actually Ex-QAR metacognitive questions as well. The point is not which is the best classification, but rather, which taxonomy is best to use in a specific situation.

Clearly, product questions are more useful for assessment. Which taxonomy should you use for instruction? Though this is currently controversial (see Allington, 1983; Durkin, 1981; MacGinite, 1983) and insufficient research has been done, it is the opinion of this author that both kinds of

TABLE 10-2 Examples of Questions Categorized According to the Process Taxonomy

CATEGORY	SAMPLE QUESTIONS
Micro	1. What word is being used in a new way?
	2. What else do you need to know to understand this sentence?
Integrative	1. How did you know what caused it to happen?
	2. How did you know who "he" was?
Macro	1. How can you decide which sentence contains the main idea?
	2. How should we go about writing a summary of this article?
Elaborative	1. What did you already know that led you to predict that this would happen?
	2. What part painted a picture in your mind? How did it do this?
Metacognitive	1. What part made this hard for you to understand?
	2. How might you go about reading this in order to achieve your goal?

questions are useful. Product questions introduce topics, guide thinking, and provide practice. Process questions can be used for more direct instruction in comprehension processes.

Let's look at parts of our history lesson again, this time adding student responses and process questions. Note the quality of comprehension instruction that can emerge when product and process questions are interleaved (a process-product processing procedure!?). Also note that when initial student answers aren't quite right, the teacher guides the students so they can see what is right and what is wrong about their answers. Finally, note that when the taxonomies are interleaved, the metacognitive product category is dropped and replaced with the entire process taxonomy.

In these examples, the teacher is asking questions that are directed toward teaching the students *how* to read for comprehension and recall. Of course, when you are first trying to teach a skill using process questions, you may need to schedule extra time for class discussion, but the goal of these discussions as modeled here is to move the students toward independence. In the third example, for instance, we would hypothesize that the

FIGURE 10-4 *A PROCESS QUESTIONING TAXONOMY*

Questions can ask what prior knowledge or processes is (are) necessary for . . .

   I. Microcomprehension
  II. Integrative comprehension
 III. Macrocomprehension
 IV. Elaborative comprehension
  V. Metacognitive comprehension

EXAMPLE 1: *TEACHING ELABORATIVE PROCESSES*

QAR TYPE	TEACHER	STUDENT
Microproduct	Who led the break from the Roman Catholic Church?	the king
Elaborative-product Elaborative-process	Why did he do this? What makes you say that?	because he was angry because when my parents changed churches, it was because they were angry
Elaborative-process	Very good! You have taken what you already know and applied it to this situation. Let's look to see if there is anything in the passage that tells you if you are right. Everyone, read the second paragraph again.	I think it was because he wanted to be head of it.
Elaborative-process	What do you know that makes you say that?	Well, it says he was the head of it. He was probably one of those people who like to be the head of everything. I know a lot of people like that.
	I do, too. That's why that was the inference I made as well.	

students would eventually move toward writing their own summaries. Then, discussion would consist of reviewing the important content and comparing summaries. (See examples 1, 2, and 3 on pp. 150-152.)

The point of all this is to show you how you can ask both product and process questions based on the model presented in this book. You will ask strictly product questions when you are trying to assess, review, or practice what students have learned, and you will mix in process questions when you are trying to teach a comprehension process as well. Both kinds of questions can be used in both reading and content-area classes.

PLANNING FOR QUESTIONING

You should probably do some planning for questioning as often as possible. Even if you do not get a chance to use all your questions, the thought processes that went into writing them will make you a better discussion leader. The point is not to ask all the questions you plan in some prespecified order. That would lead to a stilted, boring discussion. You will

EXAMPLE 2: *TEACHING MICROPROCESSES*

QAR TYPE	TEACHER	STUDENT
Micro-product	OK, then, who were the Puritans?	people who wanted to purify the church
Prior knowledge	What does it mean, "to purify"?	to make pure—better, cleaner, I guess—get rid of corruption, maybe
Micro-process	Good. You can guess the meaning because it is made from the word "pure." So what is a Separatist?	somebody who wants to separate
Micro-process	Good—did you get that from the word or from the passage?	from the word; it has "separate" in it
Micro-process	Let's look at the passage and see if you are right.	Yes, it says so. They wanted to separate from the church.
	Good. So that is a good way to learn new words in history. Look for the words they are made of and then check to see if you are right.	

need to be prepared to be flexible and to use teachable moments as they occur. However, having a stash of good questions will be a valuable resource.

For instance, you will probably want to plan to ask some prior-knowledge questions and some purpose-setting questions before reading. Cunningham (1981) points out that prior-knowledge questions must be simple and straightforward and free of technical terminology. The terminology can be checked, too, but if you try to separate concepts and vocabulary when possible, you will get a more accurate picture of what the students already know. For purpose-setting questions, it is important that you avoid focusing student attention too narrowly. Specific questions asked before reading are good for helping students retain specific information but are probably not the best if general recall is required (Singer & Donlan, 1980, p. 55).

It is possible to ask questions during reading using a study guide or a group reading strategy. (See Chapter Twelve for a description of a group reading strategy.) These may be process or product questions, and, again, they should not be so specific as to actually reduce comprehension. Questions asked after reading should be of a variety of types and should encour-

EXAMPLE 3: *TEACHING MACROPROCESSES*

QAR TYPE	TEACHER	STUDENT
Macro-process	OK, then, how can we summarize this section?	Select the main things and combine the rest into general statements.
Macro-product	What are the main ideas of this section?	"Then, in the 1530's, King Henry VIII led the people of England to break away from the Roman Catholic Church."
Macro-process	Good—the break was the first main event. But that sentence has some details in it. Let's write an easier sentence for your notes. How can we simplify it?	How about using the next sentence, "The King of England started a church for England completely separate from the Roman Catholic Church?"
Macro-process	Good—yes, that sentence seems to be more general and still captures all the main points. I like the way you substituted "the King of England" for "he." Is this better than saying "Henry VIII"?	I think so.
Macro-process	Why?	because Henry VIII is a specific name. We want the general point.
	Very good! OK. I'll write the first sentence on the board while you write it in your notes.	
Macro-product	Now, what other main ideas do we need in our summary?	etc.

age synthesis and review, depending, of course, on the purpose of the assignment.

Always consider your purpose for questioning. If you are trying to teach a reading strategy, you will ask more process questions. If you are trying to assess and review content, you will ask more product questions. If you want students to remember specific facts, you will ask more micro- and integrative questions than in other situations. If you are interested in encouraging creative applications, you will ask more elaborative questions than usual. Just remember that all comprehension processes interact. It makes no sense to say, "I'm only interested in elaboration. Their microlevel comprehension isn't important." Specific facts *are* the building blocks of elaborations! Similarly, it makes no sense to say, "I'm only interested in making sure they have the facts. I won't encourage elaboration and summarizing at all." Elaborations and summaries promote retention of specific facts!

INVOLVING STUDENTS IN QUESTIONING

Research seems to indicate that it may be useful to make students aware of whether the question is requiring that they use explicit, implicit, or prior-knowledge information (Raphael, 1981; Raphael & Wonnacott, 1981; Raphael & Pearson, 1982). Raphael (1981) taught students three question-answering strategies based on the Pearson and Johnson (1978) QAR questioning taxonomy: "Right There" (textually explicit), "Think and Search" (textually implicit), and "On My Own" (scriptally implicit). Results generally indicated that children from grades four to eight can learn these classifications and that this may improve their ability to answer questions.

Another possibility that has not yet been researched is that of teaching students to identify questions according to whether they request micro-, integrative, macro-, or elaborative information. Smith (1983) reports that this has facilitated both comprehension and writing strategies with high-ability seventh-graders. If you have been directly explaining and modeling comprehension processes to your students as recommended in Chapter Two, then teaching them to identify questions in this way may follow naturally. You might wish to simplify the terminology to "detail," "connection," "summary," and "elaboration" (heretofore called the "simplified Ex-QAR taxonomy").

Related to teaching students to identify question types is teaching students to ask the questions. Kitagawa (1982) reports success with involving fourth-and fifth-grade students with asking the questions used for discussion. As Rycik (1982) points out, teacher questioning makes the focus of control for the reader's task external rather than internal. Involving students in asking questions can get them more actively involved in their own learning. The following activities are among those that can be suggested.

Where is the answer? When you ask product questions in class, require students to tell you where they got the answer according to the Raphael (1981) categories. Or, perhaps, you may ask a different student to identify where the answer came from. (This would encourage listening.)

Information guides. For a study guide, make a list of true and false statements related to the reading. Have the students mark each of them true or false and then classify them according to the Raphael (1981) categories. Then ask them to identify the page number of the information used for the answer, regardless of the category.

What kind of information?   Make study guides consisting of questions the students must answer. Then have the students identify the type of answer given using the subprocesses renamed "detail," "connection," " summary," and "elaboration," that is, the simplified Ex-QAR taxonomy.

Write your own test.   The test-writing activity mentioned in Chapter Two for teaching selection can also be used to involve students in writing questions. If you teach your students the categories of detail, connection, summary and elaboration, you can ask them to write test questions for each category. You can then construct the test with the students' questions. (You may wish to eliminate the "connection" category, since the text is generally necessary for identifying the distinction between it and the detail category.)

Study sessions.   After teaching a question classification system (either the QAR as defined by Raphael or the simplified Ex-Qar defined herein), ask students to prepare three questions for each category while they are reading the assignment. Tell them that these questions will be used for study and review. After reading, divide the students into pairs. They can then take turns asking and answering questions.

The ReQuest procedure.   Manzo (1969) has recommended a procedure of reciprocal questioning in which the students and the teacher take turns answering the questions. This "ReQuest procedure," as it is called, is suitable for all grades and types of texts. After each sentence is read, the books are closed and the students ask the teacher questions. When the students are done, the teacher asks the students questions. This procedure gives the teacher an opportunity to praise good questions and to model question-answering strategies as well as to ask questions. When the students can predict what will be in the rest of the selection, they can read to see if they are right.

A FINAL NOTE

As you are working through these and other taxonomies, you will find that some QARs are difficult to classify, or that you and someone else, or you and your students, disagree on the classification. This is true even for the taxonomies herein that take the question-answer relationship into account. One reason may be that any taxonomy that is usable is inevitably going to be incomplete. It should not be a point of concern, however, because the purpose of the taxonomies is to provide a stimulus for writing a variety of questions. The real purpose is question creation, not question classification.

SUMMARY

Because teachers have had a tendency to ask mostly literal-level questions, taxonomies for writing a variety of types of questions have been developed. One recent taxonomy designed by Pearson and Johnson (1978) represents the first such taxonomy to focus on the relationship between the text and the answer. Because this taxonomy does not include mention of the processes discussed in this book, a similar but expanded taxonomy that includes process categories has been presented. This taxonomy should be useful for writing questions that assess and guide student comprehension. For directly teaching specific comprehension processes, a process questioning taxonomy was also suggested. In addition, some procedures for involving students in classifying and asking questions were given. Involving students in this way again encourages them to become actively involved in their own learning.

SELF-CHECK TEST

First, answer the following questions. Then, classify them according to the taxonomies presented in this chapter.[1]

a. What is the difference between a product question and a process question?
b. What should you do to find out what kind of question deals with ellipsis?
c. What were the main points of the chapter?
d. How can you go about answering question (c)?
e. How do these new taxonomies compare to Bloom's or some other taxonomy you have already studied?
f. What are the advantages and disadvantages of the QAR taxonomy?
g. What are the best ways to learn to use the taxonomies presented in this chapter?
h. Which of the two recommended classification systems would be better taught to your students? Why?
i. In general, what is a process question?
j. In general, what is the ReQuest procedure?

[1]See discussion in "A Final Note" regarding ambiguities in this exercise.

SUGGESTED ACTIVITIES

1. Classify a group of the questions used in the basal reader or in a content-area text you do or might use. What other kinds of questions would you like to ask? Write a sample lesson in which *you* write the questions!
2. Conduct a small-group discussion in which you use both product and process questions. Keep track of whether students answered the questions in the QAR that you predicted. Try to limit yourself to teaching one or two processes.
3. Write a set of questions for a short reading assignment using the QAR taxonomy. Then classify those questions according to the Ex-QAR taxonomy. Fill in other questions suggested by the expanded taxonomy.

ANSWERS TO FIGURE 10-1:

5. TE
6. SI
7. TI

ANSWERS TO FIGURE 10-3:

macro-implicit
metacognitive
elaboration prior knowledge; higher-level thinking
elaboration-prediction

REFERENCES

ALLINGTON, R. L. (1983). A commentary on Nicholson's critique of Thorndike's Reading as reasoning—A study of mistakes in paragraph reading. In L. Gentile, M. Kamil, and J. Blanchard (Eds.), *Reading research revisited.* Columbus, Ohio: Charles E. Merrill.

BARRETT, T. (1979). Taxonomy of reading comprehension. In R. Smith and T. C. Barrett (Eds.), *Teaching reading in the middle grades.* Reading, Mass.: Addison-Wesley.

CUNNINGHAM, J. W. (1981). How to ask questions before, during, and after reading. In E. K. Dishner, T. W. Bean, and J. E. Readence (Eds.), *Reading in the content areas: Improving classroom instruction.* Dubuque: Kendall/Hunt.

DURKIN, D. (1981). Reading comprehension instruction in five basal reader series. *Reading Research Quarterly, 16,* 515–544.

GUSZAK, F. J. (1967). Teacher questioning and reading. *The Reading Teacher, 21,* 227–234.

HUNKINS, F. P. (1970). Analysis and evaluation questions: Their effects upon critical thinking. *Educational Leadership, 3,* 699–705.

KITAGAWA, M. M. (1982). Improving discussions or how to get the students to ask the questions. *The Reading Teacher, 36,* 42–45.

MACGINITE, W. H. (1983). A critique of "What classroom observations reveal about reading comprehension instruction" and "Reading comprehension instruction in five basal reader series": Durkin's contribution to our understanding of current practices. In L. Gentile, M. Kamil, and J. Blanchard (Eds.), *Reading research revisited.* Columbus, Ohio: Charles E. Merrill.

MANZO, A. V. (1969). ReQuest: A method for improving reading comprehension through reciprocal questioning. *Journal of Reading, 12,* 123–126, 163.

PEARSON, P. D., & JOHNSON, D. D. (1978). *Teaching reading comprehension.* New York: Holt, Rinehart and Winston.

RAPHAEL, T. E. (April, 1981). The effect of metacognitive training on children's question-answering behavior. Paper presented at the annual meeting of the American Educational Research Association. Los Angeles.

RAPHAEL, T. E., & PEARSON, P. D. (1982). *The effect of metacognitive awareness training on children's question-answering behavior* (Technical Report no. 238). Urbana-Champaign: Center for the Study of Reading, University of Illinois.

RAPHAEL, T. E., & WONNACOTT, C. A. (December, 1981). The effect of metacognitive awareness training on question-answering behavior: Implementation in a fourth grade developmental reading program. Paper presented at the annual meeting of the National Reading Conference, Dallas, Texas.

RYCIK, J. A. (1982). What, no questions? *Journal of Reading, 26,* 211–213.

SANDERS, N. (1968). *Classroom questions: What kinds?* New York: Harper & Row.

SINGER, H., & DONLAN, D. (1980). *Reading and learning from text.* Boston: Little, Brown.

SMITH, K. J. (1983). Personal communication.

ELEVEN
INFORMAL
COMPREHENSION
ASSESSMENT

Traditional measures of comprehension ability provide general indications of how well students can comprehend as compared to their peers. Unfortunately, knowing how well a student comprehends on a test tells you little about what sort of instruction to provide. It also gives you no situation-specific information: Can the student understand fiction better than nonfiction? Was prior knowledge a problem? Is his or her comprehension improved when the purpose is stated? and so forth.

This chapter presents some informal assessment ideas that can be used to supplement the information gained from traditional tests of comprehension ability. A multiple-context approach using observations of natural reading tasks is recommended. Teachers are urged to be observant but cautious in their conclusions.

TRADITIONAL MEASURES OF COMPREHENSION ABILITY

In most traditional tests of comprehension, including diagnostic tests, group standardized tests, and informal reading inventories, comprehension is measured by a cloze task (students fill in blanks where words have been omitted), multiple-choice questions, or short-answer questions. Cloze has the problem of measuring primarily lower-level skills (McCan, 1983;

Shanahan, Kamil, & Tobin, 1982), and it is not really a natural reading task. Multiple-choice questions test recognition comprehension only, and short-answer questions lack the reliability of more objective formats. Thus no one testing format is ideal.

Moreover, these standardized testing procedures must be interpreted in light of several other serious limitations. First, because of time restraints, only short passages are generally used; this limits the degree of macroprocessing that can occur. Second, for similar reasons, all different types of passages are usually mixed together, so it is difficult to assess text-specific effects. Finally, prior knowledge is not generally assessed or controlled, so it is reasonable to assume that the students' final scores are heavily loaded on this factor (see Johnston, 1984; Royer & Cunningham, 1981). Thus, though the results of these tests are useful for providing an objective measure of general ability levels, you will probably find it useful to supplement these scores with informal observations of your students' comprehension strategies.

INFORMAL ASSESSMENT FOR THE CLASSROOM TEACHER

The classroom teacher has the chance to observe each student in a variety of situations. This allows the teacher to draw conclusions about student performance relative to type of material, task characteristics, and so on. For instance, you may discover that although Johnny scores poorly on standardized tests, he can read materials at grade level when he is highly motivated; Janice does very well in the basal reader but has trouble with content-area materials, probably because of a lack of background knowledge; Sam does very poorly on tests, probably because of anxiety, but he can answer comprehension questions in very informal or one-to-one situations; and so on. This *multiple-context approach* can help you to begin to consider a student's comprehension ability in terms of the total context involved in each task. Research indicates that students do perform differently according to combinations of such things as task and passage type (Hunter, Kendall, & Mason, 1979).

Of course, it is absolutely necessary to exercise great caution in coming to any diagnostic conclusions. There are so many factors affecting performance! A student who appears to remember nothing may simply be shy. A student who remembers only details may have concentrated attention on those only because he or she thought that was what you wanted. A student who misses literal questions may have a vocabulary problem, not a microprocessing one per se. The safest approach probably is to avoid all definite conclusions about any child and to teach all aspects of comprehension to all students as much as possible using materials at their level as determined by a combination of testing results and your observations. Of course, occasionally, specific instructional needs of specific students will become so obvious that you would be remiss in not giving those students skill-specific instruction. This is as it should be. Quite simply, it is recommended that individualized assessment and individualized subprocess instruction not be adopted as a general classroom procedure until we know more about testing and teaching than we know now.

THE COMPREHENSION ASSESSMENT CHECKLIST

One format that has been used to help remedial and classroom teachers to summarize their observations of student abilities is given in Figure 11-1. This "Comprehension Assessment Checklist" is designed to remind you to consider all the comprehension contexts that may be affecting performance. It begins by encouraging you to assess the specific text and situation that are affecting the student's performance. Only then can you assess the student's responses in relation to these. Take a minute to study the checklist. Like many of the other aids provided in this book, it follows naturally from the process approach, and, if you have read the previous chapters, you would probably have written something similar yourself.

This checklist seems to be particularly useful for working with a new or a particularly puzzling student. There are so many things to consider that it is all too easy to forget some of them! We have also found that this checklist can be a useful exercise in training yourself to be a better diagnostician. Try using it to teach yourself to think of these things automatically. Finally, this checklist can be useful in helping you plan instruction for an individual or for a whole class. Checklist results often help to point out that if you provide certain kinds of assistance, such as background knowledge or clearly stated purposes, then students will be able to comprehend better.

Figure 11-2 is a checklist completed in a fictional small-group situation. The teacher has used questioning and free recall to gather data that have been summarized here. A similar procedure can be used for a whole class. Note the comprehensiveness of the assessment that results from the use of such an instrument.

OBSERVATION IN REMEDIAL SITUATIONS

In a remedial or one-to-one situation, you can gather situation-specific information by planning and administering student-specific assessment activities in which you try to observe the student's ability to use the various comprehension processes in various realistic situations.

The first step in planning your observation is selecting a variety of contexts in which you would like to observe the student's reading behavior. You will need to consider (1) relevant aspects of texts such as content area, difficulty level, and organization; (2) different purposes relevant for that

FIGURE 11-1 *COMPREHENSION ASSESSMENT CHECKLIST*

Name or Group ⎯⎯⎯⎯⎯⎯⎯⎯⎯⎯⎯⎯⎯⎯⎯⎯⎯⎯

Assignment ⎯⎯⎯⎯⎯⎯⎯⎯⎯⎯⎯⎯⎯⎯⎯⎯⎯⎯

Date ⎯⎯⎯⎯⎯⎯⎯⎯⎯⎯⎯⎯⎯⎯⎯⎯⎯⎯

Directions: For each item, rate your student(s) according to the scale below. A rating of 3 or lower indicates a need for remediation. Remember, you are trying to understand why there have been problems in a specific situation, so be sure to answer in terms of the specific student(s) reading the specific material(s) in the specific situation.

Student(s) has(have) . . .
  5   No problems in this area.
  4   Only a few problems in this area.
  3   Some problems in this area.
  2   Many problems in this area.
  1   Very serious problems in this area.
  N/A   not applicable (for instance, several items cannot be answered if the student read silently).

SITUATION-RELATED FACTORS

___   1.   Was the *physical environment* during reading quiet, well lighted, comfortable, etc.?

___   2.   Was the *teacher/student relationship* one in which the student felt comfortable?

___   3.   Was the situation one in which the *anxiety* level was at a minimum?

___   4.   Was the *purpose* for reading clearly stated?

___   5.   Did the *teacher expect* the student to be able to understand the material?

___   6.   Was the *teacher prepared* to assess the student's comprehension (e.g., familiar with passage, questions ready)?

___   7.   Was the student able to answer in the *format* for assessment (multiple choice, analogy, free recall, written short answer, etc.) that you provided?
      Consider the following:
      a.   Did the student have prior experience with the format?
      b.   Was there an extraneous skill being tested (e.g., talking in front of a group, writing ability, reasoning beyond the passage, using new equipment) that the student has not mastered?

—   8. Were the questions and/or directions in the *assessment* themselves *understandable*?
Consider the following:
   a. Did the student understand exactly what was expected in the questions and/or directions?
   b. Did the questions and/or directions meet the criteria in the text-related factors section? (see following)

TEXT-RELATED FACTORS

—   1. Was the *readability* level appropriate for the student?
—   2. Was the *vocabulary* in the passage sufficiently concrete and familiar for the student?
—   3. Were any *sentences* unreasonably lengthy?
—   4. Were the *relationships* between individual sentences stated explicitly?
—   5. Was the *organizational pattern* sufficiently simple and explicit?
—   6. If *new concepts* were introduced, was there a sufficient description and/or a sufficient number of examples provided for each?
—   7. Was the *amount of material* to be remembered manageable (e.g., was the length of the passage appropriate)?

READER-RELATED FACTORS

Was the student . . .

—   1. *healthy* and well rested?
—   2. able to read the individual *words* accurately and easily?
—   3. able to group the words into meaningful *phrases* and read with proper *intonation*?
—   4. able to draw on adequate *prior knowledge* of this topic including a knowledge of the general and specialized vocabulary?
—   5. able to identify *main ideas* whether they were stated explicitly or not?
—   6. able to *summarize*?
—   7. able to recall the *sequence* of important events?
—   8. able to explain important *cause/effect relationships* whether they were stated explicitly or not?
—   9. more likely to recall *important details* than unimportant details?
—   10. able to identify *pronoun* referents?
—   11. able to understand the *figurative language* in the passage?
—   12. able to make *text-based inferences*?

___ 13. able to make *predictions* and/or draw *conclusions*?

___ 14. able to limit *elaboration* to those helpful in understanding and re-calling the author's message?

___ 15. able to *adjust* his or her reading *strategies* according to the purpose selected?

___ 16. able to read at an appropriate *rate*?

___ 17. able to *attend* to such a task for the required amount of time?

___ 18. aware when he or she had *not* understood something?

___ 19. *expecting* to be able to understand the material?

___ 20. *interested* in the material?

___ 21. *motivated* to try to understand and recall?

___ 22. free from *emotional* problems that might have interfered with concentration?

SUMMARY

Now, in general, what situation-related factors (if any) were causing problems?

Now, in general, what text-related factors (if any) were causing problems?

Now, in general, what reader-related factors (if any) were causing problems?

What can you do to alleviate these problems?

Source: Irwin, J.W., Pulver, C., & Koch, K. (1983). A new technique for improving reading teachers' diagnoses. Unpublished manuscript, Loyola University of Chicago.

FIGURE 11-2   *COMPREHENSION ASSESSMENT CHECKLIST*

Name or Group _____ Climbers _____

_____

Assignment _____ "Trees" read silently with oral free recall and questions _____

_____

Date __ April 9 _____

Directions: For each item, rate your student(s) according to the scale below. A rating of 3 or lower indicates a need for remediation. Remember, you are trying to understand why there have been problems in a specific situation, so be sure to answer in terms of the specific student(s) reading the specific material(s) in the specific situation.

> Student(s) has(have) . . .
> 5   No problems in this area.
> 4   Only a few problems in this area.
> 3   Some problems in this area.
> 2   Many problems in this area.
> 1   Very serious problems in this area.
> N/A   not applicable (for instance, several items can not be answered if the student read silently).

SITUATION-RELATED FACTORS

__5__   1.   Was the *physical environment* during reading quiet, well lighted, comfortable, etc.?

__5__   2.   Was the *teacher/student relationship* one in which the student felt comfortable?

__5__   3.   Was the situation one in which the *anxiety* level was at a minimum?

__2__   4.   Was the *purpose* for reading clearly stated?

__3__   5.   Did the *teacher expect* the student to be able to understand the material?

__5__   6.   Was the *teacher prepared* to assess the student's comprehension (e.g., familiar with passage, questions ready)?

__5__   7.   Was the student able to answer in the *format* for assessment (multiple choice, analogy, free recall, written short answer, etc.) that you provided?
Consider the following:

__5__   a.   Did the student have prior experience with the format?

__5__   b.   Was there an extraneous skill being tested (e.g., talking in front of a group, writing ability, reasoning beyond the passage, using new equipment) that the student has not mastered?

__4__   8. Were the questions and/or directions in the *assessment* themselves *understandable?*
Consider the following:

__4__   a. Did the student understand exactly what was expected in the questions and/or directions?

__5__   b. Did the questions and/or directions meet the criteria in the text-related factors section? (see following)

TEXT-RELATED FACTORS

__5__   1. Was the *readability* level appropriate for the student?

__5__   2. Was the *vocabulary* in the passage sufficiently concrete and familiar for the student?

__5__   3. Were any *sentences* unreasonably lengthy?

__2__   4. Were the *relationships* between individual sentences stated explicitly?

__5__   5. Was the *organizational pattern* sufficiently simple and explicit?

__1__   6. If *new concepts* were introduced, was there a sufficient description and/or a sufficient number of examples provided for each?

__5__   7. Was the *amount of material* to be remembered manageable (e.g., was the length of the passage appropriate)?

READER-RELATED FACTORS

Was the student . . .

__1__   1. *healthy* and well rested?

__4__   2. able to read the individual *words* accurately and easily?

__NA__   3. able to group the words into meaningful *phrases* and read with proper *intonation?*

__5__   4. able to draw on adequate *prior knowledge* of this topic including a knowledge of the general and specialized vocabulary?

__3__   5. able to identify *main ideas* whether they were stated explicitly or not?

__2__   6. able to *summarize?*

__NA__   7. able to recall the *sequence* of important events?

__4__   8. able to explain important *cause/effect relationships* whether they were stated explicitly or not?

__4__   9. more likely to recall *important details* than unimportant details?

__NA__ 10. able to identify *pronoun* referents?

__NA__ 11. able to understand the *figurative language* in the passage?

__1__ 12. able to make *text-based inferences?*

__NA__ 13. able to make *predictions* and/or draw *conclusions?*

_5_	14.	able to limit *elaborations* to those helpful in understanding and recalling the author's message?
_3_	15.	able to *adjust* his or her reading *strategies* according to the purpose selected?
_NA_	16.	able to read at an appropriate *rate*?
_2_	17.	able to *attend* to such a task for the required amount of time?
_3_	18.	aware when he or she had *not* understood something?
_5_	19.	*expecting* to be able to understand the material?
_5_	20.	*interested* in the material?
_5_	21.	*motivated* to try to understand and recall?
_5_	22.	free from *emotional* problems that might have interfered with concentration?

SUMMARY

Now, in general, what situation-related factors (if any) were causing problems?

Now, in general, what text-related factors (if any) were causing problems?

Now, in general, what reader-related factors (if any) were causing problems?

What can you do to alleviate these problems?

Source: Irwin, J.W., Pulver, C., & Koch, K. (1983). A new technique for improving reading teachers' diagnoses. Unpublished manuscript, Loyola University of Chicago.

student's goals; and (3) reader characteristics (prior knowledge, motivation, decoding ability) relative to (1) and (2). The use of a variety of natural tasks with passages long enough for macroprocessing will provide information not available on standardized tests.

For instance, suppose you have been asked to tutor Sally, a sixth-grade student who, on a recently administered standardized test, scored on grade level for decoding ability but at the low fourth-grade level for comprehension ability. What tasks would you like to give Sally to do so that you can observe her comprehension abilities? Well, you may want to use a fourth-grade–level story about something in which she is interested to see if she can read for fun. You may want to have her read an assignment in her classroom social studies textbook, one that she needs to read for class. You may want also to try an easier content-area book, a story she isn't interested in, or a piece of nonfiction about a familiar topic. You may wish to have something read aloud so you can listen to her intonation and fluency and so you can ask questions at selected points.

For each task you choose, you will want to prepare ways to assess the effectiveness of her processing abilities. You will want to assess prior knowledge directly. You may wish to use free recall (discussion in the next section) and/or to design questions according to the product and process questioning taxonomies presented in Chapter 10. You may wish to ask the student for self-reported information about strategies, prior knowledge, motivation, and expectations. The comprehension assessment checklist (Figure 11-1) has been used by remedial teachers as an aid for planning such informal assessment procedures.

While the student is engaged in the natural reading tasks you have provided, keep notes of your observations. Establish rapport. Make sure your directions are clear. Involve the student in his or her diagnosis. Tape-record free recall. Keep a record of reading times. Use the comprehension assessment checklist (Figure 11-1) to structure your data summary.

ANALYZING FREE RECALL

Of course, asking questions can be an effective way of assessing student comprehension. Another way of examining what a student has comprehended is to ask the student to tell you in his or her own words what was said in the passage. For a very long passage, this would give you insight into the student's macroprocessing abilities, especially his or her ability to summarize. For shorter passages, you can examine the student's ability to select important details. The theory is that what the student says in this unprompted situation is what he or she has encoded into memory, but it is important to remember that what the student says may also be affected by what he or she thinks you want to hear. Students may report only facts because they think that that is what is appropriate in a testing situation. Remember to consider the text and the total situation before drawing conclusions about the reader!

A usable procedure for analyzing free recall has been suggested by Clark (1982). He suggests dividing a passage into "pausal units" by "placing a slash wherever a good reader would pause during oral reading" (see Figure 11-3). Then, you can assign each unit a number between 1 and 3 indicating the importance of that unit in terms of the central idea of the text (see Figure 11-4). Then tape the student's recall. From the tape, record the recall by writing the number of the phrase in the student's recall in the line next to that unit (see Figure 11-4). Compute the percentage recalled, the mean of the importance of the ideas recalled, and the extent to which the ideas were recalled in sequence, as a very rough estimate of the student's awareness of the organization. In the example given by Clark (see Figures 11-3 and 11-4), Billy recalled 32 percent of the ideas, and these were in the correct sequence, but the mean importance level indicates that he may need help with selection. It would be interesting to know if Billy made any integrative or elaborative inferences or if he summarized in any way. Consider also writing down any inferences or summary statements given by the student.

Irwin and Mitchell (1983) have recommended using a holistic approach to evaluate the "richness of retellings" (p. 394). They believe that each retelling is too individualistic to conform to predetermined systems that delineate exactly what ideas the student should recall. Their system is described in Figures 11-5 and 11-6. Each retelling can be assigned a level according to these criteria. In this system, the student is given credit for including summarizing statements and other relevant "generalizations beyond text" (elaborations) and "supplementations" (inferences).

Finally, another way to examine a student's free recall is to answer the questions given in Figure 11-7. These questions direct you to try to infer

FIGURE 11-3   *SAMPLE PASSAGE (LEVEL 4)*

The three were growing tired from their long journey,/and now they had to cross a river./It was wide and deep,/so they would have to swim across./
The younger dog plunged into the icy water/barking for the others to follow him./The older dog jumped into the water./He was weak/and suffering from pain,/but somehow/he managed to struggle to the opposite bank./
The poor cat was left all alone./He was so afraid/that he ran up and down the bank/wailing with fear./The younger dog swam back and forth/trying to help./Finally,/the cat jumped/and began swimming near his friend./
At that moment/something bad happened./An old beaver dam from upstream broke./The water came rushing downstream/hurling a large log toward the animals./It struck the cat/and swept him helplessly away./

Source: Mary L. Woods and Alden J. Moe *Analytical Reading Inventory* (Columbus, Ohio: Charles E. Merrill, 1977) p.25. Reprinted by permission.

FIGURE 11-4 Sample of Recall (Billy, Grade 4)

IMPORTANCE NUMBER	PAUSAL UNIT	RECALL SEQUENCE
2	1. The three were growing tired.	1
3	2. from their long journey	2
1	3. and now they had to cross a river.	3
3	4. It was wide and deep,	
1	5. so they would have to swim across.	4
1	6. The younger dog plunged into the icy water	
2	7. barking for the others to follow him.	
2	8. The older dog jumped into the water.	
3	9. He was weak	
3	10. and suffering from pain,	
3	11. but somehow	
1	12. he managed to struggle to the opposite bank.	
2	13. The poor cat was left alone.	5
1	14. He was so afraid	6
3	15. that he ran up and down the bank	
3	16. wailing with fear.	
2	17. The younger dog swam back and forth	7
2	18. trying to help.	
1	19. Finally,	
1	20. the cat jumped	
2	21. and began swimming near his friend.	
3	22. At that moment,	
3	23. something bad happened.	
3	24. An old beaver dam from upstream broke.	8
1	25. The water came rushing downstream,	
2	26. hurling a large log toward the animals.	
2	27. It struck the cat	9
1	28. and swept him helplessly away.	

Total number of units = 28
Number of units recalled = 9
Percentage recalled = 32%
Sequence evaluation = excellent
Mean importance level recalled = 1.9 (weak)

Source: C. H. Clark, "Assessing Free Recall," *The Reading Teacher, 35* (1982), p. 437. Reprinted with permission of C. H. Clark and the International Reading Association.

what you can about the student's processing abilities. Of course, as with the aforementioned procedures, your answers will be subjective and situation specific and should *not* be used as a test score. Rather, they should help you hypothesize about instructional procedures that might help the student.

SUMMARY

Although standardized tests and reading inventories provide general measures of student comprehension abilities, they provide little situation-or process-specific information that can give clues about how best

FIGURE 11-5 Judging Richness of Retellings

LEVEL	CRITERIA FOR ESTABLISHING LEVEL
5	Student generalizes beyond text; includes thesis (summarizing statement), all major points, and appropriate supporting details; includes relevant supplementations; show high degree of coherence, completeness, comprehensibility.
4	Student includes thesis (summarizing statement), all major points, and appropriate supporting details; includes relevant supplementations; shows high degree of coherence, completeness, comprehensibility.
3	Student relates major ideas; includes appropriate supporting details and relevant supplementations; shows adequate coherence, completeness, comprehensibility.
2	Student relates a few major ideas and some supporting details; includes irrelevant supplementations; shows some degree of coherence; some completeness; the whole is somewhat comprehensible.
1	Student relates details only; irrelevant supplementations or none; low degree of coherence; incomplete; incomprehensible.

5 = highest level, 1 = lowest level.

Source: Irwin, P. A., & Mitchell, J. N. (1983). A procedure for assessing the richness of retellings. *Journal of Reading, 26,* p. 394. Reprinted with permission of the authors and the International Reading Association.

FIGURE 11-6 Checklist for Judging Richness of Retellings

	5	4	3	2	1
Generalizes beyond text	X				
Thesis (summarizing) statement	X	X			
Major points	X	X	X	?	?
Supporting details	X	X	X	X	?
Supplementations	Relevant	Relevant	Relevant	Irrelevant	Irrelevant
Coherence	High	Good	Adequate	Some	Poor
Completeness	High	Good	Adequate	Some	Poor
Comprehensibility	High	Good	Adequate	Some	Poor

The matrix describes the evaluation of retellings in a holistic fashion on the basis of criteria, similar to a procedure used to grade written compositions. This technique is an alternative to questioning for assessment of student comprehension of both narrative and expository text.

Source: Irwin, P. A. & Mitchell, J. N. (1983). A procedure for assessing the richness of retellings. *Journal of Reading, 26,* p. 395. Reprinted with permission of the author, and the International Reading Association.

FIGURE 11-7 *FREE RECALL PROCESSING CHECKLIST*

Answer each of these questions according to the following scale:

5 Yes, very well
4 Yes, more than adequately
3 Yes, adequately
2 No, not too well
1 No, poorly
NA Not applicable or can't tell

1. ____ Did the student recall a sufficient number of ideas?
2. ____ Did the student recall the ideas accurately?
3. ____ Did the student select the most important details to recall?
4. ____ Did the student understand explicit pronouns and connectives?
5. ____ Did the student infer important implicitly–stated information?
6. ____ Did the student include the explicitly–stated main points?
7. ____ Did the student create any new summarizing statements?
8. ____ Did the student use the organizational pattern used by the author?
9. ____ Did the student elaborate appropriately?
10. ____ Did the student know how to adjust strategies to the purpose given?

What effective comprehension processes were evident in the student's recall?

What comprehension processes were not evident, or seemed to be causing problems?

To what extent was the student's performance as just described affected by each of the following?

1. Limited prior knowledge or vocabulary

2. Limited motivation or interest

3. Cultural differences

4. Decoding problems

5. Difficulties in the text

6. The social context

7. Discomfort with the task

8. Other environmental influences

to help these students comprehend better. A classroom teacher can get additional information by observing students in a variety of settings in the classroom itself. A remedial teacher can select a variety of natural tasks in which to observe the student's strategies through observation, questioning, and free recall. All teachers are urged to exercise caution in drawing conclusions from informal observation, but if used with care, the comprehension assessment checklist provided in this chapter can be used to structure the planning and summarizing of observations. This should result in useful instructional information because it encourages the teacher to look at all the comprehension processes and contexts.

SELF-CHECK TEST

1. Why do you need to supplement the information gained in standardized tests and informal inventories?
2. Define the multiple-context approach.
3. List three ways of analyzing free recall.
4. Answer true or false:

___ a. The comprehension assessment checklist should be used to prescribe specific skill instruction for each student in every class.
___ b. The comprehension assessment checklist can be used to provide additional clues as to possible instructional procedures for classes and specific students.
___ c. Only short passages should be used for assessment.
___ d. Only long passages should be used for assessment.
___ e. Only content-area assignments should be used for assessment.
___ f. Only basal stories should be used for assessment.
___ g. Only motivational materials should be used for assessment.

SUGGESTED ACTIVITIES

1. For a specific student, plan three assessment sessions using natural tasks. Plan your questions and procedure for each.
2. Administer your planned informal multiple-context assessment (see Activity 1). Summarize your data using the comprehension assessment checklist.
3. Practice Clark's free recall analysis procedure. Prepare a passage, have someone (preferably a student) read and recall it, and analyze the recall protocol. Try the other two analytical procedures for the same recall. Which do you prefer? Why?
4. If you are currently teaching, use the comprehension assessment checklist for your whole class when a large part of the class is having trouble comprehending.

REFERENCES

CLARK, C. H. (1982). Assessing free recall. *The Reading Teacher, 35,* 434–439.

HUNTER, W. J., KENDALL, J., & MASON, J. (September, 1979). *Which Comprehension? Artifacts in the measurement of reading comprehension.* Paper presented at the annual convention of the American Psychological Association, New York.

IRWIN, P. A., & MITCHELL, J. N. (1983). A procedure for assessing the richness of retellings. *Journal of Reading, 26,* 391–396.

IRWIN, J. W., PULVER, C., & KOCH, K. (1983). A new technique for improving reading teachers' diagnoses. Unpublished manuscript, Loyola University of Chicago.

JOHNSTON, P. (1984). Prior knowledge and reading comprehension test bias. *Reading Research Quarterly, 19,* 219–239.

McCAN, J. (1983). *The relationship between specific processing abilities and traditional measures of comprehension skills.* Unpublished doctoral dissertation, Purdue University.

ROYER, J. M., & CUNNINGHAM, D. J. (1981). On the theory and measurement of reading comprehension. *Contemporary Educational Psychology, 6,* 187–216.

SHANAHAN, T., KAMIL, M. L., & TOBIN, A. W. (1982). Cloze as a measure of intersentential comprehension. *Reading Research Quarterly, 17,* 229–255.

TWELVE
GENERAL PROCEDURES
FOR TEACHING
COMPREHENSION
PROCESSES

Throughout this book, activities for encouraging students to develop specific processing strategies have been suggested. At this point, you may be wondering how all these activities can be incorporated into an effective program for teaching comprehension.

TOWARD A MODEL OF DIRECT COMPREHENSION INSTRUCTION

As was stated earlier, traditional comprehension instruction in reading classes has generally taken the form of providing repeated exposure subskill activities or asking product questions after a reading task. Research has shown that children are rarely told how to do the subskill or how to find the answer to the question asked (Durkin, 1981; Jenkins & Pany, 1980). It is the thesis of this book that this situation is, at least in part, a result of the fact that, until recently, we really didn't know what processes were involved; how could we tell them what to do when we didn't know ourselves?

There are still many unanswered questions about comprehension processes. In the years to come, many of the concepts presented in this book will be refined and modified. Yet we already know enough to begin to teach comprehension in a new way.

The components of the new approach suggested here have all been mentioned earlier in this book. They are

1. explication—explaining processes and strategies to the students
2. modeling—showing sample thought processes
3. questioning—asking process and product questions in which students model processes for the teacher
4. activities—providing meaningful reading experiences that require that the students use the processes

Explication is directly telling the students about the skill and why it is important. Direct explanation will probably require that you show them specific examples of when it is needed. The explanation would be most meaningful in a situation in which the skill is definitely needed to achieve another goal. It is not necessary for you to teach complicated terminology. Use everyday language like "tieing sentences together," "inferring events," "thinking about what you already know," and so on. Avoid explaining skills as if they are abstract, isolated thinking games; always show how you are helping them to understand the author's message better. Short scripts of teachers engaged in explication are given in Figure 12-1 to help you understand this step better.

FIGURE 12-1   Teachers Using E-M-Q-A Say Things Like . . .

EXPLICATION	MODELING	QUESTIONING	ACTIVITY
One of the things you can do to understand this assignment better is to try to get pictures in your mind of what the lives of these people look like. Forming mental pictures is one thing you can do to understand and remember better . . .	Let's look at the first section on Alaska. (One student reads section aloud.) Now when I read this, I picture lots of snow and ice and people all bundled up. When I picture them walking down the street in Juneau, I see the condensation of their breath and the sound of boots on snow mixed with other sounds. . . .	(After reading next section) . . . so what picture do you get in your mind when you read about the tundra? . . .	Read the rest of this section on Northern climates. Try to get a picture in your mind for each climate. When you are finished reading, draw a picture of what you would see out your window if you lived in one of these climates . . . .
Good readers don't read words one by one. They read words in groups that make sense together	I will read the next section to you, grouping the words like I do when I read to myself. Follow along in your book. . . .	Now, you read the next section to me doing the same thing	Now, here's a passage that I've "chunked" for you. Read it silently, trying to read the words in groups. . . .

Modeling involves showing the students how you do the process being discussed. As you can see in Figure 12-1, it follows naturally from explication. Indeed, it probably is the most important part of explaining, because it provides a concrete example of what you are explaining. Explication without modeling is probably not going to be very effective.

Questioning allows you to see if the students understand the skill. It also helps you to see to what extent they can do it. In this step, you require the students to model the process back to you, with either a question or an oral activity (see Figure 12-1). Both process and product questions can be used at this point.

Finally, once you have explained the skill and modeled it for the students and the students have successfully modeled it to you, then you can ask the students to perform *activities* that encourage use of that skill (see Figure 12-1). You can probably see how using the E-M-Q steps prior to assigning an activity is more likely to result in success than if those steps are omitted.

Of course, some students will still have trouble with some activities. If students perform badly on an activity, try to assess the reason creatively. Problems with other processes can interfere: For example, if students can't read the words, they can't macroprocess; if they can't chunk the words into meaningful phrases, they won't be able to elaborate; and so on. If you can determine that the problem isn't interference from other processes, then you may wish to do more explication and modeling. If you can determine that there is a problem with another process, try to create an activity in which the other processes are easier: use simpler materials, give them necessary background, and so on.

Furthermore, you need not use all four steps of E-M-Q-A each time you teach. This E-M-Q-A model simply implies that comprehension instruction should include all these steps when the skill is introduced and as many as are necessary thereafter. If you have been teaching while you have been reading this book, you are probably finding that you are already beginning to use them selectively.

To implement these E-M-Q-A steps, sometimes it will be necessary for you to conduct "group processing sessions." In a group processing session, you and the students read together, either silently or orally, discussing the reading after each section. This will result in constant interaction between you and the students during the reading. (The ReQuest activity suggested in Chapter Ten is an example of a group processing activity.) Discussion after every paragraph or section can focus on processes as well as content.

Figure 12-2 shows how a fourth-grade teacher might teach causal inference to the middle-level reading group using an E-M-Q-A approach in a group processing lesson. The teacher has planned this session because the students have been having trouble with these questions in other lessons. Figure 12-3 shows a seventh-grade teacher using E-M-Q-A to teach comprehension during a content-area lesson. This lesson was not planned but,

FIGURE 12-2   Teaching Comprehension: Fourth-Grade Reading Group

	TEACHER	STUDENT RESPONSES
	Do you know why this author puts sentences in a certain order?	because it sounds good
	Yes! And why does it sound good?	because it tells a story
Explication	Yes! The sentences fit together. They are related to each other. Good readers read more than sentences. They figure out how the sentences fit together. In order to really understand this story, you will need to understand how the sentences fit together. Often, one sentence tells why something happened in another sentence.	
Modeling	Let me show you how I do this. Everyone read the first paragraph silently while I read it aloud. [reads paragraph] Now, let's see. The first sentence tells me that Janice loved the store. The second sentence tells me that it had a lot of pretty things. Now, I ask myself, how do these sentences fit together? Well, I know that most people love pretty things. So, she probably loved the store *because* . . . Good!	it had pretty things!
Process Question	How, let's read the next two sentences. Who can tell me how these fit together?	They sold the ribbon so they could get money.
	Good! One thing was the cause of the other. Now let's read on. [They read and discuss until another connective inference is needed.]	
Product Question	Who can tell me why Janice didn't go home?	because she wanted to buy a present
Process Question	Right! But how did you get that answer? Show me where it says that.	[Student reads the next two sentences.] I just figured how they fit together, like you did.
Process Question	Right. You figured out that these two sentences fit together because one thing was the cause of the other.	

FIGURE 12-2   (cont.)

	TEACHER	STUDENT RESPONSES
Sample Activity	Now, read the next page. When you are finished I will ask you more questions about things that caused other things. Try to put sentences together as you read. You will understand the story better that way.	

rather, arose naturally because students needed to understand the text. Note how E-M-Q-A provides an easy way to teach comprehension processes in the context of content-area and other meaningful reading situations.

In working with teachers who have read the first part of this manuscript, I have found that they generally fall into two categories, which I will call (1) "focused subskill" lesson planners and (2) "meaningful, holistic" lesson planners. Teachers in the first category are very organized. They make up a list of specific processes that they want to teach and, for each, they make up a specific skill lesson. But when watching these talented teachers teaching these lessons, I have had the uneasy feeling that something is missing. Do you know what?

Teachers in the second category are fully committed to the concept of reading as a meaningful, holistic process. They select meaningful reading situations and then do everything necessary to teach the students how to comprehend in that situation. In particular, I have seen this procedure used with poor comprehenders in remedial one-to-one tutoring situations. Again, while watching, I have been plagued by the uneasy feeling that this is not the whole answer. I remember that when I mentioned this to one graduate student who was doing this, she threw up her arms and said, "I don't get it. So what *do* you want, anyway?" Does this express your feeling?

The tension between holistic and subskill approaches is clearly not new in discussions of reading methodology. It is theoretically resolved by saying that there are identifiable subprocesses but that they interact (the interactive hypothesis) in order for comprehension to occur. But how is it resolved operationally for teaching?

In my opinion, teachers need to do both. They need to be focused lesson planners like the teacher in Figure 12-2 and holistic lesson planners who teach incidentally like the teacher in Figure 12-3. Too much of the former will result in separation of the skills from the real purposes of reading. Too much of the latter will result in overwhelming students with random advice, with little opportunity for immediate reinforcement and practice. An integrated approach will result in improving skills and learning to apply them.

FIGURE 12-3   Teaching Comprehension: Seventh-Grade Content-Area Class

	TEACHER	STUDENT RESPONSES
Product question	Why did the Americans move to Mexico?	[no answer]
Process question	Well, how could we find out the answer?	Reread that section and look for clues.
Process question	Good—where does it say "the Americans moved to Mexico"?	the first paragraph on page 251
Process question	OK. Good. Everyone read it silently. What clue do you see?	Well, it says that Mexico had slavery.
Prior-knowledge question	Did Americans have slaves then?	Now, it was right after the war . . . so maybe they moved to Mexico so they could keep their slaves.
Explication	Good—there could really have been a "because" between those two sentences. Remember when we talked about how that happens a lot in this book?	
Modeling	If we were to read on, there would be other places just in this section. If I were to read on I would infer a "because" between the next two sentences: "Texas allowed slavery (because) Texas was a part of Mexico."	
Questioning	Read the rest of the page silently.	[students read]
	Who can find another place where we could insert a "because"?	The part about the Americans wanting more land. It was because of homesteading.
	Good. The author didn't use the word "because" but that was what he meant.	
Product question	OK, so what was the main point of this section?	that Americans had slaves
	That's one idea. What else?	that America wanted to keep Texas
	Yes, that too. Which of these ideas is more important?	about keeping Texas

FIGURE 12-3   (cont.)

	TEACHER	STUDENT RESPONSES
Process question	Why do you say that?	because that was what started the whole war discussed in the next section
Process question	Why else?	because all the parts of this are about that
Explication	Good. All of these paragraphs tell about why the Americans wanted to keep Texas, so that is the main point.	
	Why did they want to keep Texas?	[et cetera]

Finally, you have probably also noticed that this E-M-Q-A model involves teacher-centered comprehension instruction. Recent research seems to indicate that such direct instruction facilitates achievement (Rosenshine, 1978), and that is why it is recommended here. However, certain limitations on this approach must be mentioned. McFaul (1983) has reviewed research showing that while direct instruction is useful for some students, it may be the wrong approach for others. It seems that high-achieving task-oriented students, for instance, may do better with another approach (Peterson, 1979). Thus, although E-M-Q-A is being recommended as a general structure, its implementation must be varied according to the individual learning styles of children in your classroom.

Similarly, teachers must also remember the concepts of the "continuum of independence" and "transformation" mentioned in Chapter Two (pages 16 and 17, respectively). Students will vary in terms of their ability to perform a skill independently, and, to the extent possible, it is important for you to provide students with comprehension lessons at their level of independence. Students at the more dependent levels may need more explication and modeling (direct instruction) than students who are functioning more independently. In addition, activities designed to encourage a specific strategy can be varied according to the difficulty of the material being read or the amount of assistance included (partially completed versus blank outline, for instance).

Moreover, because many of these skills must be somewhat "transformed" to apply in different content areas and tasks, opportunities to discuss, model, and practice comprehension processes should be integrated across the curriculum and throughout all grade levels (horizontal and vertical transformation, respectively; see page 16). For example, if summarizing is taught in a basal reader lesson, then it can be remodeled and assigned as part of the social studies lesson as well. Secondary-level teachers can teach these skills in each of their classes, or, as a group, they can decide on specific skills to stress simultaneously in all classes. Repeated emphasis on active application in a variety of reading situations must accompany specific skill instruction in a total program designed to help students become active, successful comprehenders.

PUTTING IT TOGETHER: THE ACTIVE READING COMPREHENSION ACTIVITY

The final step in developing an approach to teaching comprehension based on the principles explained in this book is to put together a general lesson structure that integrates everything that has been said so far, including the E-M-Q-A approach to teaching comprehension processes. The following "active reading comprehension activity" (ARCA) does just that. ARCA is an outline of the general steps that should be followed each time you ask your students to read something in class, whether it is for reading group or for another content area. Sometimes you will follow this structure when you are teaching comprehension as a skill. Sometimes you will use it to facilitate comprehension of content-area materials.

Study Figure 12-4. Each lesson you conduct should include, in some way, the four stages indicated by the boxes. These correspond to (1) lesson selection, (2) before-reading activities (preparation), (3) during-reading activities, and (4) after-reading activities (comprehension development). If you have studied reading methods before, you will notice that ARCA is a form of the traditional directed reading activity. What makes ARCA new is the way the individual steps are carried out. Each step requires you to have read several chapters in this or a similar text.

Ideally, the first step is deciding on the objectives of the lesson. Are you trying to teach specific comprehension processes? Which ones? Or is your primary goal to teach content-area information? What information? What processes will need special attention to reach this goal? Once you have decided on your objectives, you can select the reading material to assign. To do this, you will also want to take into account everything you know about the students' abilities (Chapter Eleven) and the characteristics of the material (Chapter Eight). Of course, you may not have many choices for material selection; that is, you may be required to use a certain book and to take the chapters in order. In that case, you will still want to be aware of the possible processing problems posed by the materials, you will always want to be aware of the comprehension tasks the material requires of your students (Chapters One through Eight) for the purpose you or your students choose (Chapter Nine), and you will want to be clear about whether your instructional purpose is to teach comprehension skills or content-area information.

When you are giving the reading assignment, you will want to prepare the students to comprehend fully. If your purpose is to teach compre-

Steps . . .

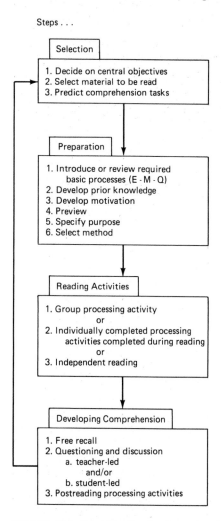

FIGURE 12-4 The Active Reading Comprehension Activity

hension skills, this will definitely involve discussing one or more basic processes (Chapters One through Six) using the first three steps of the E-M-Q-A model (Chapter Twelve). If your purpose is to teach content, you may still wish to review one or more basic processes, especially if you know they may pose a problem in this assignment. Preparing the students may also include either a review of prior knowledge or enrichment of such as well as some attention to motivation (Chapter Seven). It may include previewing (Chapter Six) and will definitely include either you or the students defining the purpose for reading (Chapter Nine). Finally you may choose to give the students a metacognitive strategy or to have them select their own (Chapter Nine).

There are several options for procedures used during reading. If you are teaching a process, this will be the activity step of the E-M-Q-A model. You may wish to have them complete individual, guided processing activities (Chapters One through Six, Ten), you may wish to conduct a group processing activities (Chapter Twelve), or you may feel that they are ready to apply the chosen reading method independently. The latter is as important as guided reading; independence is the goal of reading instruction and should be practiced whenever students are ready.

After the material has been read, you have yet another opportunity to teach comprehension processes and/or content information. You also have an opportunity to assess what they have comprehended. To do these things, you may wish to use a free recall strategy (Chapters Ten and Eleven), questioning—either by you or by the students (Chapter Ten)—or other postreading activities (Chapters One through Six). An E-M-Q-A model with process questions can be used to help students answer questions and do activities, especially for those students who are having problems (Chapter Twelve), or it can be used to teach processes that were unexpectedly difficult. Finally, the arrow indicates that information gained during this stage can be used to select the next set of objectives and materials.

To make ARCA more concrete, a short story similar to those used in reading instruction is provided in Figure 12-5. Figure 12-6 presents the les-

FIGURE12-5   THE MAGIC PRINCE (BY KENNETH J. SMITH)

In ancient China, during the years of magic, each Province had its own enchantment—a special kind of magic that could only be found in that part of the country. At the close of every decade, the most important wizards from each Province would gather together to share stories. This is one of those stories. It was told to me by a man with more years than I could count. I am telling it to you as he told it to me. I hope that you will keep it, and someday pass it on to your children. That way it will never be forgotten . . .

In one of the provinces, the people seemed happier and the land more beautiful than anywhere else in all China. Only the Emperor of this kingdom was sad. For unlike the families over which he ruled, his family was without a child. Then, one day a boy was born to him and his wife. The boy, Kim, grew to love the people and creatures in this, the most magic of kingdoms.

Many unusual plants and animals found their way into this bright-colored land of good weather and sun. The young prince's friends were not ordinary deer and horses, but kudus and zebras. Some days, the prince spent many hours in the palace gardens, running freely with a herd of strong, fleet animals—none of which was stronger or faster than the prince. He did not really speak with the animals. They all just somehow understood each other. That was a very special part of the magic of this province.

In this enchanted climate where after-shower rainbows sent ribbons of new colors across the sky, a special tree grew in the center of the palace garden. This was a cherry tree that bloomed long into the spring. When its blossoms finally fell, all the people thought it was the best of luck to catch one of the petals that glided on the warm breezes. In the summer, the cherries shone like rubies in the sunlight, and their sweet taste would linger on a person's tongue.

Whenever the prince and the animals felt like resting, they would sit very quietly under the tree. Then, when the gentle breezes blew, the ripest cherries would fall down to them. It was almost as if the tree were saying, "Here, my friends, share these with me." "Someday," thought the young boy, "I will be tall enough to pick the cherries by myself. Then I will not have to wait for the wind to pick them for us."

On the first day of Kim's tenth spring, his father called him into the royal study. "It is the custom," explained the Emperor, "for a prince to begin his tenth spring by making his first proclamation. Be thoughtful, for you must make a proclamation which shows concern not only for the people over whom you will someday rule, but also for the land and animals you will have to protect. With this proclamation your life will change."

For this, his first royal command, the boy ordered a wall built around the cherry tree. "But why?" asked the King. "Isn't it, like everything else, safe and well?"

"Yes," said his son, "for now. But what if an accident happened? The tree is the loveliest one in the land, but it is also the most fragile."

So a brick wall was built around the base of the tree. But the prince was not happy. "The tree is in more danger now than ever before. People will sit on the wall as if it were a bench. Children will walk upon its top as if they were in a playground. Build the wall higher." So the wall was built up to where the tree's branches began.

"No, that is still not tall enough. Now people will think we are hiding the tree instead of protecting it. Build the wall higher still," commanded the Prince. So the wall was made very tall, and it covered the tree almost to the top.

Animals could no longer run in that part of the garden. They were now afraid of running into the wall. Children no longer played there because they could not sit in the shade. The Prince finally seemed satisfied.

He returned to the tree after a year of travel and, thinking that he had surely grown tall enough to pick the cherries without help from the wind, unlocked the gate in the wall. He was very happy until he saw what had happened. The once beautiful tree was now barren and lifeless. The only signs of life were the few cherries growing above the top of the wall. The Prince realized what had happened. In protecting the tree from everything evil, his wall had blocked out the sunlight which the tree needed in order to grow. The Prince had the wall torn down, but he knew it was probably too late. Now the wind just whistled through the branches, making a sound almost like crying.

Many days later, the Prince sat alone by the old tree, and as had happened so many times before, the wind carried the ripe cherries down to him. This, however, was the last time the tree would be able to share its fruit, and the boy felt both sad and happy. He planted these last few cherries in an open area near the old tree. "These will take a long time to grow. If they ever bear fruit, it will be many years. But no walls. No walls, I promise," said the Prince. The people and the animals understood, for that was part of the magic of the kingdom.

LITERAL QUESTIONS

1. Where did the storyteller first hear the story?
2. Why was the emperor unhappy?
3. Why was the cherry tree so special?
4. Why did the prince say he wanted the wall built?
5. Why was the prince unhappy with the first two walls?
6. What happened to the tree after the wall was built?
7. What did the prince do after he picked the last cherries?

INFERENTIAL QUESTIONS

1. Why did the prince want to build the wall?
2. How do you think the people and animals felt when the wall was built?
3. How did the prince feel when he was too short to pick the cherries? Did you ever have similar feelings?
4. Why weren't the animals and people more angry with the prince for destroying the tree? Would you have forgiven him?
   Write a letter to the prince telling him how you feel about the wall.
5. The story begins by describing the province as "magical." What was the magic of this province?
6. What lesson did the prince learn? How did he learn it? Did you ever learn a similar lesson?

Source:_ Smith, K.J. The Magic Prince. Unpublished manuscript. Reprinted with permission of the author.

FIGURE 12-6 Basal Reader Lesson

TEACHER NOTES	PROBABLE RATIONALE
"The Magic Prince"	because it is the next story in the reader
Introduce new words	so they won't have trouble with these.
Have students read title and look at pictures. Read first paragraph aloud. "What do you think the story is about?	To get them interested, I can get them talking about magic.
Silent reading	
Ask questions: literal 1-6 inferential 1, 2, 6	to make sure they understand the story to get them to think about the story
Assign workbook pages on pronouns in the story.	

son used by a teacher using a typical basal series. Then, a sample informal lesson plan using ARCA is presented in Figure 12-7. Compare these lesson plans to see the kinds of changes that can result from using ARCA for plan-

FIGURE 12-7   ARCA Lesson

TEACHER NOTES	ARCA STEP	PROBABLE TEACHER THOUGHTS
	SELECTION	
Using "The Magic Prince," I will begin to encourage students to form mental images whle they read.	1. Decide on central objective	I am trying to teach basic comprehension processes. I hope I will be able to teach some kind of elaboration, since that is what we've been doing on the last four stories.
	2. Select material	I feel that I must use the next story in the basal: "The Magic Prince." The principal says we must use all the stories in order. Anyway, I like it.
	3. Predict comprehension tasks	This story would be much more meaningful if the students had a mental image of the kingdom and the tree. Also, predicting what might happen to the tree would be useful. I see no problems with micro-, integrative, and macroprocessing, except for a few vocabulary words.
Before Reading:	**PREPARATION**	
1. Talk about forming mental images. Read a descriptive passage and then talk about the picture I get. Also briefly review prediction.	1. E-M-Q-A	Since this is the first time I have mentioned imaging this year, I should probably model it. We've worked on prediction before, so I won't need to say much about it.
2. Introduce new words and elicit schema by discussing cherries and cherry trees.	2. Prior knowledge (motivation)	They need these words to understand the story, and thinking about cherry trees will help them image.
3. Have students read title and look at picture. Read first paragraph aloud.	3. Motivation	This will get them motivated and elicit further schema.
4. "What do you think the story is about?"	4. Previewing	
5. Tell the students that this story is for enjoyment. You want them to have a good time reading it.	5. Purpose	Enjoyment should really be the purpose of reading most of these stories!

FIGURE 12-7   **(cont.)**

TEACHER NOTES	ARCA STEP	PROBABLE TEACHER THOUGHTS
6. Ask them how to read it for enjoyment and give them strategy: "Stop and form mental images as you read. Use your imagination. Also, try to predict what is going to happen at the end."	6. Metacognitive choice of material	It will be interesting to see their answers here. I wonder if they've ever been asked this before. I will give them a method that stresses the two basic processes I want to emphasize in this story.
During Reading: 1. "After reading the fifth paragraph, stop and make a picture in your mind." Discuss the picture they get.	READING	Since we've not done too much with imagery before, it will probably be best to do this as a group for the first time. That way, I can encourage it and see if they can model it back to me. Also, their sensory descriptions will be useful to each other.
2. After reading next five paragraphs, do this again and have students predict what will happen.		
After reading: 1. Free recall; summarizing.	COMPREHENSION DEVELOPMENT 1. Free recall	Since we "processed" the story together, we really don't need to do much here. Also, their purpose was enjoyment, so asking a lot of picky questions will not be appropriate. I'll just help them to recall it.
2. What do you think the author is trying to tell you? What might the Kingdom look like in twenty years?	2. Questioning	We'll discuss the moral of the story as we have in the past. Then I'll reinforce imagery and encourage them to make more predictions using process questions if necessary.
3. Assign another story to be read for enjoyment with mental images. As they read it, they will be asked to stop to draw pictures showing their mental images.	3. Postreading activity	I definitely want to reinforce these skills right away, so I'll find other materials that are appropriate. That way they can get a chance to do this independently.

ning. The teacher's rationale is included to demonstrate the differences in the teacher's perspective.

The teacher not using ARCA does not seem to be clear about what to teach. The students do the reading with little guidance. The product questions include no mention of possible processing discussions that could ensue if a student got them wrong. Finally the follow-up activity has little to do with anything discussed while students were actually reading. Unfortunately, though this is a fictional example, it is probably not all that atypical of how comprehension is usually taught.

The most obvious difference between this lesson and the ARCA one is the teacher's awareness of what he or she is teaching. In the ARCA lesson, the teacher's instructional choices are based on the characteristics of the story. Important processing strategies are discussed and modeled. The purpose for reading is discussed and the children are encouraged to make metacognitive decisions that the teacher honors after reading by avoiding an emphasis on recall of details. The teacher is able to follow this activity with reinforcement of the same processes, because he or she knows what comprehension strategies are being taught.

Similar examples could be devised using content-area materials. If your goal is to reinforce specific reading skills, the lesson would be very similar to the one presented in Figure 12-7, except that the students would be reading in their content-area textbook. For example, suppose you have recently taught integrative inferences in reading group and you would like to reinforce this in social studies so that the students can appropriately transform the skill for that content area. For a section requiring integrative inferences (SELECTION), you would explain, model, and question about integrative inferences. Then, you would assign the next section by reviewing vocabulary and prior knowledge, previewing it with the students, and giving them a purpose and a method. Your method would stress integrative inferences (PREPARATION). During reading, students may complete a study guide asking integrative implicit questions (READING), and after reading, your discussion of this social studies chapter would focus on the inference questions and a review of the process itself (DEVELOPING COMPREHENSION).

In contrast, you might also choose to use ARCA for content-area lessons in which you simply wish to make sure they learn the content. For example, suppose you wanted to assign a science chapter on nuclear energy and you think it is generally readable in terms of micro, integrative, macro, and elaborative factors (SELECTION). You may choose to review what they already know about nuclear energy and motivate them by planning to ask a guest speaker from the local utility company to debate a local antinuclear energy leader. You may also preview the chapter by telling them what you want them to learn from each section and reminding them to use the self-questioning study technique you have already taught them (see Chapter Six for a discussion of this procedure) (PREPARATION). During reading, students make notes of their questions (READING). After reading, you assess what they have comprehended using the Ex-QAR taxonomy, and, after all seem to understand the content, you hold your debate (DEVELOPING COMPREHENSION).

Finally, similar examples could also be constructed for remedial one-to-one lessons. In that case, you will definitely be using E-M-Q before reading for those skills with which the student has problems. The reading activity stage for a given skill may move from an oral processing activity when the student is first learning the skill to an individual processing activity when he or she is more independent. Remember to make the tasks as meaningful as possible and to integrate focused subskill activities with holistic ones.

SUMMARY

Direct reading comprehension instruction should consist of explication, modeling, process and product questions, and activities (E-M-Q-A). Lessons focused on specific subskills using meaningful reading materials and incidental teaching of processes during holistic, purposeful reading assignments are both important ways to teach comprehension. Finally, a systematic approach to lesson planning, ARCA, has been presented to help teachers implement all the information provided in this book (including E-M-Q-A) when appropriate. It can be used for every lesson involving reading, whether that lesson is for reading class or for a content area and whether that lesson is designed primarily to teach reading skills or specific content-area information or both.

A FINAL NOTE: THE OUTER CONTEXT

Throughout my writing of this book, I have been aware of what Duffy (1982) has called the "outer context" affecting teacher effectiveness. By this he is referring to factors outside the classroom that affect the ways teachers can teach. This would include parental, administrative, and districtwide pressures to use specific materials in a lockstep manner. For instance, Shannon (1983) has gathered evidence to support the notion that because of the emphasis on using test scores and related scientific rationality to prove a district's effectiveness, classroom teachers feel pressure to apply basal programs stringently as if they were the only way to teach reading. He also found that this pressure to simply implement materials "alienates teachers from their reading instruction" (p. 71).

Thus, I have asked myself whether it is realistic to expect classroom teachers to use the active approach suggested in this book. I have asked teachers the same thing. The answer seems to be a resounding, "Yes." Teachers want to feel that they can use their own knowledge to increase the quality of instruction in their classrooms. It is my hope that this book will help teachers communicate new assessment and instructional ideas to parents and administrators in such a way that reading instruction becomes more than the mere management of commercial programs and content-area instruction is expanded to include content-area reading comprehension instruction as well.

SELF CHECK TEST

1. Define (in detail) each of the following terms:

explication	after-reading procedures
modeling	group processing session
questoning	horizontal transformation
activities	vertical transformation
ARCA	subskill approach
materials selection	holistic approach
before-reading procedures	integrated approach
during-reading procedures	

2. Name three situations in which you might use E-M-Q-A.

3. Name three situations in which you might use ARCA.

SUGGESTED ACTIVITIES

1. Write a prereading lesson in which you teach a comprehension skill using E-M-Q-A. Write out exactly what you would say.
2. Using ARCA, plan a *reading* lesson using a *content-area textbook* assignment.
3. Using ARCA, plan a *content* lesson using a *content-area textbook* assignment.
4. Using ARCA, plan a *developmental reading* lesson using a *basal reader* story.
5. Using ARCA, plan a *remedial reading* lesson using a *basal reader* story.

REFERENCES

Duffy, G. (December, 1982). *Context variables in reading teacher effectiveness.* Paper presented at the annual meeting of the National Reading Conference, Clearwater Beach, Florida.

Durkin, D. (1981). Reading comprehension instruction in five basal reader series. *Reading Research Quarterly, 16,* 515–544.

JENKINS, J. R. & PANY, D. (1980). Teaching reading comprehension in the middle grades. In R.J. Spiro, B.C. Bruce, and W.F. Brewer (Eds.), *Theoretical issues in reading comprehension.* Hillsdale, N.J.: Lawrence Erlbaum.

McFAUL, A. (1983). An examination of direct instruction. *Educational Leadership, 40,* 67–69.

PETERSON, P. (1979). Direct instruction: Effective for what and for whom? *Educational Leadership, 37,* 46–48.

ROSENSHINE, B. V. (1978). Academic engaged time, content covered, and direct instruction. *Journal of Education, 160,* 38–66.

SHANNON, D. (1983). The use of commercial reading materials in American elementary schools. *Reading Research Quarterly, 19,* 68–85.

THIRTEEN
DEVELOPMENTAL
AND REMEDIAL
APPLICATIONS:
Some Examples

This chapter begins with a review of what you have learned so far. Then, to encourage your own creative thinking, you will consider some fictional descriptions of classroom and remedial teachers who are beginning to use what they know about comprehension to help their students become better comprehenders. Of course, these examples cover only a very small part of what can be done on a day-to-day basis. They are designed to show you how easy it is to get started. The reader is encouraged to write a similar example describing plans for his or her own teaching situation.

A BRIEF REVIEW

What have you learned so far? Before looking at the examples, you should probably review the material to be implemented. First, you learned some general considerations in teaching comprehension. These included E-M-Q-A (Chapter Twelve) and other basic considerations (Chapter Two), such as considering horizontal and vertical transformation, differentiating activities along a continuum of independence, integrating reading and writing, and using meaningful activities and whole, natural tasks as much as possible. Make sure you understand each of these before reading on by completing Figure 13-1.

FIGURE 13-1 *REVIEW: DIRECT COMPREHENSION INSTRUCTION*

E:

M:

Q:

A:

Other considerations:

Next, you learned about the five processes that interact whenever a reader comprehends. Can you define these in Figure 13-2? If not, review Chapter One carefully.

Then you learned about what each of these processes entails and how to teach the subprocesses either incidentally or with direct instruction. Try to name each subprocess and a way of teaching each by completing Figure 13-3. If you have trouble, review Chapters Two through Six. You may also want to review Figure 1-1 (p. 4).

In Part Two, you learned about the comprehension contexts that influence comprehension. What were they? How can each of these factors influence the way you teach? You will find this information in Chapters Seven through Nine if you have difficulty with Figure 13-4.

Chapters Ten and Eleven gave you some specific procedures for asking questions and informally observing students' abilities. Can you list the categories in the Ex-QAR questioning taxonomy in Figure 13-5? What is the multiple-context approach to assessment? Review Chapter Eleven if you have trouble describing this.

Finally, Chapter Twelve included an outline for tying it all together in lesson planning. For each step of ARCA, tell what you would want to remember to consider in Figure 13-6. Now you are ready to read on.

FIGURE 13-2 *REVIEW: DEFINING BASIC COMPREHENSION PROCESSES*

Microprocesses

Integrative processes

Macroprocesses

Elaborative processes

Metacognitive processes

FIGURE 13-3   *REVIEW: TEACHING BASIC COMPREHENSION PROCESSES*

NAME   SUGGESTED ACTIVITY

  I.   Micro
       A. _____   _____
       B. _____   _____

 II.   Integrative
       A. _____   _____
       B. _____   _____
       C. _____   _____

III.   Macro
       A. _____
            1. _____   _____
            2. _____   _____
       B. _____   _____
            1. _____
            2. _____
            3. _____
            4. _____

IV.   Elaborative
       A. _____   _____
       B. _____   _____
       C. _____   _____
       D. _____   _____
       E. _____   _____
            1. _____   _____
            2. _____   _____
            3. _____   _____
            4. _____   _____

 V.   Metacognitive
       A. _____   _____
       B. _____   _____

FIGURE 13-4   *REVIEW: COMPREHENSION CONTEXTS*

  I.   Reader-related
       A.
       B.
                                    Thus, teachers should . . .
       C.
       D.

 II.   Text-related
       A.
       B.
       C.   Thus, teachers should . . .
       D.
       E.

III.   Situation-related
       A.
       B.   Thus, teachers should . . .
       C.

FIGURE 13-5 *REVIEW: THE EX-QAR TAXONOMY*

Questions request . . .
    I.
    II.
        A.
        B.
    III.
        A.
        B.
    IV.
        A.
        B.
    V.
    VI.

FIGURE 13-6 *REVIEW: ARCA*

    I.   Selection
        A.
        B.
        C.

    II. Preparation
        A.
        B.
        C.
        D.
        E.
        F.

    III. Reading
        A.
        B.
        C.

    V.   Developing comprehension
        A.
        B.
        C.

TEACHING COMPREHENSION
IN ELEMENTARY READING GROUPS

At first glance, the foregoing subheading may seem absurd: of course you teach comprehension as part of your developmental reading program! But if you are used to working with a specific reading program such as a basal series in which many of the skills and approaches described in this book are not used, you may be wondering how you can integrate these new ideas into the traditional approach with which you are familiar. Figure 12-7

(Chapter Twelve) gave an example for one specific lesson. The following example describes a teacher who began to do this throughout the year:

Ms. Venturi taught third grade in a small town in Massachusetts. Though she tried very hard and had the reputation of being an excellent teacher, she was dissatisfied with her reading groups. It just seemed as if the students left at the end of the year with the same problems they had at the beginning.

After reading this book, Ms. Venturi realized that she could do more to teach comprehension. She didn't have time to sit down and write a whole new set of lessons, so she decided to make up specific activities throughout the year whenever she thought of them. All of these activities were designed to supplement the basal series with which she was already familiar. Here is what happened. . . .

There were already a few anaphora activities in her basal series. She always found that some students found these to be easy while others stumbled through, so she made up a series of activities using the contents of the relevant basal stories. She designed this series from easy to difficult according to the steps given in Chapter Three and to considerations of independence level. After explaining and modeling with the whole class, she gave the easier worksheets to students who were having trouble. The students who were having no trouble enjoyed the more challenging ones. All the students seemed to be learning. She began to make up similar sets of supplementary activities for main idea and cause/effect inference.

Ms. Venturi also found that there were many independent learning center packets for comprehension that she could construct for students to work on in their free time after she had used E-M-Q-A to introduce the skill. She designed "create your own story" activities to encourage story grammar awareness, using basal stories as the beginnings. She cut up old books from the library sale and inserted elaboration questions for the students to answer while they were reading. She made up crossword puzzles and detective games requiring inferences about characters in basal stories. The more packets she created, the more ideas she got, and the more excited she got about introducing the skills during reading lessons.

Finally, Ms. Venturi found that the questions she asked in reading group sessions began to change. She began to ask for different kinds of information, such as connecting and slot-filling inferences. Because she used process questions, students were discussing their reasoning procedures. Several times, when they were having trouble, she modeled her own inference processes and discussed the importance of inferring while reading. She always asked students to summarize. Using EMQA and ARCA to plan her lessons, she modeled and questioned elaboration processes. For several lessons, she encouraged students to monitor their comprehension, and, when there were problems, they discussed remedies. With nonfiction materials, they discussed the three possible sources for an answer to a question, and students got involved in asking their own questions. She realized that everyone in her slowest group was bored with her word attack approach, and she began to teach this group with a meaning emphasis similar to that used in the other groups.

In the course of the year, Ms. Venturi began to see changes in reading group sessions. For one thing, they were more interesting. Everyone was actively involved in the process of comprehending. Moreover, Ms. Venturi found that her content-area lessons had become more interesting too. As she taught processes in reading groups, she found it easy to reinforce them in content lessons. Using EMQA and ARCA, she was helping students transform processes to improve their comprehension in social studies, science, and math, and it was making these subjects much easier to teach. Students were actually learning from the textbooks.

Ms. Venturi was really pleased with all these changes. They hadn't involved all that much extra work, yet she really felt as if she was teaching comprehension. It was far from perfect, but it was a start!

TEACHING COMPREHENSION IN REMEDIAL SITUATIONS

If you are a remedial reading teacher or a reading clinician, your understanding of comprehension will affect how you diagnose and how you remediate. In the fictional case study that follows, a thorough understanding of comprehension was used to guide the program. Pretend that you were the remedial teacher involved. Would you have acted as described? Why or why not?

Armando was in the third grade. He was referred to you by the classroom teacher who said that he seemed to have comprehension problems. Initial tests indicated that his word recognition skills were good, even slightly above grade level. However, on tests of comprehension, he scored at about the first-grade level. Evidently his teacher was right.

You decided to use the comprehension assessment inventory to structure your thinking about Armando (see Chapter Eleven). You noted that although Armando read words accurately, he didn't seem to use any intonation or to divide them into meaningful phrases. Although he seemed to have a good vocabulary and adequate prior knowledge when questioned, he was able to recall very little, even when prompted. He said he was interested in the topics at hand and seemed to want to do well. He also said that he considered himself to be a good reader and that he thought he had done well on the tests. When you gave him carefully selected second-grade–level short stories, you asked him to look at the pictures and guess what the story would be about. Then he read it to you. After the reading, you asked him why he had read the story. He answered, "So you could see how good I could read."

Taken together, this all seemed to indicate to you that Armando thought of "reading" as accurate word identification. Thus, by his standards, he was a good reader, and word calling without comprehending was all right. To verify this, you asked him questions about his concept of reading and found that you were right.

You decided to begin a remedial program with very simple materials in which meaning was always the focus. You began with sentences, first explaining and then showing him how to read with intonation with an emphasis on the meaning. You used sentence anagrams, and you had him write his own sentences based on what he wanted to say, so he could see the connection between reading and communication. You worked on dramatic readings together, explaining, modeling, and practicing chunking, and discussing how the characters felt and why they said what they did. You asked Armando's teacher also to emphasize phrase meaning rather than individual words when working with him.

Once Armando began to see phrases and sentences as meaningful units, you moved on to short passages. At this point, things moved fairly quickly. His teacher was reinforcing him for his answers to easy comprehension questions, and he was very excited about this. He seemed to be able to apply his knowledge of anaphora, and so on, from oral language to the written language. He was able to give you literal meanings for passages much more often, and, after modeling, discussion, and practice, he was also able to select what was important, though he still had trouble with summarizing for you. Another problem that you began to note was that Armando was still very text oriented. He now seemed to think of reading as getting the literal meaning from the page, and he was still having trouble understanding third-grade materials. By now, it was the end of the year, so it was time to write recommendations for the new teacher who would be coming in in the fall.

You recommended that Armando be encouraged to interact actively with the material, to use schema-related processes. He needed to work with easy materials on summarizing and elaborating, especially in terms of prior-knowledge elaborations and predictions. Moreover, he still needed to develop basic chunking fluency with more difficult materials, so you recommended that he be encouraged to read a book a week throughout the summer and the following year and that he be assigned someone with whom he could discuss these books. Finally, the comprehension remediation needed eventually to include content-area as well as narrative materials, because he needed to develop macrolevel skills for all types of materials to function effectively in the intermediate grades.

TEACHING COMPREHENSION IN THE CONTENT AREAS

What does all this mean to a content-area teacher? If you are currently teaching or plan to teach in a content-area classroom, you may be asking yourself this question. You may have understood the individual concepts as you read through this text, but now you may be feeling unclear about how it will all work in your day-to-day content-area activities. If you are planning to be a reading consultant for secondary teachers, you may be wondering how to translate all this information into readily accessible formats for the teachers in your school. So, let's visit a fictional high school to take a look at some content-area teachers who are beginning to teach comprehension. (Note that although these examples are from a fictional high school, they are applicable for all grades that have content-area lessons, including, generally, grades 4 through 12.)

Mr. Brown teaches an elective auto mechanics course in George Washington High School. At his other school, the only students in his class were the ones who couldn't get into the regular college-preparatory curriculum, but here things are different. Many college-bound students who own their own cars sign up on the waiting list. Even intelligent girls who are trying to break stereotypical patterns have the courage to sign up for this class. When he took this job two years ago, he thought it was too good to be true. They even let him buy the shiny new auto repair manuals shelved neatly around the room.

But now Mr. Brown is feeling discouraged. Every semester, he has assigned readings in those shiny repair manuals, and every semester he has to go back and explain everything himself, just as in the old days. "It's really too bad," he thinks to himself. "There would be so much more they could learn if they could just read!"

Mr. Brown remembers having studied this text in college. At home that night, he turns to Part Two, "Recognizing Factors That Affect Basic Comprehension Processes." In reading Chapter Seven, Mr. Brown realizes that most of his students have very little background in the industrial arts. They know very little about tools and nothing about engines. The vocabulary and the basic procedural knowledge being assumed in the manuals are unknown to them. In reading Chapter Eight, he realizes that although the text is at their level, it is poorly organized and provides little opportunity for review. The rest of that evening is spent listing basic vocabulary and mechanical processes that the students need in order to interpret the manuals.

Beginning the next day, Mr. Brown uses the advice given in Chapter Seven. He demonstrates basic procedures and lets the students practice them. He asks inferential and elaborative questions. He introduces basic vocabulary in meaningful groups and shows the students concrete examples and real engine parts. After he feels that the students are conversant in the basic terminology, he makes his first reading assignment. He remembers to preview, explain the purpose, and give them a reading method. While doing this, he shows them how the chapter is organized and how they should take notes for review using a ConStruct procedure. The students come to class the next day with their notes in hand. To his amazement, they are ready to work on their automobiles.

Ms. Garcia teaches down the hall from Mr. Brown. She fully understands his complaints: all of her students complain that their text is impossible to understand, too, and she is teaching the middle track only! For years she has tried to understand why. After all, it is a geometry text written at the ninth-grade level, according to the publisher. All of her students read at the ninth-grade level or above, according to the reading specialist. Moreover, they don't really seem to have trouble with the concepts when she explains them in class.

Mr. Brown shows Ms. Garcia the readability checklist. Perhaps it can give her some ideas. He also tells her that according to the ARCA structure, the first step in promoting comprehension is understanding the skills required by the materials. Skeptically, she goes home to analyze the textbook one more time. The first thing she notices is that only one example is provided for each concept and that new concepts are introduced rapidly in succession. She also notices that the definitions are usually more abstract than they need to be and that they are written in needlessly long sentences. There are no main ideas, introductions, or summaries, and practice problems are saved for the very end of the chapter. She is beginning to understand why they are having trouble!

Ms. Garcia decides to try an experiment using ARCA. Before assigning the next chapter section, (she has decided to assign the chapters in small sections), she provides an introduction in which she reviews important prior knowledge. She points out why the section is important and what they should learn from it. They discuss the best strategy for reading for this purpose, which includes studying examples, paraphrasing definitions, and trying practice problems while they are reading. She models these strategies while they read the first part together, and she gives them a study guide that encourages them to complete these strategies while they read.

The next day, they discuss the new concepts, and she asks them to make up their own examples. She is amazed to find out that the majority of the students seem to have learned from reading the text. She asks them how the study guide worked, and they all say it was helpful. As a class, they design a study guide for the next section. Gradually, during the semester, the students become able to use the text as a learning tool. Ms. Garcia is very pleased that she has taught them how to comprehend math textbooks. She feels that this will make a real difference in their future performance in other classes.

Finally, Mr. Stoczek is the football coach at George Washington High School. He has a new freshman on his team this year who promises to be the best thing to happen since football was invented. But there is one big problem. This promising young star is failing all his classes, and his parents are thinking of taking him off the team.

Since Mr. Stoczek is taking a required reading methods course, he immediately suspects that maybe Johnny can't read. He has Johnny do some oral reading and free and prompted recall on his assignments and finds that although Johnny identifies words very well, he doesn't seem to understand what he reads. A free recall analysis shows him that Johnny doesn't know how to select at either the micro- or the macrolevel. Using the comprehension assessment checklist, Mr. Stoczek realizes that Johnny can't identify main ideas or summarize. He is motivated but extremely anxious and he doesn't expect to succeed. A reading comprehension interview reveals that Johnny has little awareness of study strategies or how to vary his reading methods to increase recall.

Mr. Stoczek requests a brief staff meeting with Johnny's other teachers. Two teachers and the school reading specialist (all of whom have read this book) are able to meet during lunch the next day. Mr. Stoczek shares his observations of Johnny's problems, and the teachers comment that they have many students who seem to have similar needs. After much discussion, the teachers decide to work with the reading consultant to integrate comprehension instruction into their curricula. In particular, they decide to experiment with teaching microselection and macroprocessing using the hierarchal summary procedure. The reading specialist agrees to teach these skills in the content classes, and the content teachers begin to devise ways to reinforce the skills throughout the year. Also, during supervised study periods, the teachers (including Mr. Stoczek) plan to work with students (including Johnny) who are having trouble with these skills.

At the end of the year, the teachers meet to discuss the results of t heir experiment. They are very pleased with their students' progress. They feel that all the students are studying more efficiently and remembering more. They have also found that they have incidentally taught many other skills like connective inference, prediction, and metacognitive processes even though they hadn't planned to do so. "One processing discussion just led to another!" They decide to continue the program the following year, and they feel that they are ready to teach the skills without the help of the reading specialist.

Oh, yes, Mr. Stoczek is happy, too. Johnny's grades have improved, and he has been able to stay on the team. Next week, they play for the championship.

IT'S YOUR TURN!

If you found this chapter to be unnecessary, then you have probably already begun to teach comprehension strategies. If you found it helpful, then you are probably now ready to begin to apply the strategies suggested in this book. It is important that you not use the strategies described in this chapter as a template for your own decisions. Rather, you can use them to stimulate your own creativity and situation-specific responsiveness. In Figure 13-7 there is space for you to begin to write your own example. Pretend that you are describing your own classroom a year from now. In what ways are you teaching comprehension? What changes are still to be made? Skim this book (and others) for ideas. Have fun!

FIGURE 13-7   *A FINAL EXAMPLE*

Your name _____

Date (one year from now) _____

Comprehension Instruction Methods:

Results:

Changes yet to be made:

Index

A

Academic learning time, 125–26
Active reading comprehension activity (*see* ARCA)
Adams and Bruce (1980), 69
Affective responses, 76–78
    connotations, 78
    emotional response to plot or theme, 77
    figurative language, 78
    identification with characters, 77
Ambiguous expressions, 145
Analysis, 79–80
    emotionally-laden words, 81
    fact vs. opinion, 80
    fallacies of reasoning, 81
    propoganda, 81
    source credibility, 80
Anaphora, 28–32
    adjacent, 29–30
    backward, 29–30
    clausal, 28–30
    definition, 28
    direct instruction, 31–32
        anaphoric cloze, 31

make it shorter, 32
    possible lesson sequence, 32
    tieing it together, 31–32
forward, 29–30
incidental teaching, 30–31
nominal, 28–30
remote, 29–30
types, 28–30
verbal, 28–30
Anaphoric cloze, 31
Anderson, Reynolds, Schallert, and Goetz (1977), 7, 102, 104
Andre and Anderson (1978-79), 90
Antecedent, 28 (*see also* Anaphora)
Application (*see* Higher-level thinking processes)
ARCA, 181–89, 196
    compared to typical lesson, 188–89
    examples, 186–87, 200
Armbruster and Anderson (1980), 54
Armbruster and Anderson (1981), 51
Assessment (*see* Diagnosis)
Attention focusing, 92–93
Aulls (1978), 76
Automaticity, 112

B

Baker and Brown (1980), 86
Basal readers:
    ARCA, used with, 186–87
    example of lesson, 185
    supplemented with comprehension
        activities, 196
Baumann (1982), 62–63
Baumann (1984), 62
Baumann and Stevenson (in press), 31
Bibliotherapy, 78
Bloom (1956), 79
Brown and Day (1981), 61
Brown and Day (1983), 59
Burmeister (1978), 79

C

Cause/effect relationships:
    explicit and implicit statements of,
        33–35
    part of explanation organizational
        pattern, 51
    teaching example, 176–78
    used for prediction, 70
Cazden (1981), 137
Chunking, 3, 18–22
    direct instruction, 19–22
        chunked reading material, 19–20
        dramatic reading, 21–22
        paraphrase instruction, 22
        reading machines, 19–20
        sentence organization instruction,
            21–22
    incidental instruction, 19
    possible causes of disability, 18
    related research, 18
Clark (1982), 168
Classroom environment (*see* Situational
    contexts)
Clausal anaphora, 28–30 (*see also*
    Anaphora)
Cloze activities:
    teaching anaphora, 31
    teaching connectives, 36–37
    teaching story grammar, 47
Cohesion comprehension (*see* Integrative
    processes)
Collins and Smith (1980), 69, 87–88
Comprehension: (*see also* Comprehension
    processes)
    definition, 9
    model for direct teaching, 174–81 (*see
        also* E-M-Q-A)
    relationship to prior knowledge, 102

teaching, general strategies:
    ARCA, 181–89 (*see also* ARCA)
    basic principles, 15–18
    content-area example, 199–201
    elementary developmental example,
        196–97
    holistic, subskill, and integrated
        approaches, 178
    remedial example, 197–98
Comprehension Assessment Checklist,
    160–66, 197, 201
Comprehension Contexts:
    description, 7–9, 101
    examples of effects, 11
    implications for teaching, 17
    outer context, 189–90
    reader contexts, 101–13 (*see also* Reader
        contexts)
    situational contexts, 129–38 (*see also*
        Situational context)
    text contexts, 117–26 (*see also* Text
        context)
Comprehension monitoring, 87–89
    definiton, 87
    direct instruction:
        assessment, 89
        comprehension-rating procedure, 89
        remedies for comprehension failures,
            88
        taxonomy of comprehension failures,
            87
Comprehension processes:
    definitions, 2–6
    diagram, 4
    elaborative processes, 68–83 (*see also*
        Elaborative processes)
    general example, 10–11
    integrative processes, 27–40 (*see also*
        Integrative processes)
    macroprocesses, 44–63 (*see also*
        Macroprocesses)
    metacognitive processes, 86–97 (*see also*
        Metacognitive processes)
    microprocesses, 18–24 (*see also*
        Microprocesses)
Comprehension-rating procedure, 89
Concept of reading, 18, 198
Connective cloze, 36–37
Connectives:
    description, 33–35
    direct instruction, 36–37
        connective cloze, 36–37
        finding implicit connectives, 37
    explicit cues, 34
    implicitly stated, 33, 35 (*see also* Cause/
        effect relationships)
    incidental instruction, 36
    related research, 33
    table of common types, 34

Connotations, 78
ConStruct procedure, 56–57, 90, 199
Content areas:
  as defined herein, 17
  teaching comprehension in, 16–17
    examples, 23–24, 30–32, 36–37,
      52–59, 61, 75, 82, 88, 90, 92–96,
      176, 178–79, 188–89, 197, 199–201
Context pyramid, 8
Continuum of independence, 16, 180
Control mode reliance, 105
Crafton (1983), 106
Critical reading (*see* Analysis)
Cromer (1970), 18
Cultural differences, 111–12

D

Davey and Porter (1982), 89
Davidson (1982), 54
Decoding fluency, 112–13
Deletion (*see* Macrorules)
Demonstrative pronouns, 28, 32 (*see also*
  Anaphora)
Denotations, 78
Diagnosis, 158–72
  comprehension assessment checklist,
    160, 161–66
  free recall, 167–71
  informal classroom observation, 159–60
  multiple-context approach, 159
  remedial observation, 160, 166–67
  standardized tests, 158–59
Difference readers, 18
Direct reading activity, 181 (*see also*
  E-M-Q-A)
Dramatic reading, 20–21, 198
Duffy (1982), 189
Duffy and Roehler (1982), 16
Dulin (1978), 110
Durkin (1981), 146

E

Elaborative processes, 68–85, 90, 196
  affective responses, 76–78 (*see also*
    Affective responses)
  definition, 5–6, 68
  general teaching suggestions, 82–83
  higher-level thinking responses, 78–82
    (*see also* Higher-level thinking
    responses)
  inappropriate vs. appropriate, 69
  mental imagery, 74–76 (*see also* Mental
    imagery)
  predictions, 69–71 (*see also* Predictions)

prior-knowledge elaborations, 73–74
  (*see also* Prior-knowledge
  elaborations)
  types, 68–69
Ellipsis, 28–30
E-M-Q-A, 175-178
  activities step, 176
  definition, 175
  example, 175
  explication, 16, 36, 175
  modeling, 16, 23, 61, 71–72, 74–75, 83,
    92, 103, 176–77, 179, 186, 196
  questioning, 176
Episode, 45 (*see also* Story grammar)
Evaluation (*see* Higher-level thinking
  responses)
Explication (*see* E-M-Q-A)
Expository structures (*see* Organizational
  patterns in expository materials)
Ex-QAR taxonomy, 142–48 (*see also*
  Questioning: expanded QAR
  (taxonomy)

F

Fact vs. opinion, 80
Fallacies of reasoning, 81
Figurative language, 78
Flexibility in using processes, 96–97
Frayer, Frederick, and Klausmeir (1969),
  109
Frayer model, 109–10
Free recall, 167–71 (*see also* Diagnosis)

G

Goodman and Burke (1980), 18
Group processing session, 176

H

Hafner (1977), 78
Herber (1970), 16, 107
Hierarchical summary procedure, 52–54, 90,
  92, 201
Higher-level thinking responses, 78–82
  analysis, 79–81 (*see also* Analysis)
  application, 79
  evaluation, 82
  synthesis, 82
Hildyard (1979), 102
Holistic approach, 17–18, 178
Horizontal transformation, 16–17, 180
How short can you make it? 61–62

I

Imagery (*see* Mental imagery)
Important information defined, 23
Incidental instruction, 19, 23, 30, 36, 58, 61, 71, 74, 77, 88
Inference:
  anaphoric inference, 28–32
  causal inference, 33, 36–37
  main idea inference (*see* Invention)
  related to elaboration, 68
  related to schema theory, 103–4
  relationship to comprehension, 27
  slot-filling inference, 37–39
  story category inference, 45
Informal comprehension assessment (*see* Diagnosis)
Information guides, 153
Integrative processes, 27–40
  anaphora, 28–32 (*see also* Anaphora)
  connectives, 33–37 (*see also* Connectives)
  definition, 3, 5, 27
  global connections, 39
  interaction with macroprocesses, 44–45
  local connections, 39
  related research, 39
  slot-filling inferences, 37–39
Interactive hypothesis, 5, 10–11, 76, 178
Invention (*see* Macrorules)
Irwin and Mitchell (1983), 168
Irwin, Pulver, and Koch (1983), 160–66

J

Jenkins and Pany (1980), 15–16
Johnson and Pearson (1978), 107–8
Johnston (1981), 7–9

L

LaBerge and Samuels (1974), 112
Locative pronoun, 28, 32 (*see also* Anaphora)

M

Macrocloze task, 47
Macroprocesses, 44–67
  definition, 5, 44
  interaction with other processes, 44–45
  macrorules and summarizing, 58–61 (*see also* Macrorules and Summarizing)
  macroselection, 57–62 (*see also* Macroselection)

organizational patterns in expository materials, 48–52 (*see also* Organizational patterns in expository materials)
story grammar, 44–48 (*see also* Story grammar)
subprocesses, 5
variety in the use of, 45
Macrorules, 58–61
  definitions, 58–59
  deletion, 59
  invention, 60
  selection, 60
  superordination, 59
  direct rule instruction, 61
  example, 60
  related research, 60–61
Macroselection, 57–62
  definition, 57
  direct instruction, 58
  which one? 58
  write a fair test, 58
  related research, 58
Magic Prince, 183–85
Main idea/detail structure, 52, 62, 196
  mapping, 54–55
  relationship to macrorules, 61
  skill hierarchy, 63
Make it shorter, 32
Mapping, 54–55, 108–9
Mason and Kendall (1978), 18
Matching students with materials, 124–25
McCutchen (1982), 39
McFaul (1983), 180
McNeil (1984), 107–8
Meaningful context, importance of, 17
Mental imagery, 74–76
  incidental instruction, 75
  related research, 75
  remedial intruction, 75–76
Metacognitive processes, 86–100
  comprehension monitoring, 87–89 (*see also* Comprehension monitoring)
  definition, 6, 86
  direct instruction, 89
  incidental instruction, 88–89
  study skills, 89–96 (*see also* Study skills)
Method for reading, 130–33
  definition, 130
  examples, 131–133
Meyer, Brandt, and Bluth (1980), 48–49
Microprocesses, 18–24
  chunking, 18–22 (*see also* Chunking)
  definition, 3
  microselection, 22–24 (*see also* Microselection)
Microselection, 3, 22–24
  definition, 22–23

direct instruction, 23–24
  selecting what to study, 24
  selective paraphrase, 23–24
  write your own test, 24
  incidental instruction, 23–24
  related research, 22–23
  relationship to macroprocessing, 23,
      44–45
Modeling (*see* E-M-Q-A)
Moore and Arthur (1981), 110
Mosenthal (1984), 8, 9, 134
Mosenthal and Na (1980), 136
Motivation, 110–11
  motivation ratio, 110–11
  teaching suggestions, 110–11
Multilevel reference books, 125
Multiple-context approach, 159 (*see also*
      Diagnosis)
Multitext approach, 124–25

N

Narrative sructures (*see* Organizational
      patterns in narrative materials)
Ngandu (1977), 110
Nominal anaphora, 28–30 (*see also*
      Anaphora)
Note-taking, 93–94

O

Organizational patterns in expository
      materials, 48–56
  categorization, 50–51
  direct instruction, 52–56
  examples, 52
  examples of use, 49–50
    ConStruct Procedure, 54–56
    Hierarchical Summary procedure, 52–54
    main idea/detail structure, 62–63
    mapping, 54
    study guides, 52–53
  main idea, 52, 62–63 (*see also* Main idea/
      detail structure)
  related research, 48–49
  relationship to macroselection, 57
  relationship to prediction, 70–71
  types, 51
Organizational patterns in narrative
      materials (*see* Story grammar)
Outer context, 189–90 (*see also* Situational
      context)
Outlining (*see* Organizational patterns in
      expository materials)

P

Paraphrase instruction, 22
Pauk, 94–95
Pearson and Johnson (1978), 22, 28, 32,
      80, 102, 107–8
Phrase reading, 20
Possible sentence lesson, 110
Predictions, 69–70
  definition, 69
  incidental instruction, 71
  remedial instruction, 71–72
  types, 70
Prediction task for story grammar awareness,
      47
Previewing, 92, 103
Prior knowledge, 102–103 (*see also*
      Schema theory)
  building prior knowledge, 106–7
  facilitating usage, 103
  related research, 102
  relationship to comprehension, 102
  used for connective inference, 33
  used for prediction, 70
  used for slot-filling inferences, 37–39
Prior-knowledge elaborations, 73–74, 104
  incidental instruction, 74
  judging appropriateness, 73
  related to purpose, 74
  remedial instruction, 74
  teacher monologue, 75
Processability, 118–20
Process questioning taxonomy, 146–50
  examples, 149–52
Pronomial anaphora, 28–30 (*see also*
      Anaphora)
Pronouns, types of, 28–32 (*see also*
      Anaphora)
Propoganda, 80–81
  examples of types, 81
Proverb, 28, 32 (*see also* Anaphora)
Pulver (in press), 36
Purpose for reading, 130–33
  definition, 130
  examples, 130–33
  relationship to metacognitive processes,
      97
  relationship to prior-knowledge
      elaborations, 74

Q

QAR Taxonomy, 142–43 (*see*
      Questioning: QAR taxonomy)
  examples, 143
Questioning, 141–57
  activities involving students, 153–54

information guides, 153
ReQuest procedure, 154
study sessions, 154
what kind of information? 154
where is the answer? 153
write your own test, 154
expanded QAR taxonomy, 143–46
examples of use, 147–48
types of information, 145
planning for questioning, 150–53
process questioning taxonomy, 146–53
QAR taxonomies
scriptally-implicit information, 142
textually-explicit information, 142
textually-implicit information, 142
taxonomies, 142–50 (*see also*
Questioning: expanded QAR
taxonomy, process questioning
taxonomy, QAR taxonomy)

R

Readability, 121–23, 200
Readability checklist formulas, 118
misuse, 118–19
Reader context, 7, 101–13
cultural differences, 111–12
decoding differences, 112–13
prior knowledge, 102–3 (*see also* Prior
knowledge)
schema theory, 103–6 (*see also* Schema
theory)
vocabulary, 103–6 (*see also* Vocabulary)
Reading comprehension interview,
134–36
Reading group, possible effects, 137
Reading machines, 19–20
Reading purpose (*see* Purpose for
reading)
Recall as defined herein, 11–12
Reciting, 94
Reder (1978), 73
Rehearsal, 93
Repeated exposure model, 16
Repeated reading, 112
ReQuest procedure, 154
Reviewing, 94
Rosenshine (1980), 2
Rubin and Gentner (1979), 47–48

S

Sanders (1966), 79
Scardamalea and Bereiter (1983), 39
Schema theory, 103–5
control-mode reliance, 105
schema availability, 105

schema-based vs. text-based processing,
105
schema maintenance, 105
schema selection, 105
Scrambled stories for story grammar
awareness, 47
Scriptally-implicit information (*see*
Questioning: QAR taxonomy)
Select the best, 62
Selecting what to study, 24
Selection (*see* Macrorules)
Selective paraphrase, 23–24
Self-questioning, 90–91
Semantic maps, 108–9
Semantic paraphrase, 22
Sentence anagrams, 21-22, 198
Sentence combining, 37
Sentence organization instruction, 21–22
Sequencing (*see* Time-sequence
connectives and Organizational
patterns in expository materials)
Shank (1982), 107
Shannon (1983), 189
Simplified Exc-QAR taxonomy, 153 (*see
also* Questioning)
Situational context, 8–9, 129–38
assessment task, 134
classroom environment, 137–38
comprehension task, 129–30
reading comprehension interview,
134–35
reading purpose and method, 130–34
social context, 134–37
Slot-filling inferences, 37–39
Smith and Barrett (1979), 76
Smith (The Magic Prince), 183–85
Social context (*see* Situational context)
Source credibility, 80
Spiro (1979), 106
Spiro and Tirre (1979), 105
Stein and Glenn (1977), 45–46, 49
Steingart and Glock (1979), 74
Stevens (1981), 18
Story grammar, 44–48, 196
episode defined, 45
example, 47
instructional procedures, 46–48
macrocloze task, 47
prediction task, 47
scrambled stories, 47
story maker, 47–48
relationship to summarizing, 46
table of categories, 46
used for prediction, 70
Story maker, 47–48
Strange (1980), 106
Study guides:
definition, 52
examples, 53, 59

suggested uses, 52–53, 59, 90–93
Study sessions activity, 154
Study skills, 89–96
  comprehension processes used for, 90
  specific strategies:
    attention focusing, 92–93
    ConStruct procedure, 90 (*see also*
      Organizational patterns in
      expository materials)
    elaborations, 90 (*see also* Elaborative
      processes)
    hierarchical summary procedure, 52–54,
      90, (*see also* Organizational patterns
      in expository materials)
    imaging, 90 (*see also* Mental imagery)
    note-taking, 93–94
    previewing, 92
    rehearsal, 93
    reviewing, 94
    self-questioning, 90–91
    underlining, 93–94
  study systems, 92
  teaching in the elementary school, 96
Subskill approach, 2, 178
Substitution, 28 (*see also* Anaphora)
Summarizing, 58–62 (*see also* Macrorules)
  direct summarizing instruction, 61–62
  direct rule instruction, 61
  how short can you make it? 61–62
  select the best, 62
  example, 60
  incidental instruction, 61
  related research, 60–61
Superordination (*see* Macrorules)
Syntactic paraphrases, 22
Synthesis (*see* Higher-level thinking
  responses)

T

Taylor (1982), 52–53, 92
Taylor (1979), 102
Taxonomies for questioning (*see*
  Questioning: taxonomies)
Taxonomy of comprehension failures, 87
  (*see also* Comprehension
  monitoring)
Text context, 7, 117–26
  processability, 118–20

readability checklist, 121–23
readability formulas, 118
Textually-explicit information (*see*
  Questioning: QAR taxonomy)
Textually-implicit information (*see*
  Questioning: QAR taxonomy)
Tierney and Pearson (1981), 105
Tieing it together, 31–32
Time-sequence connectives, 35
Top-down vs. bottom-up strategies, 105
Transformation of skills, 16, 180

U

Underlining, 93–95

V

Vaughan, 56–57
Verbal anaphora, 28–30 (*see also*
  Anaphora)
Vertical transformation, 16–17
Vocabulary, 107–10
  relationship to comprehension, 107
  teaching, 107–10
    Frayer model, 109–10
    possible sentence lesson, 110
    principles, 107–8
    semantic mapping, 108–9

W

Warren, Nicholas, and Trabasso (1979),
  69
Weaver (1979), 21
Whaley (1981), 47
What kind of information? 154
Where is the answer? 153
Which one? 58
Wixson, Bosky, Yochum, and Alvermann
  (1984), 134–36
Word-by-word reading, 18–19
Word identification (*see* Decoding)
Write a fair test, 58
Write your own test, 24, 154
Writing/reading activities, 17, 23–24, 32,
  37, 47–48, 57, 61–62, 77, 82